For permission requests, contact the publisher at:

Executive Excellence Publishing
1806 North 1120 West
Provo, UT 84604
Phone: 1-801-375-4060
Toll Free: 1-877-250-1983
Fax: 1-801-377-5960
www.eep.com

For Executive Excellence books, magazines and other products,
contact Executive Excellence directly. Call 1-877-250-1983, 801-375-4060
fax 1-801-377-5960, or visit our website at www.eep.com.

First edition.
Printed in the United States of America
10 9 8 7 6 5 4 3 2 1

$24.95 USA
Business Ethics/Corporate Responsibility
ISBN 1-930771-30-4

Credits: Photographs—Kenneth Linge Photography, visit www.kennethlinge.com
          Architectural Renderings—Kinateder & Associates, visit www.kinateder.com
          Cover design—Van Schelt Design, LC., visit www.vanschelt.com

This book is printed on acid-free, re-cycled paper.

"Freedom is not the last word. Freedom is only part of the story and half of the truth. The positive aspect of freedom is responsibility. That is why I recommend that the Statue of Liberty on the East Coast of the United States be supplemented by a Statue of Responsibility on the West Coast."

—Viktor E. Frankl, M.D., Ph.D.
Author, *Man's Search for Meaning*

Dedication

We dedicate this book to those valiant souls who
strive to meet their personal responsibilities in life
and who apply the principles of responsible leadership
in their families, teams, organizations, and communities.

STATUE OF RESPONSIBILITY®

Foundation

www.SORfoundation.org

Contents

Sea to Shining Sea

by Warren Bennis

For several years now, I've lived within a short iron golf shot of the Pacific Ocean in an idyllic gated Southern California community.

Indeed, from my bedroom window, I gaze out over the ocean. And, even with traffic congestion, I'm only a short, 20-minute drive from my office on the manicured campus of the University of Southern California. On a good day, I might sing with the Beach Boys, "I wish we all could be California gurus." My personal brand is my sun tan. Life's been good. Liberty, albeit Los Angeles style, abounds.

My roots, however, are eastward, and in recent years, I've been teaching at Harvard Business School and the Kennedy School of Government, Cambridge, Massachusetts. I fly coast to coast in six hours, sleeping or reading en route.

At age 82, having been an academic professor and university administrator most of my adult life, I suppose that I could be excused if I failed a current events quiz. Yet, inexplicably, I still feel compelled to keep up (and comment) on the events, issues, and personalities of the day, especially as they relate to my field—leadership.

This compulsion was rendered comedic, last year, in a special tribute to me sponsored by the Kennedy School of Government at Harvard, when my daughter and her husband sang to the Beatles' tune, "Will you still need me, will you still read me, when I'm 94." I keep vowing never to write another foreword, yet here I am.

Why this *Foreword*? The notion of a Statue of Responsibility on the West Coast, conceivably visible from my bedroom window, strikes my fancy. I'm even more taken by the idea when I realize that it has roots in Viktor Frankl's

7

logotherapy work. Indeed, the west coast Statue of Responsibility would serve as a bookend logo, a flip-side twin, of New York's Statue of Liberty. In a way, my whole life's work has revolved ideologically around this statue, even though I'd never heard of it until recently.

Do we really need this thing? Yes, on about the same order as we need oxygen. Why? In today's complex world, people at every age and stage, in every position and organization, and especially managers and leaders, need to be reminded daily of their basic responsibilities to stakeholders—meaning anyone who has a stake in their success or failure as a person or business.

For Americans, addicted to freedom and liberty and rights, this medicine goes down like liver oil. We'd rather consume "snake oil" or motor oil than learn co-responsibility in marriages, families, teams, great groups, and creative coalitions. After all, we have a proud heritage of lone rangers, solitary wolves, charismatic leaders, and John Wayne mavericks.

Like old dogs, accustomed to snoozing in the soft lap of liberty and the feather-bed of freedom, we are hard-pressed to learn "new tricks" of collaboration and community, responsibility and accountability. It all sounds like heavy labor—something we would rather outsource than internalize.

Yet it can be done. Sure, we have our share of freeloaders, but frankly I've been impressed that so many senior leaders have learned not only difficult new technology but more importantly new styles and mindsets. Some have had to shed old prejudices, biases, and habits; grow new perspectives; and expand their capabilities.

Unfortunately I must also say that many senior executives have remained rather insulated, isolated, and even protected from learning new tricks. The old way, their way, is not only the best way—it's the only way, other than the highway. When leaders become static, they often become autocratic or toxic. That all-too-familiar style sends many followers to the exits looking, often in vain, for real leadership: somebody or something worthy of their loyalty and trust.

Help Wanted

Today, responsibility-oriented leadership is more important than ever. In effect, I see a sign posted in every organization I enter: "Wanted: Great Leaders." We're all desperately seeking CEOs—a Moses to lead us out of bondage and blight into the abundance and beauty of a promised land.

I have spent much time over the past 50 years up close with leaders, trying to learn what they do, what their direct reports think of them, and gaining a prismatic view to tease out of them or to discern their characteristics, and identify a cluster of competencies or qualities that exemplary leaders manifest.

Beyond qualities, however, I've also looked for judgments, actions, crucibles, learning experiences—what leaders do to rise to the top and what they must learn and do to stay there. Remarkably, many old dogs have an amazing regenerative capacity for learning new skills and mastering new tricks. Even when they are thought by some to be washed up, over the hill, all bark and no bite, the best of them reinvent themselves and come back strong to lead their organizations to new heights. (And sometimes they know that they're considered at the top of the field, but not at the top of the game.)

Like many of you, I gained some poignant early lessons in leadership from my childhood and teenage years. I grew up in a family of three boys. My older brothers, 10 years older than I am, are identical twins. During their long lives, they were impossible to tell apart. We gave them a surprise birthday party on their 82nd birthday, and I had to squint to see who was who.

Growing up in that family was, to say the least, very interesting. When I was about seven years old, I began noticing the pattern of leadership and followership. One of my brothers seemed to have "the right stuff." Whatever he suggested, my friends and I would follow automatically—going to a game, playing a sport, doing a picnic, going to a movie, ditching school—whatever it was, we followed; yet when his twin, his double, suggested the same thing, we curiously declined. Nothing happened. It was like acoustical dead space.

I began wondering, "What is the difference between people who seem to have the capacity to enroll people in their vision, and those who don't?"

As a 17-year-old kid, I joined the army and entered World War II, playing for mortal stakes, and I observed many different leaders there. War, while hell, draws leadership portraits in bold relief.

Perhaps my best learning experience was being a university president. That was a daunting experience, and I can't claim I was a great success, but I sure learned a lot.

Now, what does all this have to do with the Statue? Symbolically, it's a "leaders wanted" sign—an open invitation for all of us to step up and lead out. It's the identical twin of the Statue of Liberty—and yet, like my brothers, so very different, more like a polar opposite. And yet between anode (the positive electrode) and cathode, we have transmission. We value both leadership and followership. And we accept the conditions of each, even when that might mean joining the Army and fighting a war or being the president for a season.

I can't predict what paths *responsibility* might take you, but as an old dog, I know this much: It will likely take you from sea to shining sea, Atlantic to Pacific, USC to Harvard, and back to my beloved USC and the Pacific Ocean.

The responsible life is one amazing ride.

Warren Bennis, contributing editor to Leadership Excellence, *is a distinguished professor of business administration at USC and an advisor to Harvard Business School and the Kennedy School of Government.*

Freedom Isn't Free

by Mark Victor Hansen

You were coded at a DNA level to be free. Once you are free and love it, you want to help free every person everywhere.

Abe Lincoln freed the American slaves in 1865. Yet today, over half the world's population is politically enslaved. More are economically enslaved. Most are enslaved by a lack of thinking and a belief that they are not enough and cannot be it, do it, or have it.

The Statue of Responsibility is an irresistibly compelling project that deserves to take its place on the West Coast, and by doing so, will harmoniously balance the Statue of Liberty on the East Coast.

One of the most inspirational books of all time, *Man's Search for Meaning*, was written by a WWII prisoner of war and holocaust survivor, psychologist, Dr. Viktor E. Frankl. Frankl, some 40 years ago, wisely proposed his visionary and enlightened idea that the world needs a Statue of Responsibility. Now, we are manifesting that idea in reality.

You need to go online and see our introductory DVD to get a 360-degree view of our dream coming true. We expect it to inspire you, and millions of other people, to support this worthy project.

Jack Canfield, Senator McGovern, Stephen R. Covey, Mrs. Elenore Frankl, and other giants, present a simple message that will touch your soul, give you hope, and help make a brighter, better future for all.

Freedom endures, Frankl taught, when we understand the relationship between rights and responsibility.

When we become a licensed driver, we have the right to drive. Imagine for a moment that our highway system is the greatest democracy in the world. While we have the right and privilege to drive anywhere and anytime—we also have the responsibility to be adept, alert, sober, and careful. We drive a safe machine, or a lethal weapon, it all depends on what we do behind the wheel.

We hope that you will drink in the idea that Frankl inspired, that the principles of liberty (rights) and responsibility are harmonically linked.

Let's marry rights and responsibilities so every driver on the highway of democracy, drives with wisdom to be totally and preeminently responsible. That is the driver with whom we all want to share rush hour with.

In truth, we all want a hand up, not a hand-out. To do so, America, and other freedom-loving countries, must move from a weakening entitlement mentality to a strengthening empowerment mentality. This move begins with you and I. Art Linkletter and I wrote about how to become totally accountable in our book, *How to Make the Rest of Your Life the Best of Your Life*. We identified 10 new ways to make people truly free.

Companies that practice and promote social responsibility generate maximum business impact in society, which translates to the bottom-line.

One such example is Paul Newman. Newman first created a salad dressing and donated the profits to support his philanthropy. He then opened a restaurant in his hometown of West Port, Connecticut, that offers delicious, organic, healthy menu items. People choose his products and eat at his restaurant, knowing that they are supporting a business that supports charitable and worthy causes. Millions and millions of dollars every year are sent to comfort forgotten and hurting children around the world, all because a business chose to act socially responsible first.

The "Golden Rule" is more than a great idea. It is the rule that will get you the gold, create a legacy, and have you feel terrific along the way.

I know you will enjoy your reading adventure. As you pursue and walk your own path of responsibility, your soul will thank you.

Mark Victor Hansen is the bestselling co-author of the Chicken Soup for the Soul *series of books.*

Freedom's Call

by Daniel Louis Bolz

Why This Book?

As Dr. Viktor Frankl stated, *"Freedom is not the last word. Freedom is only part of the story and half of the truth. The positive aspect of freedom is responsibility."*

There comes a time in a nation's history when its core values must be revisited, re-energized, and re-enthroned, in order for that nation to endure. We live in such a time. We all know what America stands for. Our beacon of hope and freedom reaches out to all. For democracy to thrive under the banner of freedom, responsibility must co-exist with liberty. This message applies to all freedom-loving people and countries. Freedom is the umbrella under which all other positive human endeavors can flourish. Albert Einstein said, *"Everything that is really great and inspiring is created by the individual who can labor in freedom."*

Responsibility 911 is offered to "Friends of Freedom" as a rallying cry to the principles of freedom, liberty, and responsibility. This book provides a united voice from many authors to underscore the message of the Statue of Responsibility monument: *"With great liberty come great responsibility."* This anthology defines the role responsibility plays in our lives. Whether you use this book for personal enlightenment, corporate training, family discussion, or as a springboard for dialogue—I hope your reading inspires you to preserve your freedom.

The Idea

A noble idea was proposed some 40 years ago by Viktor E. Frankl, a man who lived through the most intense deprivation of personal freedom imaginable.

He challenged America to keep its light of hope and freedom burning brightly to future generations by declaring that liberty must be embraced with responsibility to maintain freedom. To stand as a visual reminder of his idea, Frankl declared that the Statue of Liberty on the East Coast be supplemented with a Statue of Responsibility on the West Coast. The Statue of Responsibility Foundation is committed to the realization of this poignant idea.

While we pay respect to Dr. Viktor E. Frankl, the Statue of Responsibility monument will not be a shrine to him. Rather, his sublime idea that responsibility must go hand in hand with liberty will be enshrined in the monument.

The Cause

No cause is more timely, or more needed. The Statue of Responsibility monument will firmly and boldly declare to our country, and to the world, the sublime message that with liberty and great power comes great responsibility.

Civilizations leave their legacy to future generations by the monuments they build. Great monuments lift the human spirit, crystallize inner beliefs, encourage discussion, and lead to strengthened resolve and renewed action.

Like millions of others, I first became aware of the magnificent idea to build a Statue of Responsibility while reading Viktor Frankl's book, *Man's Search for Meaning*, during my college days in the 1970s. From that time to the present, my life's journey has shown me the critical role freedom plays in allowing people to pursue meaning-filled lives that result in their happiness. Once freedom has been declared, once freedom has been won, and once order has been implemented to guide it, it becomes the duty of each successive generation to preserve it. Responsibleness lives in the act of preserving freedom.

The Foundation does not advocate a uniform way to act responsibly. Our hope is that the monument will stimulate an international discussion on the role responsibility plays—hand in hand with liberty—in maintaining freedom. Individuals must cultivate their own commitment to live a responsible life.

The Statue of Liberty has served as a symbol of liberty, both in America and around the world. Its counterpart, the Statue of Responsibility, will likewise serve as a symbol—a visible representation and call to responsibility—both in America and abroad. These two principles—liberty and responsibility—when linked together, will help engender and secure freedom for our generation and for generations yet unborn, wherever a thirst for freedom exists. Only by balancing Liberty with Responsibility can Freedom be sustained.

The Message

Freedom is global in scope. The International Monument Pathway at the base of the monument will allow visitors to experience artistic representations of responsibility and freedom as sculpted by selected artists from many countries. These sculptures, up to 30 feet in height, will provide an international experience to the powerful message of the Statue of Responsibility monument. Each participating country will receive a 30-foot-tall version of the Statue of Responsibility to place in their country. The message of the Statue of Responsibility is a message that belongs to freedom-loving people worldwide.

I hope you will give thoughtful consideration to the words in this book. They come from authors who are passionate about improving the state of mankind while preserving the fundamental liberties of all. Their united message is that by engaging in responsible thoughts and actions, the highest ideals of civilization will be secured. For freedom to endure, the twin pillars of liberty and responsibility must become firmly entrenched in the workings of society, and in the hearts and deeds of its citizens.

For too long, our discussion and application of freedom has focused solely on our liberties, or our rights. The Statue of Responsibility will provide a visual reminder that the discussion and application of freedom needs to include both liberty and responsibility.

The Challenge.

We know that some critics will scoff at our cause, and skeptics will cast their shadow of uncertainty. We anticipate that others will ridicule the design of the monument. Throughout all time, critics have nipped at the heals of those engaged in worthy undertakings, and skeptics have pointed their finger of doubt. Such is the path we are on. Our resolve to succeed in our mission is fixed, our determination unshakable, and our inner conviction impenetrable.

The Statue of Responsibility will be a gift to America by Americans, and by "Friends of Freedom" from around the world. It will stand 300 feet tall. It will be cast in stainless steel. The sculptor, Gary Lee Price, was commissioned in 1997. The final design was approved by the Foundation and has now moved beyond the prototype phase and into the engineering phase. Photos and architectural renderings appear in this book. It will stand on the West Coast of America as a proud bookend to Lady Liberty. It will be built by individuals who willingly take a stand for freedom as we journey into the 21st Century.

I invite you to become a "Friend of Freedom" to this ambitious cause. Help support this project in ways that only you can. Help us build this mighty monument to all that is good and to all that is right in the world.

Rarely does a project of such magnitude, importance, and timeliness present itself. The Statue of Responsibility is such a project! I invite you to join us in building the Statue of Responsibility!

Daniel Louis Bolz is president and CEO of The Statue of Responsibility Foundation. Visit www.SORfoundation.org.

Personal Responsibility

"Everything that is really great and inspiring is created by the individual who can labor in freedom."

—Albert Einstein

The New 3Rs: Respect, Responsibility, and Rights

by Gary P. Waterworth Owen

To educate and entertain, emotionally engage and intellectually stimulate, to delve into the depth of things, and confront the significant problems we face is no easy task. E.F. Schumacher wrote: "The volume of education continues to increase, yet so do pollution, exhaustion of resources, and the dangers of ecological catastrophe. If still more education is to save us, it would have to be education of a different kind: an education that takes us into the depth of things." And Albert Einstein noted: "The significant problems we face cannot be solved at the same level of thinking we were at when we created them."

So hats off to those in the film industry who have produced such movies as: *An Inconvenient Truth, The Constant Gardener, Syriana, The Lord of War,* and *The Last King of Scotland.* Their plots and content seem to have been extracted straight off global media headlines. They have addressed significant social, environmental and economic issues, made millions of people globally think a little deeper, and certainly been a boon to those whose mission it is to promote the need for relevant education, social entrepreneurship, sustainable development, and corporate social responsibility.

However, when I watched these movies, I recalled Theodore Roosevelt's observation: "A man who has never gone to school may steal from a freight car; but if he has a university education, he may steal the whole railroad."

Respect

At the time of this writing, it was declared on BBC News that:

• Heroin should be prescribed to drug addicts to tackle crime.

• Staff at 60 percent of supermarkets in Nottingham tested in an undercover operation have been caught selling alcohol to kids under 18.

• More schools in England have been judged "inadequate" by inspectors, and several fall into the most serious category where schools are put into special measures and where school leadership is deemed incapable of achieving change.

• Britain's teenagers are the most badly behaved in Europe.

But who is really to blame, an under-18 youth buying alcohol or an adult selling alcohol to someone underage?

No one can deny we owe our children a brighter future, but we also owe our future brighter children. Our present educational system at best barely prepares young people for present and future challenges. At its worst, it is the subject of spurious headline initiatives, like the one being put forward now: "Super nannies"—the UK Government Home Office's latest innovation aims to assign full-time "super-nannies" to 6,000 problem families. It is said that they will bring serenity, order, and early bed times where before there was only chaos, cursing, and juvenile career criminals. Sadly, however, the plan is flawed in one vital respect: The Home Office is not sending in nannies; it's a newsy euphemism for social workers.

African wisdom states, "It takes a whole village to make a man." Present trends in society reveal a severe breakdown of family and community. As a result, we are witnessing a slow-but-sure disintegration of society and an overwhelming sense of rootlessness and hopelessness in the most pampered and educated regions of the world.

A 200-page report entitled "Freedom's Orphans: Raising Youth in a Changing World" reveals that in 2006 more than 1.5 million Britons thought about moving away from their local area due to young people "hanging around." About 1.7 million admitted to not going out after dark as a direct result of "youths gathering."

Britons were also three times more likely to cite young people "hanging around" as a problem than they were to complain about noisy neighbors. Adults have become fearful of children. British adults are more likely than their other European counterparts to say that young people are predominantly responsible for anti-social behavior, and cite "lack of discipline as the root cause of anti-social behavior." These adults tend to turn a blind eye or cross over on the other side of the road rather than intervene in the discipline of another person's child, often because they fear they might be attacked or verbally abused. Now 15 percent of Britons are planning to emigrate. What a sad reflection on a once great nation.

Of course, this social dilemma is not restricted to the UK alone. Delivering the Steve Biko memorial lecture at the University of Cape Town, Bishop Tutu questioned why a respect for the law, environment, and even life are missing in South Africa. "What has happened to us? It seems as if we have perverted our freedom, our rights into license, into being irresponsible. Rights go hand in hand with responsibility, with dignity, with respect for oneself and for the other. The fact is, we still depressingly do not respect one another. I have often said black consciousness did not finish the work it set out to do."

Bishop Tutu went on to say present government officials often acted like former officials during the Apartheid era—treating people rudely. He said South Africa should oppose xenophobia and act sensitively when place names were being changed rather than appearing to gloat and ride roughshod over the feelings of others. He also made a plea for people to pick up litter, to care for their own environments and for their fellow citizens.

"Perhaps we did not realize just how Apartheid has damaged us, that we seem to have lost our sense of right and wrong, so that when we go on strike, as is our right to do, we are not appalled that some of us can chuck people out of moving trains because they did not join the strike, or go on the rampage. The best memorial to Steve Biko would be a South Africa where everyone respects themselves, has a positive self-image filled with a proper self-esteem, and holds others in high regard," extolled Bishop Tutu.

Limited to the privileged few throughout most of recorded history, the 3 Rs of education (Reading, wRiting, aRithmetic + Read, Remember and Repeat) became an obligatory element of general education and the main task of elementary school. Everyone agrees on the value of education, but in addition to solid, marketable skills, education has always included subjects about which most people say later in their life: "This hasn't been of much use to me since I left school!"

However, exposure to subjects not directly related to any material benefit can be of great value. The consequence of learning cannot be measured only in monetary terms. If so, we are the poorer for it. In a fast-changing world, mastery of today's curriculum may not be of much value when new thinking is needed. Our precious school years should be reinforced with knowledge of sustainable value and essential life skills.

If the 3 Rs of education is not the "be and end all" of vocational success in the future, what are the foundational skills for the future?

Humanity has reached a crucial tipping point. "The future is a race between education and catastrophe," said H.G. Wells. We need a universal agreement for an education in values. The Green revolution spawned the 3 Rs of Reduce, Reuse and Recycle, which was a step in the right direction. But why do we have waste in the first place? We designed it in. Now we have to design it out. This requires a new way of thinking.

"Respect" is a new UK government initiative, albeit a knee-jerk reaction to a festering problem. It is about central government, local agencies, local communities and ultimately every citizen working together to build a society in which people can respect one another—where anti-social behavior is rare and tackled effectively, and communities can live in peace together. It's not about going back to the past or returning to the days of "knowing your place."

It's about nurturing and, where needed, enforcing a modern culture of respect, which most people want. It's about showing tolerance, acceptance, and common decency towards people, family, friends, and peers—people who are older or younger, people from different walks of life or who follow different cultures or religions. It's about being considerate of the consequences of behavior towards others.

For most cultures, this is automatic and ingrained in the habits of everyday lives. But when respect for self, others, and the community breaks down, antisocial behavior takes hold. Making offensive and threatening remarks, participating in violent behavior, and urinating in the street is clearly inconsiderate or disrespectful. Irresponsible marketing has played its role in perpetuating the myth of the Brand, promoting to the youth market unhealthy food and overpriced fashion items, creating champagne tastes for people with beer money. It seems we have been led to believe that the only way we can avoid being a nobody is to have somebody else's name on our clothes and a myriad of seasonal fashion accessories. We seem to know the cost of everything and the value of nothing. We are building bigger and better houses but are living in broken homes.

Responsibility

"Stop the world; I want to get off" is the wish of many feeling disillusioned with the manic "society of speed" we have created, or perhaps lacking the necessary courage, pray to find themselves lucky enough to be thrown clear of the collision. This need for speed pervades entire cities and many societies, every crook and granny—from fast food, to fast communications, faster cars, and even faster women. As revealed in the movie *The Constant Gardner*, "The pharmaceuticals industry is right up there with the arms dealers." New cures are dispensed before costly and time-consuming tests can be responsibly completed and then recalled with no responsibility accepted for the damage caused. There seems to be never enough time to do the job right, but always enough time to do the job over. Investors and shareholders, obsessed with quarterly thinking, demand higher and quicker returns, pushing business leaders to bend the rules and burn out at a frenzied Enron pace, revealing the lack of moral compasses and providing evidence that possible "ethical by-passes" were conducted at birth. Faster and faster broadband is demanded in case a single dollar is lost. The saying "Speed Kills" springs to mind.

Many companies recognize the risks associated with degrading ecosystems and are trying to adapt, but most fail to balance the maintenance of healthy ecosystems with their quarterly returns. A collective business response is needed to address the scale of environmental change currently taking place. The implications that water scarcity, climate change, nutrient overloading, biodiversity loss, habitat change, overexploitation of oceans, and the resulting escalation of poverty and social breakdown will have for the future of business are issues that have to be addressed now.

The scarcity of raw materials, higher operating costs, government restrictions and reduced flexibility are issues companies need to factor in now and prepare for these risks by transparently and honestly measuring their impact and dependence on ecosystem services, taking advantage of emerging business opportunities and reducing their operational footprints. This needs a drastic program of unlearning and relearning.

We all acknowledge that modern mainstream society intoxicated with over-consumption and unbridled growth is toxic on every level: physical, mental, emotional, and spiritual. With the growth in China and India, western economies have stepped up a gear, moved into overdrive and are accelerating on a collision course that can be avoided. The economic losses caused by the degradation of ecosystems and the vital services they provide is proving that the elephant is truly in the room and does not want to leave.

We, the consumer, and business must develop and enhance our Response-ABILITIES—our Abilities to Respond effectively to the realities of the fragility of the Earth's ecosystems and the effect it is having on global societies. The final result of this scenario is anything but clear. Whether we are in agreement about global warming or global cooling, there is climate change. Nature bats last.

The best that most of us achieve individually (and it does make a difference) is some minute demonstration of personal ethics and concern by recycling our unwanted plastic, glass, and paper. The resulting plastic, glass, and paper mountains around European landfill sites are proof of our individual efforts. Excuse the cynicism following: Many do purchase the odd energy saving light bulb, savor occasionally, premium-rated organic produce, take the odd walk after launching a serous attack on the Sunday roast beef and Yorkshire pudding—hopefully contemplating and calculating the air miles incurred to have the luxury of such a lunch.

Some do invest in the latest hard-to-find and even-harder-to-fill hybrid hydrogen powered car and some fortunate enough to live in cities with excellent public transport systems, do away with cars altogether and enjoy the extra income derived, by purchasing the latest range of labor-saving electrical and electronic devices available. Unwanted slow mobile phones and even slower laptops are donated to worthy causes in Africa, provided the recycling point is convenient and on the way to work. However many feel skeptical about whether such items will ever reach their "in need" beneficiaries, or end up in some container destined for some other port of call in a developing country with lax environmental recycling law. But when it comes to planning the annual family sun, sea and sand holiday, we know deep down inside that getting to the destination by walking or by bicycle is not only impossible, but will not gain many favorable votes from the rest of the family. Our outward manifestations of these actions are the green badges by which we recognize each other. Learning to live sustainably within an oil-driven economy, without oil, is a huge challenge and often seems beyond all of us. But it can be done.

Rights

Understanding and adopting a decent code of behavior is what makes society function as a whole. John Ruskin noted: "Education is not about teaching people what they do not know; it is teaching them to behave as they do not behave." B.F. Skinner showed how much of behavior is based on conditioning. In *Escape from Freedom*, Erich Fromm makes a convincing argument that much of human behavior is based on avoidance of responsibility. Conditioning creates our Beliefs, Beliefs create our Attitude, Attitude governs our Behavior, and Behavior delivers our Results. If we want to change our Results, we have to work on our Conditioning and resultant Behavior.

To comprehend whether or not these behavioral experiments, and this theory of humanity accurately reflects how we are formed, we have to confront one of the most sensitive philosophical issues: Where do we come from? What are we? Where are we going? Is there indeed such a thing as free agency? If not, then we are, in fact, products of psychic and environmental determinism—our cruel or caring parents, our ruthless or nurturing state, our religion or lack of religion, or our class or caste status at birth. If there is no such thing as free agency, then we have to accept that Al Capone, Charles Manson, Idi Amin, Saddam Hussein, and Robert Mugabe are just unfortunate victims reacting inappropriately to challenges in their environment—that they are mere pawns in a pervasive system, rather than the creators of their own private power-crazed agendas and responsible for the consequences of their actions.

Accepting responsibility for our own lives liberates us from our past and frees us to move forward. Abandoning blame, shame, and regret from the perceived fate of our birth, from the burden of class and caste that has kept so many in bondage for so long, is liberating and essential for sustainable growth. J. Rousseau suggested: "Man is born free, yet everywhere he is bound in chains. We cannot escape from a prison if we don't know we're in one." Too many of the chains binding people are mind-created realities. We do have the ability to control our own lives, and we can free ourselves from the past and wrong doings. Only dead leaves go with the flow. We do not have to be swept along with the current. The environment we choose to be in will have more of an effect on us than will our very genetic make-up. The people we choose to mix with, the companies we choose to work for, the clubs we choose to subscribe to, will affect our lives and results. But it is our choice, based on free agency, and conscious, value-based decision-making.

So which ideology should we hold fast to: Personal responsibility, or psychic and environmental determinism? There is much evidence to prove that both schools of thought have an influence on an individual's life. We are, indeed, the products of the conditioning and belief systems we have unconsciously swallowed since birth. Did you choose your name, the school and church you attended when a child? Some societies do enjoy more freedom and transparency, are safer, value creativity and innovation, respect human rights and are more prosperous than others. Those that are repressive and cruel, where the mass is poor and the leadership does not respect human rights, have their cross to bear.

Many years before his election as President, Abraham Lincoln said: "At what point shall we expect the approach of danger? By what means shall we fortify against it? Shall we expect some transatlantic military giant to step the Ocean, and crush us at a blow? Never! All the armies of Europe, Asia and Africa combined, with all the treasure of the earth (our own excepted) in their military chest; with a Bonaparte for a commander, could not, by force, take a drink from the Ohio, or make a track on the Blue Ridge, in a trial of a thousand years. At what point then is the approach of danger to be expected? I answer, if it ever reach us, it must spring up amongst us. It cannot come from abroad. If destruction be our lot, we must ourselves be its author and finisher. As a nation of freemen, we must live through all time, or die by suicide."

In this congested Information Age and amid all this velocity, slow down for a moment, and take time out to consider how these 3 Rs can be implemented in your life, society, and business. These 3 Rs are worth investing in and fighting for, and can defend us from the enemy within. Only when we have Respect for ourselves and others, the planets fauna and flora, accept personal Responsibility for our lives and the society we choose to live in, can we earn, demand and be worthy of our Rights.

Gary P. Waterworth Owen is the founder of the ResponseABILITY Alliance, London, England. Email gary@responseabilityalliance.com or visit www.responseabilityalliance.com.

2

The Success Principle

by Jack Canfield

One pervasive myth in American culture today is that we are *entitled* to a great life—that somehow, somewhere, someone (certainly not us) is responsible for filling our lives with continual happiness, exciting career options, nurturing family time, and blissful personal relationships—simply because we exist.

The truth is there is only one person responsible for the quality of the life you are living, and that person is you! If you want to be more successful, you have to take 100 percent responsibility for everything that you experience in your life. This includes the level of your achievements, the results you produce, the quality of your relationships, the state of your health, your income, your debts, your feelings—everything!

This is not easy. Most of us have been conditioned to blame something outside of ourselves for the parts of our life we don't like. We blame parents, bosses, friends, media, co-workers, clients, spouses, weather, economy, money—even our astrological chart. We never want to look at the real source of the problem—ourselves.

To achieve what you truly want, you must assume 100 percent responsibility for your life. Nothing less will do.

100 Percent for Everything

Back in 1969—only one year out of graduate school—I had the good fortune to work for W. Clement Stone, a self-made multimillionaire worth $600 million. As the publisher of *Success* magazine and the author of two books, Stone was also America's premier success guru.

When I was completing my first week's orientation, Mr. Stone asked me if I took 100 percent responsibility for my life.

"I think so," I responded.

"This is a yes or no question, young man. You either do or you don't. Have you ever blamed anyone for any circumstance in your life? Have you ever complained about anything?"

"Yes, I have."

"Okay, then. That means you don't take 100 percent responsibility for your life. Taking 100 percent responsibility means you acknowledge that you create everything that happens to you. It means you understand that you are the cause of all of your experience. If you want to be really successful, you will have to give up blaming and complaining and take total responsibility for your life. That is the prerequisite for creating a life of success. It is only by acknowledging that you have created everything up until now that you can take charge of creating the future you want. If you realize that you have created your current conditions, then you can un-create them and re-create them at will. Do you understand that?"

"Yes, sir, I do."

"Are you willing to take 100 percent responsibility for your life?"

"Yes, sir, I am!"

Give Up All Your Excuses

If you want to create the life of your dreams, you need to take 100 percent responsibility for your life. That means giving up all your excuses, all your victim stories, all the reasons why you can't and why you haven't up until now, and all your blaming of outside circumstances.

You have to take the position that you have always had the power to make it different, to get it right, and to produce the desired result. For whatever reason—ignorance, lack of awareness, fear, needing to be right, the need to feel safe—you chose not to exercise that power. However, all that matters now is that from this point forward you choose to act as if you are 100 percent responsible for everything that does or doesn't happen to you.

If something doesn't turn out as planned, you will ask yourself, "How did I create that? What was I thinking? What did I say or not say? What did I do or not do to create that result? How did I get the other person to act that way? What do I need to do differently next time to get the result I want?"

A few years after I met Mr. Stone, Dr. Robert Resnick, a psychotherapist in Los Angeles, taught me a simple formula that made this idea of 100 percent responsibility even clearer to me: **E + R = O (Event + Response = Outcome)**.

The basic idea is that every outcome you experience in life (whether it is success or failure, wealth or poverty, health or illness, intimacy or estrangement, joy or frustration) is the result of how you've responded to earlier events in your life.

Two Basic Decisions

If you don't like the outcomes you get, you can make two basic choices:

1. You can blame the event (E) for your lack of results (O). You can blame the economy, weather, money, education, racism, gender bias, government, your wife or husband, your boss's attitude, the lack of support, and so on. No doubt all these factors do exist, but if they were the deciding factor, nobody would ever succeed.

Jackie Robinson would never have played major league baseball, Denzel Washington would have never become a movie star, Dianne Feinstein and Barbara Boxer would never have become U.S. senators, Erin Brockovich would never have uncovered PG&E's contamination of the water in Hinkley, California, and Bill Gates would never have founded Microsoft. For every limiting factor you can identify, there are hundreds of people who have overcome them, so it can't be the limiting factors that limit us.

It is ourselves! We think limiting thoughts and engage in self-defeating behaviors. We defend our self-destructive habits (such as drinking and smoking) with indefensible logic. We ignore useful feedback, fail to continuously learn new skills, waste time, eat unhealthy food, fail to exercise, spend more money than we make, fail to invest in our future, avoid necessary conflict, fail to tell the truth, don't ask for what we want—and then wonder why our lives don't work.

2. You can instead simply change your responses (R) to the events (E)— the way things are—until you get the outcomes (O) you want. You can change your thinking, and you can change your behavior. That is all you really have any control over anyway. Most of us are so run by our habits that we never change our behavior. We get stuck in our conditioned responses. We need to regain control of our thoughts and behaviors. Everything you think, say, and do needs to become intentional and aligned with your purpose, values, and goals.

If You Don't Like Your Outcomes, Change Your Responses

A friend of mine owns a Lexus dealership. When the Gulf War broke out, people stopped coming in to buy Lexuses. They knew that if they didn't change their response (R) of continuing to rely on newspaper and radio ads to bring into the dealership to the event (E) of nobody coming into the showroom, they'd get the same outcome (O) of decreasing sales. So they tried some new things. The one that worked was driving a fleet of new cars out to where the rich people were—country clubs, marinas, polo grounds, fundraisers and parties in rich areas—and inviting them to take a spin in a new Lexus.

Have you ever test-driven a new luxury automobile and then got back into your old car? Your old car was fine, but suddenly you knew there was something better—and you wanted it. After test-driving the new car, many people bought or leased a new Lexus.

The dealership kept changing their response (R) to an unexpected event (E)—the war—until they got the outcome (O) they wanted—increased sales. They ended up selling more cars per week than before the war broke out.

If you keep on doing what you've always done, you'll keep on getting what you've always got. The day you change your responses is the day your life will begin to get better! If what you are currently doing would produce the "more" and "better" that you are seeking in life, the more and better would have shown up! If you want something different, you'll have to take responsibility for doing something different!

You have to give up blaming. You will never succeed as long as you blame someone or something else for your lack of success. You have to acknowledge the truth—you took the actions, thought the thoughts, created the feelings, and made the choices that got you to where you now are.

You are the one who ate the junk food. You are the one who didn't say no! You are the one who took the job. You are the one who stayed in the job. You are the one who chose to believe them. You are the one who ignored your intuition. You are the one who didn't take care of it. You are the one who decided you had to do it alone.

You have to give up complaining. Let's take a moment to really look at complaining. In order to complain about something or someone, you have to believe that something better exists. You have to have a reference point of something you prefer that you are not willing to take responsibility for creating. If you didn't believe there was something better possible—more money, a bigger house, a more fulfilling job, more fun, a more loving spouse—you couldn't complain. So you have this image of something better and you know you would prefer it, but you are unwilling to take the risks that would be required to create it.

We only complain about things we can do something about. We don't complain about the things we have no power over. Have you ever heard anyone complain about gravity? Never. Why not? There is nothing anyone can do about gravity, so we just accept it. We know that complaining will not change it, so we don't complain about it.

The circumstances you complain about are, by their very nature, situations you can change—but you have chosen not to. You can get a better job, find a more loving partner, make more money, live in a nicer house, live in a better neighborhood, and eat healthier food. But all of these things would require you to change.

You could: Learn to cook healthier food. Say no in the face of peer pressure. Quit and find a better job. Take the time to conduct due diligence. Trust your own gut feelings. Take better care of your possessions. Reach out for help. Take a self-development class.

You don't do those things because they involve risks. You run the risk of being unemployed, left alone, or ridiculed and judged by others. You run the risk of failure, confrontation, or being wrong. You run the risk of your mother, your neighbors, or your spouse disapproving of you. Making a change might take effort, money, and time. It might be uncomfortable, difficult, or confusing. And so, to avoid risking any of those uncomfortable feelings and experiences, you stay put and complain about it.

Complaining means you have a reference point for something better that you would prefer but that you are unwilling to take the risk of creating. Either accept that you are making the choice to stay where you are, take responsibility for your choice, and stop complaining—or take the risk of creating your life exactly the way you want it.

So make the decision to stop complaining, to stop spending time with complainers, and get on with creating the life of your dreams.

The Statue of Responsibility

Remember, you always have the freedom to choose—the freedom to think, say, and do something different, the freedom to take responsibility for creating your life the way you want it. Few countries on this planet have given people so much freedom. We refer to ourselves as "the land of liberty and justice for all." Liberty and the rule of law must be accompanied by each of us taking full responsibility for making our life and the lives of communities work. These qualities of liberty and responsibility are foundational principles of our country. That's why I am excited about the building of the Statue of Responsibility on the West Coast as the companion to the Statue of Liberty on the East Coast to remind us to take personal and social responsibility for our lives.

Just as the Statue of Liberty on the East Coast reminds all who enter New York Harbor of the great sacrifices that have been made to ensure the personal liberties we all cherish, the Statue of Responsibility on the West Coast will remind all who see it of the personal responsibility that is required to preserve those liberties—and hence our freedom.

Jack Canfield is the bestselling co-author of the Chicken Soup for the Soul *series of books. Visit www.jackcanfield.com.*

3

The Kite: From Freedom to Responsibility

by Claudio García Pintos

From the beginning, freedom has been an open question to mankind. Liberty has inspired so many individual fights, revolutions, wars, crises and conflicts. Anyway, the "real fight," the real conquest of mankind, is still waiting to be fulfilled.

The question about whether we are free or conditioned may distract us from the real point. Any answer will probably be partially correct. If we think that we are absolutely free from conditionings, we are talking about an angel or a superhero. And if we think that man is absolutely conditioned or driven, we are talking about a machine or automaton. In both cases, human nature is lost.

Viktor Frankl wrote: "In the spare space among conditionings, man is absolutely free. Freedom must be understood as the capacity of man to decide what to do or what to create to solve his conditionings." Frankl didn't deny conditionings but confirmed the human capacity to *do* and to *be* in spite of them. That's why he could say: *Man is not under the control of conditionings; conditionings are submitted to his decisions.* He noted: "We talk about the human being as responsible, precisely because of man's natural freedom. And the relationship between liberty and responsibility reveals that freedom is not only to *be free from* but to *be free to*, and to assuming responsibility means what the man is free for."

We can understand this concept by focusing on the image of a kite. Sometimes when we see a kite flying, we feel the yearning for experiencing this freedom. The kite flies high, making colorful pirouettes. It flies and dances, higher and higher, freely. But, let us ask: How can the kite fly so high, dancing with this colorful liberty? Because it makes use of the wind, and it is tied. Yes, it is tied by the string that was pulled by the hand of the child who makes it fly. The hand that pulls it firmly, demanding more and more, obtains from it its best performance.

What would happen if we cut up the string—or if we didn't pull it firmly? The kite would not fly; it would fall to earth. Without flying, it would not be a kite anymore.

Now, let us think of human being, using the analogy of the kite. Life presents us circumstances that tie us—commitments that become themselves conditionings. Some of them are freely given, like being a woman or a man, the family in which we were born, our race, our nationality and others. We can call them "native conditionings".

But other conditions are chosen by us. They are products of our personal decisions—like having a baby, for example. Parenthood is an optional commitment—one that I choose to assume. I'm not obliged to be a father or mother. Once I have a baby of my own, however, it is a conditioning because my life, after having the baby, is not the same as before. Whether given or chosen, biological, sociological, psychological or spiritual conditionings exist. Being a man means to unfold and mature, in spite of them. These conditionings are like the string of the kite.

On the other hand, our existence consists of being linked to each other. Our relationships build our existence. You and I are created for others, and our humanity is fulfilled by the relationship with a "you" and a "You." This auto-transcendent characteristic is represented by the child's hand, which pulls the string firmly, expecting to see the kite fly.

Then, we have found the answer. Man is like a kite. His possibility of flying—of being free—depends on two circumstances: To be tied, conditioned, and to respond in a better way to the firm demand of those who expect something from him, who needs something from him.

I borrowed this kite analogy from a poem by a Brazilian friend, Luiz Falcao. He ends his poem saying: *"To be free is a challenge When your life is Always tied by a thread."*

Man can become a person when he is capable of assuming this challenge—not victimizing himself because of his conditionings, but deciding to face them responsibly.

Being Responsible, Living Responsibly

We all want to be free, even though sometimes we do not know how to achieve liberty or we are frightened to achieve it. But not all of us want to be responsible, perhaps because we tend to see responsibility as a burden. That is why we tend to avoid it, presuming that by doing so our life will be easier.

However the weight of responsibility lets us stand firmly in life and fulfill our existence. Frankl used the image of a Roman arch. When it is weak, architects do not keep out load from it. They decide where to locate the correct load just to keep the rocks firmly, keeping the arch in use. That is the effect of responsibility: It strengthens us.

Sometimes I accept to be responsible, but I do not know how to be responsible.
Therapists see this daily. Sometimes people want to live responsibly, but they
do not know how to do so. Today, we live in the name of "freedom," meaning:
"I only have to do whatever I want to do." We confuse the sequence of the
concepts, since "freedom" must be understood: "I want to do whatever I have
to do." It's no small difference.

Leonardo Da Vinci once said, "*Tie your wagon to a star.*" Let us suppose that
life means to carry our wagon to the top of a mountain. To carry up our "life-
wagon," loaded with all circumstances we have lived. If we try to pull it or to
push it, we run the risk of sliding down to the starting point. Sometimes we
find people who, after some failed and laborious attempts trying to climb the
mountain with their wagon, are frustrated, hurt, tired or disappointed because
they feel that they are still at the starting point. The answer is found in
Leonardo's advice: Tie your wagon to a star. This star could be a value that lets
us face the effort of living, or maybe a person to whom we offer it as a gift.
This star, in times of depression and frustration, will help us stand again, hitch
our wagon, and continue our climbing.

Now, we can understand the vertical design that Gary Price has given to
the statue. This star (a value or someone to whom we related the daily effort of
living), not only receives from us a meaningful gift, but it also promotes a
meaningful living for ourselves. This is the key to understanding responsibility. Man finds meaning offering his life to enrich others' lives, and to promote
solidarity between people, and, doing so, he enriches his own life.

In this necessary and profound dialogue between freedom and responsibility, man can find his humanity. In this dialogue between the Statue of Liberty
and the Statue of Responsibility, the whole human race will be motivated to
discover new and necessary solutions to answer the eternal search for a meaningful living for all.   ॐ

*Claudio García Pintos, Ph.D., is director of CAVEF (Cátedra Abierta Viktor Emil Frankl) Center of
Logotherapy Studies, Buenos Aires, Argentina, and author of 10 books. Email: cavef@yahoo.com or visit
www.geocities.com/cavef.*

4

Freedom and Responsibility

by Paul T. P. Wong

America is the envy of the world. What is the secret of the American dream? I propose that freedom and responsibility are the twin pillars of the good life in the United States and elsewhere.

Never in the history of humanity had so many freedoms been won for the individual in so many countries. Yet, liberty without responsibility poses the greatest threat to democracy—it can lead to self-indulgence, decadence and even anarchy.

Dr. Viktor Frankl has long contended that meaningful living is predicated on the exercise of freedom of choice and personal responsibility. To Dr. Frankl, responsibility entails responding to the demand of meaning unique in each situation.

The relationship between freedom and responsibility is complex and so much hangs in the balance. The challenge facing politicians, policy makers, and educators is: How to foster responsible, meaningful choices without imposing undue limitations on individual freedom. Any progress in addressing this question will contribute to the welfare of the individual and the society as a whole.

The real issue in life is not what happens to us, but how we choose to react; not what circumstances we are in, but how we choose to live in these circumstances. It is in choosing that we reveal our humanity or lack of it.

How liberating the gift of freedom! How sobering the awesome responsibility of freedom! Since we have the capacity and freedom to do the choosing, we are responsible for the consequences of our actions. The immutable law of action and consequence operates in the natural realm as well as in the spiritual sphere.

Accept Full Responsibility

We have the responsibility to decide how we want to live and what we want to become. Will we make something of ourselves, or will we spend the

rest of our lives as quitters, losers and whiners? Just think about all the excit-
ing choices before us:
  • Happiness is a choice
  • Health is a choice
  • Success is a choice
  • Serenity is a choice
  • Faith is a choice
  • Relationship is a choice
  • Integrity is a choice
  • Optimism is a choice

Better still, we choose not only our daily life but also our destiny. Making
responsible choices is a daily discipline. Good intention is never good enough.
We need to follow through with action.

Once we have decided on the direction of our future, we begin to do what
is necessary in order to overcome problems and achieve our goals. Be prepared to fight the uphill battle all alone. Practice tough-mindedness and the
occasional teeth-clenching determination. There can be no turning back.

Assuming responsibility can be a lonely and terrifying job. In our inner
secret chamber, we alone make the decisions. Others may point a gun to our
heads and force us to do their bidding. They may even subject us to physical
torture. But they cannot kill our spirit. Nor can they gain entry to our inner
most sanctuary. We choose; therefore, we exist.

Accountability is the only way to ensure the proper exercise of responsibility. No sooner had we thought that we could do whatever we want without
having to give account to anyone, than we begin the slippery road to perdition.
Freedom flourishes only within the boundaries of the law and constraints of
personal responsibility.

Love Our Neighbors

We are responsible not only for ourselves but also for our neighbors. Jesus
says: "Love your neighbor as yourself." When asked, "Who is my neighbor?"
Jesus tells the story of a Samaritan—one of those half-bred, despised and shun
by the Jews (Luke 10: 25-37). The implication is that the neighbor is someone
to whom we extend love and help.

Buddhism teaches that we need to have compassion towards all sentient
beings. We have the responsibility to spread the message of enlightenment and
deliver them from the sea of suffering.

All faith traditions and moral philosophies teach the importance of helping
the needed. The underlying assumption is that we are all interconnected. No
one can live independently of others. The law of cause and effect operates collectively because of our interdependence. Thus, we come full circle, back to
the first step of responsibility.

The Others are not strangers; they are Us, because we all participate in human suffering. Our civilization cannot long survive without realizing the imperative of responsibility towards others.

While advocating individual freedom, Frankl also emphasizes social responsibility. We are responsible for the disadvantaged and disfranchised. Our humanity is measured and judged by our commitment to helping those who are unable to help themselves.

The Statue of Responsibility

The Statue of Liberty is such a powerful symbol. Thousands upon thousands of "boat people" have been moved to tears as they caught the first glimpse of that magnificent Lady in New York harbor. At long last, America, land of the free!

On July 4, 1986, America celebrated the 100th birthday of Lady Liberty. With a glowing sunset in the background, President Ronald Reagan declared, "We are the keepers of the flame of liberty; we hold it high for the world to see."

How are we going to defend the flame of liberty? If the major drama in the last century was the triumph of democracy over totalitarianism, what then will be the story of the 21st century? How can we win the war against international terrorism? Is it possible that the exercise of responsible and compassionate freedom may be more powerful than military might?

One of Dr. Frankl's unfulfilled dreams is to erect a Statue of Responsibility on the West Coast of America, to remind people that liberty cannot be separated from responsibility. Freedom without responsibility is like a ship without a rudder, heading towards shipwreck.

Can you visualize the Statue of Responsibility of two intertwined hands? It symbolizes one person helping another person. This Statue is a powerful reminder of all the victims of oppressions, the dying children in AIDS-ravaged sub-Sahara Africa and all the starving people in poverty-stricken countries. They are our neighbors. They are Us.

When we learn to fully appreciate the gift of freedom, not only as an inalienable human right, but also as the innate human capacity, then we are on our way towards creating compassionate, responsible society.

Old values have been jettisoned and authority figures rejected, with nothing to replace them. The enduring themes of history have given way to the trivialities of Reality TV. Long forgotten are the true heroes who have moved the nations with their words, and changed the course of history for the better with their deeds. In their place, we have installed celebrity icons who dispense trinkets to adoring fans for millions of dollars in return.

In this epochal cultural shift, responsibility has become the first casualty. People clamor for rights without duties, benefits without contributions, and comforts without sacrifices. Politicians feed into this mentality of entitlement in order to buy votes. In the midst of this moral vacuum, a general call to responsibility seems just as good a remedy as any of the more ambitious paradigms for social change.

When one dares to choose responsibility, one needs to be prepared for the arduous journey ahead. It is never easy to live responsibly, but the alternative is much worse. Only through carrying out our responsibility toward self and others, can we find fulfillment and selfhood.

From a larger perspective, we need to embrace the heart of darkness, the unbearable burden of our history, the horrors of a million innocent deaths, the unspeakable evils of tyranny, the bottomless abyss of human suffering—the endless drumbeats of terrors and killings hammer a thousand nails into our hearts. But that is part of being human.

We need to own up what is wrong in order to fix it. It is our willingness to accept the enormity of the human problems that test our resolve and courage to move forward. But accepting our responsibility without affirmation will eventually lead to discouragement and despair. To Frankl, affirmation is a deep-seated conviction that there is something good in life that is worth fighting for, and there is positive meaning to be fulfilled. Hope springs from the affirmation of meaning and purpose.

We have the power to recreate and transform ourselves, but we need to assume full responsibility for our own future. Even when we seek help from professionals or pray to God for healing, it is still because we choose to. Yes, there are always risks involved in taking charge of our own lives, but the alternative is no life, no future. The choice is yours.

A sense of responsibility demands that we love our neighbors, even those in remote corners of the world. Only in embracing this global vision, can we save Ourselves and Others. The exercise of responsible and humanistic freedom may be our best guarantee against terrorism.

Paul T.P. Wong, Ph.D., is president, International Network on Personal Meaning; professor of psychology and business administration and chair, Division of Social Sciences and Business Administration, Tyndale University College, Toronto, Ontario. This paper was originally posted as the INPM president's column on www.meaning.ca. You are invited to visit this website.

5

Broken Windows

by Michael Levine

When is a dirty bathroom a broken window? This question could determine your success or failure. Answer that question correctly—and use that answer as a beacon—and your business could dominate its competition indefinitely. Ignore the answer, and you will condemn your business to failure in a short time.

The "broken windows" theory was first put forth by criminologists James Q. Wilson and George L. Kelling, concentrating on petty criminal acts like graffiti, purse snatching, or jay walking, and how they can lead to bigger crimes such as murder. The theory states that something as small and innocuous as a broken window sends a signal to those who pass by every day. If it is left broken, the owner of the building isn't paying attention or doesn't care. That means more serious infractions—theft, defacement, violent crime—might be condoned in this area as well. At best, it signals that no one is watching.

If a window in a building is broken and left unrepaired, all other windows will soon be broken because the perception that the broken window invites is that the owner of this building and the people of the community around it don't care if this window is broken: They have given up; anarchy reigns here. Do as you will, because nobody cares.

Broken Windows in Business

That same theory applies to the world of business. If the restroom at your business is out of toilet paper, it signals that management isn't paying attention to the needs of its people. Certainly, the perceptions of consumers are a vital part of every business, and if a retailer, service provider, or corporation is sending out signals that its approach is lackadaisical, its methods halfhearted, and its execution indifferent, the business in question could suffer severe—and in some cases, irreparable—losses.

When broken windows in business are ignored, fatal consequences can result. Small things make a huge difference. A messy reception area might lead customers to believe that the company as a whole doesn't care about cleanliness or quality. We all bear some responsibility to stand up for what we want and have every right to expect from a company to which we give our hard-earned money.

In a capitalist society, we can assume that a company that wants to succeed will do its best to fulfill the desires of its consuming public. If the company sees sales slipping but doesn't have data from consumers as to what made them decrease their spending, the company will not know what to fix.

Still, businesses that don't notice and repair their broken windows should not simply be forgiven because their consumers don't make a fuss. Leaders are responsible to tend their own house—and the time to repair broken windows is the minute they occur.

Prevent Broken Windows

It's better, however, to prevent broken windows to begin with, since small things can snowball into large problems. A smart business owner prevents them at—or before—the first sign of trouble.

In a business, the broken windows can be literal or metaphorical. Sometimes a broken window really is a broken window, and a new pane of glass needs to be installed quickly. However, most of the time, broken windows are the little details, the tiny flaws, the overlooked minutiae that signal much larger problems either already in place or about to become reality.

Companies that fail to notice and repair their broken windows suffer greatly. Those that make it a priority to attend to every *potentially* broken window win.

People want to feel that the businesses that they work for and those they buy from *care* about what they want. Consumers are looking for businesses that anticipate and fulfill their needs and do so in a way that makes it clear the business understands the consumers' needs or wants and is doing its best to see them satisfied.

Broken windows indicate to the consumer that the business doesn't care—either that it is so poorly run it can't possibly keep up with its obligations, or that it has become so oversized and arrogant that it no longer cares about its core consumer. Either of these impressions can be deadly to a business.

Tiny details—the smaller, the more important—can make a big difference in success or failure. A broken window can be a sloppy counter, poorly located sale item, randomly organized menu, or an employee with a bad attitude. It can be physical, like a flaking paint job, or symbolic, like a policy that requires consumers to pay for customer service.

Broken windows are everywhere, except at the best businesses. I invite you to take the *Broken Windows for Business Pledge*. It's a serious statement outlining the tenets of the broken windows for business theory.

The Pledge

I hereby pledge to do the following:

• I will pay attention to every detail of my business, especially those that seem insignificant.

• I will correct any broken windows I find in my business, and I will do so immediately, with no hesitation.

• I will screen, hire, train, and supervise my employees to notice and correct broken windows in the least amount of time possible.

• I will treat each customer like the only customer my business has. I will be on constant vigil for signs of Broken Windows hubris and never assume my business is invulnerable.

• I will mystery shop my own business to discover broken windows I hadn't noticed before.

• I will make sure every customer who encounters my business is met with courtesy, efficiency, and a smile.

• I will exceed my customers' expectations.

• I will be sure always to make a positive first impression and will assume that every impression is a first impression.

• I will make sure that my online and telephone customer service representatives do everything possible to solve a customer's problem perfectly the first time.

• I will be obsessive and compulsive when it comes to my business.

If you live up to the promises in the pledge and make them second nature, you will discover your business—and maybe your life—running more smoothly and efficiently than ever before. But no matter what, I can definitely guarantee one thing: You will never look at a broken window—or an unbroken one—the same way again.

Michael Levine is the founder of Levine Communications Office and author of Broken Windows, Broken Business: How the Smallest Remedies Reap the Biggest Rewards, *from which this article has been adapted. Visit www.LCOonline.com.*

6

American Anagram

by Tom Schaff

The need for the Statue of Responsibility monument is a lot like an anagram: It's self-evident when you have the answer but hardly obvious before you see it.

Anagrams are made by rearranging the letters of a phrase to form another phrase. Take "Attaineth its cause, Freedom" for example. You could work on this for weeks before you found out that these 24 letters spell out a most beautiful and awe-inspiring phrase, "The United States of America." Just because most people can't figure out the anagram, doesn't mean its answer isn't necessary. Imagine what our lives would have been like had the good old USA and our brand of Freedom never existed! But what wasn't obvious was self-evident, at least to one group of patriots. Collectively, their insight led to foresight, realized through personal sacrifices that created a way of life never known in the history of mankind.

Maybe you'll do better with the anagram, "Built to Stay Free." If the answer isn't immediately obvious to you, you're not alone. Rearrange the letters and eventually you'll see the solution is "Statue of Liberty," but it wasn't always quite that clear. Especially to American citizens in 1884.

Finished and waiting in France for America to raise the money for its pedestal, the 100th birthday gift from our allies was a symbol for all American people. But the youthful nation didn't see the need. They thought it was a lighthouse for New York City until Joseph Pulitzer decided to do something about it. As publisher of *World* newspaper, he convinced all Americans, rich and poor, that they had a responsibility to make donations, no matter how small. Today, refurbished under the leadership of Lee Iacocca, it stands among the seven wonders of the modern world, the world's unequivocal symbol for freedom.

At first glance, the Statue of Liberty appears to be enough for us. Her torch serves as our beacon of democracy to the seven continents represented by her spiked crown. Her tablet reminds us of the good fortune this democracy has enjoyed since July 4, 1776. It isn't yet obvious that something is missing. Yet the signs are all about us. Something is amiss in America.

Have you read the papers? Our national debt continues to increase, while literacy plummets. Voting, once considered a right, is often considered a hassle. Obesity skyrockets as the number of children with a father's name on the birth certificate decreases exponentially. Don't even get me started on the environment, Rwanda or the AIDS epidemic in Africa.

We've been taught to revere liberty—and well we should. Yet perhaps there are greater questions than those that reveal our entitlements. H.L. Mencken, a cynical man of letters from our past, commented, "Most people want security in this world, not liberty."

Maybe it's time for our nation to enter a new exploration of questions, including but not limited to: Can our way of life continue to sustain itself? Where do our rights intersect with our obligations? What is the continuing price of liberty without regard to responsibility? The answers to these vexing questions are found simply in my submissions to the Anagram Hall of Fame, "Points at issue of liberty" or "So built to inspire safety." The answer to both of course is, "Statue of Responsibility"

"Points at issue of Liberty" reminds us true freedom has, is and will always require responsibility. Freedom hasn't, isn't and never will be free. We have obligations and duties that have been neglected far too long. The pendulum has gone too far and needs to sway back. More than ever, America is threatened by enemies the like we have never seen. The enemies are ourselves. Without a significant increase in responsibility coast to coast, what we have taken for granted for some time will one day be uncertain. Clearly, it is evident that it's time to create a pedestal for responsibility.

"So built to inspire safety" is a reminder that our nation needs a new bookend monument to the Statue of Liberty. "Inspire" means "to breathe life." "Safety" is the state of being safe, the condition of being protected against physical, social, spiritual, financial, political, emotional, occupational, psychological or other types or consequences of failure, damage, error, accident, harm or any other event which could be considered not desirable. Even though responsibility has most often been associated with duty and obligation, a new inspirational Statue of Responsibility will breathe life into the concept and help to transform our nation's thinking to see the opportunity it truly represents. As we progressively embrace responsibility, our influence will go up in all areas of life and among all nations, giving us choices currently unavailable, insuring our vitality and sustainability.

Without a Statue of Responsibility, our citizens risk a spiral downward, threatening our refuge, security and shelter. Unmitigated, we become a nation at risk of the most dangerous of dangers—a nation that becomes complacent, unaware that the seeds of debacle are sowed and growing under our very eyes.

While not obvious, it's evident that things can't continue the way they are.

And thanks to the Statue of Responsibility monument, they won't. Monuments constantly remind us of a higher ideal, a higher mission for our lives, and a grander purpose for living. In a busy world cluttered with multiple messages, monuments can give us pause. Their art encourages us to ponder finer thoughts. Their message invites us to reflect upon noble ideals.

Monuments can steer us to truth. The Statue of Liberty has steered generations towards the truths of liberty and rights, truths that help us stay free. The Statue of Responsibility will steer generations towards the truth of responsibleness that is inherent with rights, inspiring our safety from ourselves. Two grand monuments to the two grand principles of freedom, liberty and responsibility will soon border our country on the east and on the west. The need for the monuments isn't any more obvious than their anagrams nor any less self-evident of an opportunity when their truth is revealed.

To the degree we embrace this opportunity, we protect and preserve the tremendous democracy we have inherited. Safety makes us invulnerable and secure, providing shelter and refuge to those willing to accept responsibility for safeguarding freedom.

Responsibility is like an umbrella. In times of storm, it protects us from harms way, sheltering us from the cold, cruel forces that threaten our well-being. In good times, umbrellas discreetly spare us from the overdose of extreme doses of things that serve us quite nicely in moderation. As we navigate the world of change while living in the land of prosperity, responsibility is indeed our opportunity.

Freedom isn't free and the Statue of Responsibility won't be either. In a nation that routinely builds corporate sports arenas for numbers now exceeding a billion dollars, it's time to ante up a pittance for the life of privilege we enjoy. Collectively, it's time to join hands and raise the $300 million required to build the Statue of Responsibility. We must do this immediately.

My final anagram, derived from "The United States of America," summarizes my thoughts about the Statue of Responsibility and has much in common with the way this article started. The anagram, "The Dream: Fine Cause, Toast It!" isn't any more obvious than the others. The need for your support for the dream and promise of the Statue of Responsibility is self-evident in retrospect. Your donations, support, volunteer hours and prayers for this cause will help protect something we can all toast, *"The United States of America!"*

Tom Schaff is a sales trainer, speaker and consultant who serves on the board of the Statue of Responsibility Foundation and as its corporate giving director. The reflection of The Gateway Arch in his hometown, St Louis, Missouri, reminds him why monuments are important. Visit his blog at www.responsibility911.com. Email tschaff@expgrowth.com.

7

Responsibility Is a Choice

by Bob Proctor

Responsibility is a choice. I often refer to it as being the key to freedom. Your future can be everything you have ever dreamed about—and then some. You have the talent and tools to experience one beautiful day after another. I believe that is what the Architect of the Universe had in mind for you when you were created. If not, you would have never been endowed with such awesome powers.

My good friend and mentor, Val Van De Wall, wrote, "When people take responsibility for their life and the results they obtain, they will cease to blame others as the cause of their results. Since you can't change other people, blame is inappropriate. Blaming others causes a person to remain bound in a prison of their own making. When you take responsibility, blame is eliminated and you are free to grow."

Those who haven't taken responsibility for their results and their life often find themselves in a mental prison. In many ways, a mental prison is a much worse place to live than a federal prison or penitentiary. Mental torment can destroy everything that is necessary for a meaningful life: Self image, self respect, relationships and many other attributes. It will even cause a person's physical health to deteriorate.

Responsibility opens the door and permits you to walk into freedom. If you find yourself confined to such a mental state, understand there is a way out. Escape is encouraged and possible.

The master key that fits the lock is clearly marked and is within everyone's reach. It is responsibility. The people we respect the most are those who accept responsibility for every aspect of their lives. These individuals rarely duck responsibility by blaming someone else. When faced with an unfavorable situation, they are usually aware they have attracted the negative circumstance and know everything happens for a reason. They merely learn their lesson and keep reaching out, above and beyond to the new frontier, taking responsibility for whatever happens, every step of the way.

When people refuse to accept responsibility for their life, they reject their uniqueness and they turn all of their special powers over to other people, situations, or circumstances. They are then no longer in control of their future. They hope something good will happen, but because of past experiences they likely expect something they do not want to happen. When you accept responsibility for your life and for the results that you alone determine, you will develop confidence that your dreams can be realized and your plans can be carried out.

Awareness of this magnificent truth is one of the greatest, if not *the* greatest thing that can happen in your life. It's Aladdin's lamp, a magic wand, and the tooth fairy all wrapped up in one.

Dr. Rollo May, a distinguished psychiatrist, once wrote, "The opposite of courage in our society is not cowardice, it is conformity." It requires great courage to take responsibility for your life. It's so much easier to blame someone else or something outside of you.

George Bernard Shaw said, "People are always blaming their circumstances for what they are. I don't believe in circumstances. The people who get on in this world are the people who get up and look for the circumstances they want, and, if they can't find them, they make them." I believe Shaw was right. In my opinion, those who win big in life take responsibility and create their own destiny. Freedom brings with it certain responsibility, and responsibility brings with it certain freedom.

There is a vast difference between being responsible "for" and being responsible "to." For some, this concept may be life-altering, and it has the power to free you of unnecessary mental weight that you may carry around with you. This concept has been misunderstood by many people and has single-handedly ruined many lives. Ignorance of this principle will cause a person to experience the destructive emotions of anger, guilt, and resentment. It seems so simple, but don't let its apparent simplicity fool you.

It's common to hear parents blame themselves and assume responsibility for something that has happened to their child, and the child might be 40 years old! "If only we ..." Or, "I should have ..." Often we inappropriately assume responsibility for something, when in fact our real duty to the person may have ended 20 years ago. Unfortunately, many people carry that baggage around with them for life, never realizing they have a choice.

The correct interpretation of this is: You are responsible *for* your feelings and your results—not another person's. You may be responsible *to* another person for one thing or another, but not *for* another person. The exception, of course, is when you choose to take on the responsibility of raising children until they reach the age of maturity. In that case, you are both responsible *to* and *for* them, until they become responsible for themselves.

At times, it might be appealing to contemplate having another person take on our responsibilities for us. We could even trick ourselves into believing that by doing this, we would be more free to play, have fun and do the things we wanted. Without serious thought, it might never enter our mind that exactly the opposite would happen.

When you permit others to take on your responsibilities, you become dependent on them. They become the giver and you become the receiver. Your well-being is dependent upon their generosity. Hopefully, at some point, it becomes clear that this behavior only leads to a life of lack, limitation, resentment, and confusion on the parts of both the giver and the receiver.

I've never witnessed anything positive that has come from the misuse of responsibility. When you take on the responsibility for another person's feelings, results, or actions, you destroy their self-reliance and self-respect.

You are responsible for all of the results in your life. You are responsible for your happiness. You are responsible for your health. You are responsible for your wealth. You are responsible for your emotional state.

Regardless of what has happened in the past, the future lies ahead with an open slate, waiting for you to take control and create a wonderful life for yourself.

Winston Churchill, who certainly knew something about responsibility, said, "Responsibility is the price of greatness."

Here's a marvelous affirmation that you can verbalize every night before you go to sleep and every morning as you step out of bed:

I am responsible for my life . . . for my feelings . . . for my personal growth . . . and for every result I get.

Bob Proctor is chairman of LifeSuccess Productions. Visit www.BobProctor.com.

8

Who Is Responsible for Good Work?

by Howard Gardner

The great psychiatrist Viktor Frankl, who escaped the death camps of World War II and became a leading thinker of the 20th century, believed that responsibility must go hand in hand with liberty. He had a vision that one day a large statue would greet visitors, including immigrants, to the western shores of America. That statue would remind us of the responsibilities that all human beings should assume by virtue of their being human.

Efforts to construct such a statue are under way, and perhaps by the time you read these words, the Statue of Responsibility will already be in place. Meanwhile, such a monument—envisaged to be a 330-foot structure, with the hand of liberty clasping the hand of responsibility—serves as a virtual icon for the topic of this book.

Most of us think in terms of our *rights* of life, liberty, and the pursuit of happiness and a comfortable life. Yet, we all have certain responsibilities. We're expected to assume responsibility for our health and welfare; for those who depend on us—spouses, offspring, and as they age, grandparents and parents; for those at our workplace, profession, neighborhood, community, and society. No wonder we are more comfortable with rights: The areas for which we could assume responsibility threaten to overwhelm us.

Most of us spend at least half of our waking hours at work. For many of us, work entails burdens; for a fortunate few, work is a privilege, garlanded with rewards. This is especially true for professionals—individuals who are accorded status, prestige, and a comfortable livelihood, in return for which we are expected to offer high-level services and clear-minded judgment. Today, issues of responsibility have taken on new urgency. Across the professions, examples abound of work that is clearly irresponsible.

Four Key Concepts

I comment on four key concepts:

1. Work. For most of history, we've worked long hours so that we could eat, have shelter, survive, be secure, and protect our families. Most laborers have little time for leisure. Today we see an increasing division of labor and hierarchization and specialization of work. Those in power have latitude in how they approach their work and allocate time. Those with special knowledge form prestigious professions.

2. Responsibility. To have an open and fair society, we must be prepared to carry out crucial actions: We must act toward others in the way in which we would want all others to behave, and avoid other actions—however tempting. The classical view of politics entails a commitment to act as a responsible citizen, and the classical view of a profession entails a commitment to act as a responsible worker.

3. Work and responsibility. A notion that marks the intersection of work and responsibility is that of *vocation* or *calling*. These words imply that the work we carry out is work that we have been "called" to execute carefully and responsibly. When work is considered "just a job," the responsibility is circumscribed—we carry out the letter of our job description, nothing more. We get paid for what we do, as long as we do it. And when a better opportunity arises, or when our organization decides that our services are no longer needed, we move on. Today, life centers around work we want to do, like to do, and feel needs to be done well. Our work needs to be "good."

4. Good work. Good work is of excellent technical quality, ethically pursued, socially responsible, engaging, and enjoyable. Of course, such work is not easily achieved. Not all work is executed at a level of excellence, carried out ethically, and engages the passions of the worker. Still, we strive to become good workers and to encourage good work. A nagging question arises: How do we discourage or prevent work that does not meet these criteria of good work? Who is responsible for good work?

The Good Work Model

Good work entails four elements:

1. The individual worker. Relevant here are the worker's belief systems, motivation for doing good work, and personality, temperament, and character. These determine whether the person will hold to high standards or cut corners, "go along," or engage in compromised or irresponsible work.

2. The domain of work. All professions and most other lines of work have a set of core values and beliefs that are known to workers and carry a certain degree of force. For example, for more than 2,000 years physicians have tried to adhere to the core commitments of the Hippocratic Oath.

3. The field forces that operate on the domain. Mediating the core values are social entities: Gatekeepers who determine entry, individuals who provide or deny opportunities or prizes, and evaluators who assess the merit of the work. Think of the field as the individuals and institutions that hold power and make decisions. The sum of the domains (all professions, arts, crafts, and disciplines) constitutes the culture; the sum of the field entities constitutes the society.

4. The larger social reward system. Individuals, domains, and fields are embedded in the society and economy. This broader society embraces various rewards and sanctions, and these exert influence over and above the signals that permeate a domain or profession.

Good work is most likely to emerge when these four elements are aligned. This does not guarantee good work, but when workers' beliefs and values coincide with those of the domain, field, and society, they are free to work in ways that make sense to them.

Each individual must decide whether to behave in a professional manner. Many "professionals" aggrandize themselves, cut corners, and benefit parasitically from colleagues. And many humble tradesmen behave in ways that are highly professional. In standard professions, explicit responsibilities have emerged; professionals are expected to know these and to act in accordance with them. In less professional work, the burden of delineating these responsibilities falls more on the individual practitioner.

Values, Ethics, Morality

Good workers honor the core values of their profession rather than succumb to pressures of their supervisors or seductive lures of the marketplace. We withhold the epithet "good worker" from those who use their positions to enhance their pocketbook, achieve credit unfairly, or abuse others.

Not all ethical issues and judgments of quality are clear cut—some involve right versus right or shades of gray: Is it better for a physician to serve a large population or initiate a concierge practice, in which enrolled patients are well served but only those with the means to pay for it are beneficiaries? Should the lawyer give her all for a client, no matter how nefarious the client, or draw on a broader sense of justice?

Recognizing the complexity of ethics is not the same as embracing relativism. That the answer is not always clear or that judgments may be controversial is scarcely license for "anything goes." In most cases, one path is superior to another: Bribery may be part of doing business somewhere, but few would defend a system of bribery as superior to one that bans or punishes bribery.

In ethical work, workers have a set of values that draw on the enduring values of the domain. They operate according to those values, even when these clash with immediate self-interest. They recognize issues of moral complexity, wrestle with them, seek advice and guidance, reflect on what goes right, and seek to right the course. They take the challenges of responsibility seriously and seek to behave in as responsible a way as possible.

Still, we regularly encounter examples of irresponsibility. Clearly we find it too easy to shirk responsibility and behave in ways that may be good for us, but not healthy for society. Matters conspire to undermine responsibility. We are not born moral or ethical—these virtues need to be nurtured, often against the odds. Those who start on the right track can deviate. Pressures and seductions are powerful. The material rewards for irresponsibility sometimes dwarf the plaudits for responsibility. Intrinsic motivation becomes essential in a milieu where ambient signals diminish ethical sense.

The sense of responsibility of those who do an exemplary job extends to other individuals, to the core values of their domain, to the benefit of society. The decision to enter a caring profession, go against the odds, persevere, and navigate uncharted domains characterize individuals who embrace responsibility, sometimes to the point of exhaustion, and model it for others.

Professionals are buffeted by powerful market forces. The crucial variable is the extent to which people in that vocation take on the responsibilities they deem important, whether or not support is available from others or from the values of the domain.

Here are six takeaways: 1) Know the mission of your occupation and your role in it; 2) relate your beliefs and goals to your occupation and roles; 3) work with individuals and institutions that take responsibility seriously; 4) set priorities, be alert to limits and boundaries, and balance responsibilities; 5) broaden your sphere of responsibility in your profession or community; and 6) support youth, the future good workers.

Most people have not internalized the need to act responsibly. Leaders need to portray what it means to be responsible, to model responsibility, and to pass on a sense of responsibility to future stewards of the workplace.

Howard Earl Gardner is the Hobbs professor of cognition and education, Harvard GSE, and author of Five Minths for the Future. *Call 617-496-4929 or visit www.howardgardner.com.*

9

100% Responsibility

by Taylor Hartman

When was the last time you accepted full responsibility for a problem? When was the last time you heard anyone say, "That's completely my fault. I am *100 percent responsible* for what happened and will do whatever is necessary to make it right!"

We have created a society of victims with a cultural backdrop that actually promotes *blame, denial* and *rationalization* rather than responsibility and ownership. Today, if you smoke three packs of cigarettes a day for 40 years and die of lung cancer, your family blames the tobacco company. If your child misbehaves in school, you give him the label ADHD and medicate him. If your neighbor crashes into a tree while driving home after too many drinks at the bar, he blames the bartender.

When something goes wrong, it is rare that someone steps forward to take ownership for creating the problem. Even more rare is the person who takes 100 percent responsibility for creating the problem and accepts ownership for providing a solution. Those individuals and companies that pay their dues by exposing their vulnerability (*"It was my fault!"*) and accept ownership for resolving the problem (*"How can I make it right with you?"*) earn the privilege to become members of the *100 % Responsibility Club*. This club is highly exclusive and holds its members in strict adherence to principles that far exceed social expectations.

The State of What Is

Unfortunately many of us have been raised in a victim society. We have been taught by countless role models that our problems are not our own doing and that we, in fact, have been wronged. For many reasons—misunderstood, abandoned, and neglected—we have spent more energy seeking strategies for getting off the hook rather than facing the music when we make mistakes.

Think President Bill Clinton and Monica Lewinsky, most partners during divorce proceedings, driving while under the influence, Enron, public education, major airlines. We have learned our lessons well. We excuse and devalue ourselves (think many sports figures, politicians, and celebrities) rather than value ourselves by stepping up to our problems and finding viable solutions. Denying ownership weakens us until we no longer have the strength to even identify the truth, let alone face it.

We've become so accustomed to fear-based thinking that it now serves as our native tongue. Do these excuses sound familiar?

Victim: "*I forgot.*"

100% Responsibility: "*Why didn't you write it down?*"

Victim: "*I didn't have a pen;*" or "*I did write it down, but it didn't do me any good because I threw the paper away;*" or "*You can't seriously expect me to remember the details when I've got so much to do.*"

100% Responsibility: "*So, you didn't care enough about me to keep your promise. And based on your current excuse I can't count on you to care about me to keep your future promises either. You care more about your self than others.*"

Or how about this scenario?

Victim: "*It's not really anyone's fault!*"

100% Responsibility: "*How convenient. Now neither of us are accountable for what happened, and we have no responsibility for resolving the problem, and we're noble because we are playing nice and letting each other off the hook.*"

Victim: "*Well, it's just one of those things that happens, you know . . .*"

100% Responsibility: "*No, I don't know how, nor do I want to be in a relationship where things just happen without genuine cause or reasonable consequence.*"

People get in their cars late for a meeting, jump on the freeway and call ahead on their cell phone indicating they will be late as if this excuses them for leaving late. They left their office late, but somehow calling from a cell phone on the freeway excuses that!

Our current culture promotes *blame,* *denial* and *rationalization* as our native tongue. Far more people speak, understand and accept this way of thinking than 100 percent responsibility. We have succumbed to and accept excuse-making over keeping our promises. Accepting this brutal truth can move us to take the necessary steps in overcoming it. Joining the *100% Responsibility Club* is a great start.

Membership Requirements

Membership in the Club requires a commitment to getting the desired results regardless of the consequence. It requires performance over excuses— empowerment to resolve problems over justification for mistakes.

You must first be willing to be wrong and admit it when you are wrong to others. Second, you must be willing to make right whatever you did wrong.

Membership dues in the *100 % Responsibility Club* are tough to pay because we've spent a lifetime convincing ourselves that being right was more important than performance and achieving the desired results. Whatever relationship you want, you can have, if you will take 100 percent responsibility for getting it. You cannot, will not, must not, let any excuses, blame, or justification exist for explaining it away. Being right is far less important than building legitimate relationships—both personally and professionally. A lifetime of "being right" produces weak people and limited transactions. A lifetime of taking 100 percent responsibility for building legitimate relationships makes strong leaders.

Club Motto

Until you can recite the Club Motto with conviction, you can't be in the club. Club members understand and accept this motto without excuse or exception.

"I am 100 percent responsible for every relationship in my life. I will do whatever is necessary to achieve the desired results. This is not a 50-50 proposition. It is not 100-100, both equally and fully responsible in order for the relationship to work. I am 100 percent responsible for creating what I get. And I get exactly what I deserve."

Membership Rewards

By taking 100 percent responsibility for every relationship, we expand our options. We increase our control over ourselves and all factors that have an impact on the relationship. Take anything less than 100 percent and we limit our options to creating high performance and getting the desired results. Wouldn't you rather be in charge of your destiny than have someone else control your life? Value yourself enough to be wrong. Respect yourself enough to own the problem. Trust yourself enough to seek proactive resolutions for solving problems and building legitimate relationships.

Being 100 percent responsible frees you to act, create solutions, and win! As long as you give any percentage of responsibility away to someone else, they can hold you hostage. If they don't behave as you expect them to, they own you. A long time ago, someone probably lied to you and suggested that the best way to navigate life was to assume as little responsibility as possible. Know that they did you a huge disservice. Now is the time for you to become 100 percent responsible for yourself and your relationships. Step up and seek 100 percent responsibility as a way of life—the way you choose to live!

Taylor Hartman, Ph.D., is a business consultant, CEO of Hartman Communications, and author of The Color Code: A New Way to See Yourself, Your Relationships and Life. *Visit www.colorcode.com.*

10

The End of Excuses

by Kate Ludeman and Eddie Erlandson

When things are sailing along smoothly, we rarely ask, "Who's account-able for this?" In most companies, accountability means to "account for" what I have done in the past, instead of defining what I will do now and in the future. Business today demands a new kind of proactive accountability that allows people to influence events before they happen, rather than create a defense after the situation cannot be altered.

Have you ever made these excuses? "I didn't know you needed it right away." "It's not my job." "They wouldn't listen to me." Somehow, we have caused people to feel more responsible for explaining their results than for achieving them. When things go wrong, we hear excuses offered in injured tones implicating other people, events and external obstacles. Many people think an adequate explanation can excuse a poor result. We often operate by the maxim: Every problem has a scapegoat—convincingly point a finger and you're off the hook. It seems as if we don't have to keep our promises—as long as we provide a good reason for falling short of what we said we would do.

It spells disaster for our companies when we become an "I didn't mean to" culture, squeaking by on "Where can I pin the blame?" It's time for every employee and manager to step out of blame into accountability. Here's a sim-ple formula to transform your life: Solid Agreements + 100 Percent Responsibility = Accountability. This means the end of excuses.

Four Ways to Shift into Accountability

1. Stop blaming and hold others accountable only after you first own your part of the problem. When you complain and explain, you pretend you're not responsible for your failure and they do nothing to change the reality—in fact, you contribute to poor results. Explanations mean you're dead in the corporate water. Conversely, telling ourselves and others the impeccable truth about how we get in our own way, and then clearing the path, is the only route to success.

We witnessed a dazzling example of accountability in action when we coached the executive team at the Defense Logistics Agency (DLA), an organization which supplies everything from food to fuel for the armed services. When Vice Admiral Keith Lippert took over as director in 2001, DLA was a loose collection of fiefdoms with infighting and blame passing between headquarters and business units.

At the beginning of the first executive offsite, we asked participants to write down issues that concerned or irritated them about their teammates, all of whom were present in the room. Their list encompassed pet peeves and grudges they'd held for 15 years or longer, and even derogatory nicknames they'd made up on the sly. Then we had people explore how they contributed to the very problems that led to their irritation. After gaining insight into their contributions to the problems, we had them share their accountability discoveries in one-on-one conversations. We gave them two hours to walk around the room and discuss their biggest issues with people and own their contribution. Some revealed anger towards people who'd they perceived had broken agreements, and then they owned up to how their own communications had led to the breakdown. Others admitted frustration with how decisions had been made, and their own reluctance to speak frankly when they had the chance.

The combination of accountability and transparency brought observable lightness and warmth to people's faces. This process helped the team take a giant step forward in eliminating blame, denial, and withholding, and also freed up enormous energy for creative problem solving. Over the next few years, they banded together to transform the agency. When Hurricane Katrina hit, DLA's new efficiencies and speed allowed them to deliver $309 million in supplies, including 58 million meals, 4.5 million gallons of fuel, and $7.5 million in medical supplies. Today, the agency is viewed as so cost effective and customer oriented that the 2005 Base Realignment and Closure Commission significantly broadened the agency's scope, at the very time that similar organizations are being significantly reduced in size.

2. Invoke the Rule of Three. In our coaching, we find the Rule of Three useful when monitoring a person's commitment to responsibility. For example, if someone in the group interrupts and talks over me once, I'm not responsible. But if the same person does it three times, or if three different people interrupt me, it's wise to wonder what I can do to change it. If someone gets irritated with you once, it's their problem. By the third time, *you* are also responsible for taking corrective action. If someone doesn't keep a commitment with you, they're 100 percent responsible the first time. If someone in the group discards or discounts your intuition once, they're 100 percent responsible. By the third time, they're 100 percent responsible, and so are you—for consistently producing that result in your life. Unless we use the Rule of Three, most of us believe our problems come from "out there." This attitude guarantees that problems don't get corrected. As long as someone doesn't address her part of an issue, the situation or problem will return again and again.

3. Notice the gap between what's wanted and what's created—the commitments and the deliverables. Winners are not whiners. They're willing to look squarely at the gaps they've created, invite feedback, and shift into curiosity about what they can do to close the breach. Here are some questions that help narrow these gaps and invite accountability: What is it about my attitude or behavior that keeps this going? Do I have a hidden, unexamined personal agenda? Is there anything I'd like to communicate but haven't? Have I broken or missed any agreements?

4. Make and keep solid agreements. Agreements range from the profound (the merger of two behemoths) to the mundane (turning in expense reports on time), and behind every accountability lapse is a broken agreement. When you break an agreement, face it head-on. Take responsibility. Let go of excuses and ask yourself, "In what ways am I responsible for what occurred?"

People frequently go first to the fact that they have too much to do, got over-committed, or said they would do something they didn't have the time or resources to do. But usually there's more significant learning behind this. It's more likely that you don't keep agreements because you agreed to do something you really didn't want to do just to get the person off your back.

Only make agreements with which you feel a strong alignment. Put all major agreements and all controversial ones in writing and scrupulously keep them. Recognize when agreements aren't working and renegotiate them before they "default."

Here are four lessons for making sold agreements: First, only make agreements you feel completely aligned with and committed to. Second, when you feel you have no choice about an agreement, remind yourself that honesty and directness are *always* choices. Share your feelings and speak candidly about your own internal experience without blaming or complaining. Third, keep your agreements. Fourth, the moment you see the need for a change, let those who will be affected know and renegotiate the agreement.

As you work with the new accountability, you'll no longer make excuses or blame others. Instead, you'll ask how you can be more, better, faster, smarter—and then you'll make it happen. You won't prepare defenses when feedback is offered. Instead, you'll move powerfully and joyfully upward. And, you'll make no excuses—you'll be too busy reaching the top rung.

Kate Ludeman, Ph.D., and Eddie Erlandson, MD, are authors of Radical Change, Radical Results *and* Alpha Male Syndrome. *They have coached more than 1,000 senior executives; their company, Worth Ethic Corporation, is based in Austin, Texas. Call 512-493-2300 or visit www.worthethic.com.*

11

God Has a Plan for You

by Desmond Tutu

You would not be normal if you were not depressed by all the news reports that we get today—news of war, conflict, violence, poverty, and horrendous diseases. When we look at the state of the world sometimes we wonder whether God had any plan at all. You may wonder, couldn't God have organized this slightly better?

It almost seems as if human existence is just meaningless gibberish. But is that in fact the whole picture? Haven't we in our time seen the Berlin Wall collapse? The shackles of Apartheid in South Africa fall? That remarkable spectacle of Nelson Mandela emerging from prison? Haven't we seen a small, little woman dispense compassion and caring and love for derelicts in Calcutta? And didn't that somehow make you feel exhilarated?

I used to go to university campuses and college campuses and meet up with students who ought to be worried about grades and degrees of that sort. No, they were worrying about people 10,000 miles away.

Our lives are not atomistic. We are connected with those who have gone before, as we will be connected with those who come after.

This is God's world, and God is in charge. In the darkest moments of our struggle against Apartheid, we sought to uphold the morale of our people. We sought to keep the light of hope burning by telling them, "Hey the perpetrators of injustice, however powerful they be, have already lost." And we would say to them, this is God's world. God is in charge. Of course there were many, many moments we wish we could whisper in God's ear, "God, for goodness sake, we know you are in charge. Why don't you make it slightly more obvious?" And then, Apartheid collapsed, and freedom arose as a phoenix from the ashes.

The upholders of Apartheid never in their wildest dreams imagined that they would ever lose power. They thought that God was a kind of accident that happens to somebody else, never to themselves, and they strutted the world stage. They never thought that this is a moral universe, and because it is a moral universe, right and wrong matter. The demise of Apartheid, the collapse of communism, and all of that ugliness—that is proof positive of the fact that this is, in fact, a moral universe. That even an injustice can never have the last word.

You and I are rightly appalled when we hear, or read, of this or that other awful occurrence. When something like the outrage in Madrid happens. When you get the things in Baghdad. When you hear of the molestation of a child. You are quite rightly outraged. I have not, as yet, ever heard anyone stand up and blatantly announce, "I am a child molester." "I am an abuser of women." Even the worst possible dictator will never say, "I violate human rights." None of them ever says that. Why are we appalled when something awful happens? Because we acknowledge that evil is not the norm. Injustice is not the norm. Poverty is not the norm. War is not the norm. It is one of the most almost incontrovertible pieces of evidence . . . that those are the aberrations.

The norm is goodness, compassion, and gentleness, because that is what we are made for. Isn't that fantastic? When you have done something gratuitously good, when you have been nice to someone when you needn't have been, you have a wonderful glow inside of you.

When you have done something lousy, your body tells you. You feel it in your stomach and the anger and resentment affect you. Your blood pressure goes up because our nature is in fact to be good. We are fundamentally good.

Isn't it extraordinary that people we hold in high regard are not aggressively macho? You could say a lot of things about Mother Teresa. Macho is not one of them. She was minute like salt. You could put her in your back pocket more or less and forget about her. But, you can't, you couldn't, because she seemed to have an aura and charisma, because she was good.

Who is the most admired state person in the world today? It is not someone heading a country that is militarily powerful or economically prosperous. Almost without any doubt Nelson Mandela is regarded everywhere as a remarkable human being. He was a president of a country that even in my wildest moments of patriotism, I couldn't say was anything more than just very small—militarily, economically. And yet, in the presence of this shuffling old man, people's knees buckled, because they knew they were in the presence of an extraordinary human being.

When the world expected that after 27 years of incarceration he would emerge consumed by bitterness, resentment, and anger, he awed the world by an exhibition of quite extraordinary magnanimity. He invited his white jailor to his presidential inauguration. "Come as a VIP guest to my inauguration," he said. Throughout his time as president and since, he has always been an icon of what most of us would like to be. He has been someone who has said, "We will walk the path not of retribution or revenge but the path of reconciliation and forgiveness." (Mohandas Ghandi)

You are fundamentally good. God thinks so. He has the highest regard for you. To God, you are special, with a specialness that is not replicated. God loves you as if you were the only person on earth. Your name is engraved on the palms of God's hands. You don't have to earn God's love for you. He loved you even before you were. In the Bible, He told Jeremiah the prophet, "Long before I formed you in the womb, I knew you." From all eternity, Jeremiah was part of His divine plan.

The same goes for you. From all eternity, you have been part of God's plan. You aren't an afterthought, and God gives up on no one.

God's best collaborators dream that it is possible for this world to become a better world. When God sees the kind of things we do to one another—when He sees the Holocaust, genocide in Rwanda, Apartheid, and racism—God weeps. But when God sees you go out to poverty stricken places, where you don't get any publicity, building schools, clinics, and serving others, He smiles. Remember, God has no one, except you.

Archbishop Desmond Tutu is a human rights activist and a Nobel Peace Prize winner for his work against Apartheid in South Africa. This article is adapted from his speech at American University.

12

You Needn't Be Superman

by Christopher Reeve

All of us have different strengths and insecurities. Truly courageous people (leaders) put aside their doubts and fears and say, "follow me."

Even though I had once played the movie role of Superman, after my horseback riding accident in 1995 at age 42, I was left paralyzed with no more than a 50-50 chance of living. My identity as an actor, husband, and father was centered around doing things. I was very hands-on. I enjoyed a very active life. Suddenly, I could do nothing for myself. After the injury, I had to learn a new way of living with my wife and three children (then ages 15, 11, and 3) and working with others.

Ten Painful Lessons

From my experience over the past nine years, from my efforts to overcome paralysis and recreate my life, I have learned a few lessons:

Lesson 1: Figure out a new way of leading and living. An essential element of good life management is knowing how to go to Plan B very quickly. I learned something about crisis management. I had to learn a new way of living, leading, communicating, and parenting. I could do nothing for myself. I thought, "I'm no longer qualified to be a husband or father. I'll only be a terrible burden on my family." I had to learn a new way of leading my family and living my life.

Lesson 2: Remove guilt, self-doubt, and fear. I had bad case of survivor guilt and depression. So, I had to learn to forgive myself for being injured. In a position of leadership, you need to remove self-doubt, fear of failure, and any feelings that you might not be up to the task, or that people will see through you and find you deficient in some way. My new job was not to be self-pitying, not to whine, not to replay the accident, not to live in the past. People around me were looking to me for assurance that life would go on in some way. Suddenly I was a member of a club I didn't want to join—and I was like the president of the club without even running for office.

Lesson 3: Never let anyone tell you that it cannot be done. I had to over-come the gloomy prognosis of the doctors who initially gave me only a 50-50 chance of living, and virtually no chance of recovering motion or continuing my career. So, my rule #1 is, Never accept ultimatums or people telling you it can't be done. I had learned this lesson years earlier in my acting career. For years I had been told that I wasn't right or ready for certain roles. I had experi-enced a lot of rejection.

Lesson 4: Base hope for the future on a sold foundation. For centuries, medical doctors believed that the spinal cord could not regenerate. But in the 1990s, doctors agreed that it could regenerate under certain conditions. I relied on that finding to lead my family and pull me out of depression. It gave me hope, which is different than optimism. Hope is built on logic and plausibility. To take your life and your company forward, you can't just blindly say, "It's all going to work out for the best." You must be able to say, "Here's what possible, and here's what we are going to do. Here are our goals."

Lesson 5: Lead by vision, voice, and trust. I taught my five-year-old son how to ride his bike without training wheels by telling him not to look down at the pedals but to look straight ahead where he wanted to go. Within a few min-utes, he was doing tricks. And I told my teenage daughter not to let my freak accident stop her from riding horses. I was later gratified to learn that she not only regained the confidence to resume riding, but she was also named captain of her college polo team. Leadership is based on other people's trust and con-fidence in your vision and your voice.

Lesson 6: Involve others in the mission. You need to empower the people around you so they feel their contributions are vital to the success of the mis-sion. As a director, I have an idea of where I want a scene to go, but if I try to impose my ideas, I take away the actor's incentive to share insights. It's a mis-take to be heavy handed. Great leaders provide guidance and direction but wel-come ideas from their people. If people feel that their opinions are valued, they will bust a gut for you. Everyone will give 100 percent and work together if they know that the mission is larger than the individuals doing it.

Lesson 7: Make your life work inspiring. This past summer, I was in New Orleans directing a movie that chronicles the life of Brooke Ellison, an 11-year old girl who in 1991 was hit by a car. Almost every bone in her body was bro-ken, and she was paralyzed. But with the help of her family, especially her mother, she earned a bachelor's and master's degrees at Harvard and will enter law school this fall. It's hot working on the set, and we have a tight schedule and budget. We're only making the schedule because everyone wants to be there and is very involved. Also, they are inspired by the story. So, make your work inspiring, and others will be attracted to it.

Lesson 8: Do something for others who are less able than you. I was lucky in the sense that I had the resources to access the latest medical technology and receive the best care. But many disabled people are handicapped further by the high cost of health care. After my injury, my insurance company denied payment for a back-up ventilator that I needed to breathe. I became more aware of the cost pressures on health insurers and sponsors of heath benefits and how adversarial the relationship is between patients and the insurance companies. Determined to do something about the high healthcare costs for others less able than myself to pay for care, I partnered with a major insurance company to help educate families and children about healthy lifestyles and nutrition, and thus cut healthcare costs.

Lesson 9: After a setback, regroup and then set new goals. If you feel paralyzed in your progress toward your goals or life mission, I encourage you to go forward and set new goals based on the solid foundation of hope in some future possibility that is within the realm of plausibility. You may have to learn a new way of influencing other people. I've learned that I can have even greater influence with my children not by doing things with them or for them, but just by being there for them, listening to them, and loving them for who they are. Soon after my accident, my wife told me, "You are still you, and I love you." That's all I really needed to know to keep living and learning.

10. You can't just sit back and do nothing about a situation you can influence. Given the disabilities or weaknesses that we all have, it's easy for us to think that there is nothing we can do about certain situations that adversely affect us. But I have learned that when I stop and think about the situation, I can usually think of one or two ways I might have some direct or indirect influence. I find that the key to changing a situation or at least having influence on the decision is to show sincere interest in arriving at a fair, win-win solution.

Christopher Reeve was an actor, director, advocate for the differently abled, and speaker. This article is adapted from his speech at the 2004 Society for Human Resource Management (SHRM) conference in New Orleans. Visit www.ChristopherReeve.org.

13

Contemporary Morality

by Pope John Paul II

I give thanks to God for the immense gift of faith in Jesus Christ, which gift has been welcomed and treasured by the people of many countries. Our Lord's call to "Come, follow me" is as valid today as it was on the shores of Lake Galilee some 2,000 years ago. The joy and hope of Christian discipleship mark the lives of countless faithful men and women who together strive to respond to Christ's call and bring his truth to bear on the life of their family, community, and nation.

Yet, it is also true that the pernicious ideology of secularism has found fertile ground. At the root of this disturbing development is the attempt to promote a vision of humanity without God. It exaggerates individualism, sunders the essential link between freedom and responsibility, and corrodes relationships of trust that characterize genuine social living. Media reports describe the destructive consequences of this eclipse of the sense of God: The undermining of family life, a drift away from the church, and a limited vision of life that fails to awaken in people the sublime call to direct their steps toward a truth that transcends them.

Have No Fear

In the face of such challenges, when the winds are against us, the Lord calls out: "Courage! It is I! Have no fear." Remaining firm in trust, you too can dispel fear and apprehension. Especially within a culture of the "here and now," we must forever stand out as fearless witnesses and servants of the hope of Christ.

In proclaiming this hope, I'm confident that you will lead men and women from the shadows of moral confusion and ambiguous thinking into the radiance of Christ's truth and love. Indeed, it is only by understanding humanity's final destination—eternal life in heaven—that the multitude of daily joys and sorrows can be explained, enabling people to embrace the mystery of their own life with confidence.

Any weakening in Sunday observance weakens Christian discipleship and dims the light of witness to Christ's presence in our world. Sunday is the "supreme day of faith," "an indispensable day," "the day of Christian hope!" When Sunday loses its meaning and becomes subordinate to a secular concept of "weekend" dominated by such things as entertainment and sport, people stay locked within a horizon so narrow that they can no longer see the heavens.

Rather than being truly satisfied or revitalized, they remain entrapped in a senseless pursuit of the novel and deprived of the perennial freshness of Christ's "living water." Although the secularization of the Lord's day causes us much worry, you can draw comfort from the faithfulness of the Lord who continues to beckon his people with a love which challenges and calls the faithful—and in a special way the young people—to remain faithful to the celebration of Sunday worship.

I suggest that you give priority to programs that instruct the faithful about the true meaning of Sunday and inspire them to observe it fully. People are easily overshadowed by shallow sociological understandings of community. As a remembrance of a past event and the celebration of the living presence of the Risen Lord amid his people, Sunday also looks to the future glory of his return and to the fullness of Christian hope and joy.

Work the Vineyard

Sent by the Lord into the vineyard—into homes, workplaces, schools, and civic organizations—disciples of Christ find no room for "standing idle in the marketplace," nor can they be so deeply immersed in the internal organization of church life that they are distracted from the command to evangelize others actively. Renewed by the strength of the Risen Lord and his Spirit, Christ's followers must return to their "vineyard," burning with a desire to "speak" of Christ and to "show" him to the world.

In expressing my appreciation of your tireless service, I encourage you always to listen to your priests as a father would listen to a son. Help your priests to appreciate that their spiritual identity must shape all their pastoral activity. The priest is never a manager or mere defender of a particular point of view. In imitation of the Good Shepherd, he is a disciple seeking to transcend his own personal limitations and rejoice in a life of intimacy with Christ. A relationship of deep communion with Jesus, in which the priest habitually talks "heart to heart" with the Lord, will nurture his quest for holiness, enriching not only himself but the entire community he serves.

It is in embracing the universal call to holiness that the particular vocation to which God summons every individual is found. Your initiatives to promote a culture of vocation and to treasure the states of ecclesial life, which exist so that "the world may believe," will bear fruit. As for the young men who generously respond to God's call to the priesthood, I again affirm that they must receive your every assistance as they strive for a life of simplicity, chastity, and humble service, in imitation of Christ, the Eternal High Priest, of whom they are to become living icons.

The contribution of consecrated men and women to the mission of the church and the building up of civil society has been of immeasurable worth to nations. Innumerable people have benefited from the selfless commitment of pastoral ministry and spiritual guidance as well as to education, social and medical work, and care of the elderly. We admire men and women whose "gift of self for love of the Lord Jesus and, in him, of every member of the human family" enriches our communities.

The evangelical counsels of chastity, poverty and obedience, embraced for the love of God, splendidly illuminate the fidelity, self-possession, and authentic freedom necessary to live the fullness of life.

Safeguard Human Rights

I proclaim my solicitude for fundamental human rights whose expression we find clearly taught in the Gospel message. I resolve to promote, in a clear, authoritative and effective manner, respect for the fundamental rights and liberties of individuals.

I would hope that the *Covenants of the Universal Declaration of Human Rights* become more operative in the world. In this way, the *Declaration* would echo the expression of people everywhere to promote by legal safeguards the rights of all men and women without discrimination of race, sex, language or religion. We still see too many examples of injustice and oppression and a growing divergence between the *Universal Declaration* and a massive increase of human rights violations in the world.

Today individual persons and civil powers violate basic rights of the human person with impunity: Rights such as the right to be born, right to life, right to responsible procreation, right to work, to peace, to freedom and social justice, the right to participate in the decisions that affect people and nations? And we still face forms of collective violence—like racial discrimination against individuals and groups and the use of physical and psychological torture against prisoners or political dissenters. We see instances of the sequestration of persons for political reasons and acts of kidnapping for material gain that attack so dramatically family life and the social fabric.

What criteria can we use to see that the rights of all persons are protected? What basis can we offer as the soil in which individual and social rights might grow? That basis is the dignity of the human person. We must accept that each individual is truly a person. As such he has rights and duties which together flow as a direct consequence from his nature. These rights and duties are universal, inviolable, and inalienable. The preamble of the *Universal Declaration* says: "The recognition of the inherent dignity and of the equal and inalienable rights of all members of the human family is the foundation of freedom, justice and peace."

It is in this dignity of the person that human rights find their immediate source. And it is respect for this dignity that gives birth to their effective protection. The human person, even when he or she errs, always maintains inherent dignity and never forfeits his or her personal dignity. Every human being has of his or her destiny, and all rights derive from the dignity of the person who is firmly rooted in God.

Religious freedom is at the basis of all other freedoms and rights—especially the right to freedom of thought, of conscience and of religion—and is tied to them all by reason of the dignity in the human person. True freedom is the salient characteristic of humanity: It is the fount from which human dignity flows; it is the exceptional sign of the divine image within man. It is offered to us and conferred on us as our own mission.

Today men and women have an increased awareness of the social dimension of life and have become ever more sensitive to the principle of freedom of thought, conscience, and religion. However, with sadness we must also admit that forms of government still exist under which, even though freedom of religious worship receives constitutional recognition, the powers of government deter citizens from the profession of religion and make life difficult and dangerous for religious communities.

Men and women thirst for dignity. I solemnly ask that, in every place and by everyone, religious freedom be respected for every person and for all peoples. I make this solemn appeal because of the conviction that, even aside from the desire to serve God, the common good of society may profit by the moral qualities of justice and peace which have their origin in man's faithfulness to God and to his holy will. The free exercise of religion benefits both individuals and governments. Therefore, the obligation to respect religious freedom falls on everyone, both private citizens and civil authority.

Why then is repressive and discriminatory action practiced against vast numbers of citizens who suffer all sort of oppression, even death, simply to preserve their spiritual values, yet who despite all this have never ceased to cooperate in everything that serves the true civil and social progress of their country? Should they not be the objects of admiration and praise rather than considered as suspect and criminals?

How can a state call for trust and collaboration while proclaiming itself atheist and taking up positions against the faith and beliefs of its citizens?

Justice, wisdom and realism all demand that the baneful positions of secularism be overcome. Every person must have the opportunity within the context of our life together to profess his or her faith and belief, alone or with others, in private and public.

While insisting on the vindication of human rights, we are obliged to exercise our basic rights in a responsible and ethical manner. Every man and woman has the duty to respect in others the rights claimed for oneself. We must all contribute our share to the building up of a society that makes possible and feasible the enjoyment of rights and the discharge of the duties inherent in those rights.

I hope that you will continue tirelessly to promote the defense of the human person and of his dignity in the spirit of the *Universal Declaration.*

Uphold Marriage and Family

I'm pleased to acknowledge your steadfast efforts to uphold the uniqueness of marriage as a lifelong covenant based on generous mutual giving and unconditional love. The church's teaching on marriage and stable family life offers saving truth to individuals and a sure foundation upon which your aspirations can be anchored. Incisive and faithful explanations of Christian doctrine regarding marriage and the family is of utmost importance in order to counter the secular, pragmatic, and individualistic outlook which has gained ground in the area of legislation and even a certain acceptance in the realm of public opinion. Of particular concern is the growing trend to equate marriage with other forms of cohabitation. This obfuscates the very nature of marriage and violates its sacred purpose in God's plan for humanity.

Raising families according to the splendor of Christ's truth is a sharing in God's work of creation. It lies at the heart of the call to promote a civilization of love. The deep-seated love of mothers and fathers for their children is also the church's, as is the pain experienced by parents when their children fall victim to forces and trends that draw them away from the path of truth, leaving them disoriented and confused. Parents, despite the often bewildering social difficulties of today's world, are in a position to exercise great influence and offer broader horizons of hope. It is the bishop's particular task to ensure that within civil society—including the media and entertainment industries—the values of marriage and family life are supported and defended.

Vigilant concern for the poor, the abandoned, and the mistreated, and promotion of charity will do much to indicate a path of genuine development.

With affection and gratitude, I assure you of my prayers as you seek to shepherd the flocks entrusted to you. Go forward now in hope!

Pope John Paul II was Holy Father of the Catholic Church. This article is adapted from his speeches to The Bishops of Australia and to The Secretary General of The United Nations.

14

Answers to Life

by Harald Mori

In the preface to Viktor Frankl's autobiography, *Recollections,* Dr. Joseph Fabry writes about the great variety of dimensions and aspects of Frankl's life as follows: "There is another Frankl (beside the medical doctor, philosopher, scientist and founder of the 3rd Viennese school of psychotherapy, Logotherapy) . . . behind his philosophy stands a very human man."

In his book, *The Will to Meaning,* Frankl says: "Freedom threatens to degenerate into mere arbitrariness unless it is lived in terms of responsibleness. I like to say that the Statue of Liberty on the East Coast should be supplemented by a Statue of Responsibility on the West Coast."

We live in a time that shows us in brutal clearness what happens when so-called human beings do not learn what it means to live with responsibility or when they start to rush into a very selective view of what they think they should do. Terrorism is one of the worst threats of our time—terrorism of a group of people or of fanatical individuals. Globalization has consequences that allow more and more people to travel around and bring much harm or much good to others. Former U.S. Vice President Al Gore expressed his sorrow about the developments in the world as follows: "Much more important than the ecological crisis and the economic crisis in the world is the crisis about meaning!"

Logotherapy contains the Greek word "logos," which denotes meaning. Frankl found that every individual's highest goal, more or less, is to find meaning in life. Of course it is important to combine the very personal interest in life with the longing for the meaning of a whole population or generation. In a world of many possibilities, we must ask ourselves how to behave in this world, how to react, and how to create new situations. In every single situation of life, man is challenged to give answers, answers to life—to his or her own life in all its singularity and uniqueness.

To answer means to respond, to respond means to live responsibility at its best. Every single situation in life is a question: How we decide to go on,

65

which choices we make, which decisions we make. To act with responsibility is not a burden, it is a possibility and an opportunity, a gift of life. It depends on us, which values we create in life. Does love have a place in our hearts? Does courage and a hope for the future exist within us?

Independence and freedom are human rights that should be defended. Every women, every man, and every child should have the ability to live in a free country, in a free society, and in a free world. It is a pity that for many people in our world, freedom will only be a dream. Sometimes the path to freedom is a path of suffering.

Viktor Frankl saw responsibility not so much as a moral imagination or a question of certain laws—but he wanted to show us that every person creates a part of the world and in that way leaves a trace of himself and a legacy of his values. Frankl taught that every life will experience the "Tragic Triad"—meaning that each of us will experience suffering, guilt and death. Possessing a personal meaning of life will give strength to us as we experience this triad.

Every situation in our life is a question that only we can answer. We must create these decisions for ourselves. Frankl gave a definition of living with meaning. He said, "To choose from the possibilities of life means to exist—but to choose the best of all possibilities means to live meaningfully."

What can we do to make the world better, to find the right answers? How can we live with meaning? It is not an easy path, but it is the way of daily felt responsibility. Responsibility for what? Responsibility for a sense of time, of our brief existence here. Responsibility for a belief in something bigger than ourselves. Religion may be helpful for some, but even the non-religious man has some imagination concerning that which he cannot explain.

As a practicing psychotherapist, I see many people who are confronted with two types of existential questions. One is about the personal meaning in life, the personal aims in life. The second asks for a higher meaning, a greater context in which people want to find a place in this world. To find answers to the questions of life seems to be connected with giving answers! To say "Yes to Life" means to say *yes* to our future and the future of our children.

As a logotherapist, I am trained to search for solutions. Problems have challenged mankind from the beginning of time. Taking personal responsibility is to find solutions and answer questions. To take responsibility is to take a stand for a hopeful future.

Good education, teaching of real human values, and honoring virtues are necessary to give mankind a better chance to realize a hopeful future.

As our youth learn that success follows finding a reason to live, then, to a large extent, we have succeeded in our personal responsibility to them.

Responsibility means that every single individual in the world is important, and that every individual shall respect the freedom of others. The Statue of Responsibility needs to be built. In reality the monument will only be a symbol for what is going on in man's inside. About the hunt for luxury and money Viktor Frankl wrote very wise words in his book, *The Will to Meaning*, which I quote here: "To those people who are anxious to have money as though it were an end in itself, 'time is money.' They exhibit a need for speed. We need new types of leisure which allow for contemplation and meditation. To this end, man needs the courage to be lonely."

We can be sure that the more people find meaning in their life, the higher will be the probability for peace in the world.

I had the great opportunity and honor to be a graduate student and personal assistant of Viktor Frankl in the last 10 years of his life. Frankl himself was a man, a most human neurologist and psychiatrist who not only dissected and analyzed the human psyche and behavior, but who also tried successfully to daily live what he was teaching. He always cared to avoid reductionism and, even while in the Nazi concentration camps during World War II, was in search for meaning in life.

I express my deep conviction that there always can be a better world, when we help to open people's eyes to the beauties and values, especially the existential values, in the world. When we find peace in our hearts, we will have peace in the world. When we care about others, we will be protected by others.

Responsibility is not only a word—it is an attitude towards life. If we all work together in industry, in politics, in education and in humanity—if we choose to live out our liberties in terms of responsibleness, then there is a chance that our freedoms can be preserved. This is the role the Statue of Responsibility will play in our individual lives and in the world.

In my opinion, it was Viktor Frankl who—as a witness of the 20th century—brought to our awareness this remarkable point, that it is so very necessary to long for responsibility within liberty. In his most famous book, *Man's Search for Meaning*, he wrote:

"So, let us be alert—alert in a twofold sense:
Since Auschwitz we know what man is capable of.
Since Hiroshima we know what is at stake".

Harald Mori is an international lecturer and an Austrian Ministry of Health board-certified psychotherapist. Mori is founder and president of VFA (Viktor Frankl Association), visit: www.viktorfrankl.at; and co-founder of ABILE, Training Institute for Logotherapy and Existential Analysis, visit: www.abile.org.He worked as a personal assistant to Professor Viktor E. Frankl from 1987 to 1997.

Rights & Responsibilities

"Without personal and collective responsibility, there can be no democracy, no real freedom. I feel privileged to have an opportunity to help make the Statue of Responsibility more than an idea. It is an idea whose time has come!"

—Dr. Alex Pattakos
from Prisoners of Our Thoughts, Viktor Frankl's Principles at Work

15

The Statue of Responsibility

by George S. McGovern

All Americans take pride in our freedom. In Jefferson's words written into our *Declaration of Independence*, "life, liberty and the pursuit of happiness," are identified as "the unalienable rights" of the people. The authors of our *Constitution* state in the preamble that a major purpose of that founding document is to "secure the blessings of liberty to ourselves and our posterity."

In the crucial debates preceding the decision of the 13 colonies to revolt against further British rule, the eloquent Patrick Henry concluded an address to his fellow Virginians with the cry: "Give me liberty or give me death."

With the considerable help of the French, General George Washington and his soldiers defeated the British forces and gained their freedom from foreign rule.

In later years the French government presented the American people with the Statue of Liberty that has stood in New York City Harbor as a treasured monument to our freedoms.

Freedom is not free; it requires a keen sense of citizen responsibility if it is to be achieved and if it is to flourish and survive.

I support the creation of a Statue of Responsibility because I see it as the natural and essential ally of our Statue of Liberty.

When we pledge our allegiance to "liberty and justice for all," we must be aware that this is a tall order. It is not easy to insure liberty and justice for all.

A democratic society, a strong economy, a creative culture, a healthy and educated citizenry, an environmental ethic, and a government that serves the public interest honestly and openly—all of these are essential to a good society. None of them can flourish without responsible citizens.

I am a concerned citizen who believes that America has benefited from both major political traditions—liberalism and conservatism. Since the days of Thomas Jefferson and John Adams coming down to Franklin Roosevelt and Dwight Eisenhower, and more recently John Kennedy and Lyndon Johnson, the senior George Bush and Bill Clinton—these and other American presidents have borrowed noticeably from both liberalism and conservatism.

The creative tension between authentic conservatism and authentic liberalism is the genius of American politics. I respect the insights and principles of both of these traditions. I tend to distrust neo-conservatives and neo-liberals—in part because they lack reliable or identifiable historical roots. In politics, as in the whole of life, a measure of authenticity is valuable. "Neo" is an added and confusing modifier that is fast developing a bad name.

One of the requirements of citizen responsibility is to think and communicate responsibly. If you are a conservative, say so. Likewise if you are a liberal, as I am, who also has strong conservative positions as well, say so, and don't let any critic or opponent falsely put you so far out in left or right field that most people see you as irrelevant.

America urgently needs a revival of personal and public responsibility in us as citizens and on the part of our leaders. Both our leaders and the citizenry must work harder to separate fact from fiction, to think and speak rationally, to avoid groundless fears and exaggerated emotionalism in evaluating public issues. There is still wisdom in President Franklin Roosevelt's declaration: "The only thing we have to fear is fear itself." Likewise Tom Paine's historical call for "Common Sense" remains necessary for self-government.

Currently our political process is clogged by charges and counter-charges based on irresponsible appeals to our baser instincts. Reason and clear thinking are clouded by the excessive use of brief one-liners on television, by the superficial dependence on polls and focus groups, and by heavy dependence on political consultants who frequently place winning at any cost, including the sacrifice of truth and common sense.

There is also an urgent need for more responsible guidelines in the funding of political campaigns. As matters now stand, special interests with huge funds at their disposal have come to dominate much of our political discourse. Many of our most thoughtful students of politics believe that campaign finance reform is vital to the health of American democracy.

Jefferson long ago declared that those who expect freedom and ignorance to exist together "expect what never has been and never can be." Citizens and politicians have a responsibility to be informed on public issues. Needless to say, we have a serious responsibility to follow political campaigns and go to the polls as well informed as is possible. It is a weakness of democracy and the protection of freedom that only half of eligible voters use the right to vote even in a general election for the Presidency and the Congress. A much smaller percentage vote in primary elections or in state and local elections.

One final note on responsibility. A citizen should seek to make his or her own way when possible and practical in the work force. We all, of course, derive a wide array of government assistance in such ways as public education, social security, health care, pure food and medicines, civil rights, national defense, environmental protection, highways and many other government services. Beyond such vital services, no responsible citizen should dishonestly evade taxes or needlessly seek government aid as a substitute for employment on his or her own initiative.

America needs a Statue of Responsibility.

George S. McGovern was a United States Senator, Democratic Presidential nominee, 1972; U.S. Ambassador to U.N. Food and Agriculture, Rome; and is currently U.N Global Ambassador on Hunger.

16

Life, Liberty, and the Pursuit of Meaning

by Alex Pattakos

The introduction to the *Declaration of Independence*, signed on July 4, 1776, notes: "We hold these truths to be self-evident, that all men are created equal, that they are endowed by their Creator with certain unalienable Rights, that among these are Life, Liberty and the pursuit of Happiness." These powerful words help to establish a platform upon which all democratic societies may be built.

True freedom in a democracy can't be found in, nor can it rest solidly upon a foundation comprised only of "unalienable Rights," no matter how well intended. Within the USA, the expectation of "Liberty and the pursuit of Happiness" as unalienable Rights has overshadowed, if not totally ignored, an important corollary of true freedom and participatory democracy—*Responsibility*.

The notion that responsibility is necessary for participatory democracy has deep roots. It can be traced to Ancient Greece where the rights *and* responsibilities of citizenship were not taken lightly. The relationship between responsibility and true freedom also has a history that should remind us that freedom is not something that we should take for granted or about which we should ever become complacent.

Viennese psychiatrist Viktor Frankl warns: "Freedom threatens to degenerate into mere license and arbitrariness unless it is lived in terms of responsibleness." And even though Dr. Frankl enjoyed his time spent in America and admired much about it, he was not shy about criticizing the popular understanding of some cherished American values, such as our notion of freedom. He took exception, for instance, to what appeared to be a commonly accepted view of equating freedom with a license to do virtually anything that one wants. To Dr. Frankl, freedom without responsibility is an oxymoron. That is why he said: "The Statue of Liberty on the East Coast should be supplemented by a Statue of Responsibility on the West Coast."

I've always been intrigued by this idea for a "Statue of Responsibility." Such a monument makes sense to me and, in my view, would be more than just a "book-end" to the Statue of Liberty. It could serve, among other things, as an important reminder to everyone of what is required to safeguard true freedom and a democratic way of life. Moreover, I can't imagine a sustainable democratic system founded on liberty alone. In the absence of personal and collective responsibility, there can be no democracy, no real freedom, and as Dr. Frankl would say, no authentic *will to meaning*.

True freedom is not "just another word for nothing left to lose," as the late singer Janis Joplin once opined. The word *freedom* implies that we have *everything* to lose, especially if we don't take our role in a democratic society seriously. It is a fundamental value that must be cherished and protected by each and every one of us. And this necessary pre-condition of democracy can only—and will only—exist if we hold ourselves, and others, *responsible*.

We can all benefit from the wisdom and experience of Nelson Mandela, who ends his autobiography, *Long Walk to Freedom*, with the words: "But I can rest only for a moment, for with freedom come responsibilities, and I dare not linger, for my long walk is not yet ended." Freedom's cry, especially in today's world, is a call for responsibility that should be heard loud and clear.

The American concept of democracy can be traced to Ancient Greece, where citizenship and civic education were essential building blocks for both community and society. In no small way, they formed the basis for government structure and guided political discourse. And while we certainly could debate the extent to which Greek democracy reflected the "power of the people," the design of any democratic regime, by definition, has had to focus attention on this core principle ever since.

However, like the role of freedom in a democracy, the "power" of the people is only *part* of what it takes to make a true democracy. Viktor Frankl argued that true freedom is more than liberty *per se*; it requires responsibility as well. True democracy is more than people power *per se*; it requires *people wisdom* as well.

In this regard, I'm indebted to my friend and colleague, Dr. Alexander Christakis, who introduced me to the term *demosophia*—the "wisdom of the people"—and who is perhaps the world's leading authority on helping people harness their collective wisdom and power to construct democracy in a responsible, sustainable, and meaningful way. It is through open and focused dialogue that demosophia can be brought to life among a "community of stakeholders." In addition to uncovering the root causes of problems and, concomitantly, the drivers needed to effect positive change, the explicit focus on the "collective wisdom" provides a structure for understanding the embedded values that influence decision-making. In a democratic context, such value clarification and aggregation are vital to the formulation of meaningful public policy. Political scientist David Easton, a recognized authority on political systems and decision-making, defines public policy as "the allocation of values for a society."

The importance of dialogue can be extended directly into our discussion of freedom and responsibility. The concept and process of dialogue can be linked both to civic education and "good government." The word "dialogue" comes from the Greek *dialogos*—made up of the root words *dia* ("through") and *logos* ("the meaning"). Through authentic dialogue, we can access a larger pool of common meaning that cannot be accessed individually. Note the similarities between common meaning, collective wisdom, and demosophia. Also, recognize that Viktor Frankl's system of psychotherapy, known as "Logotherapy," also builds upon the same root word, *logos*, and therefore can be loosely referred to as "therapy through meaning."

The root *logos* is also commonly used in the original Greek to mean *spirit*, which alters the translation of dialogue. This twist in meaning suggests that dialogue is more than "collective thinking"—often an all-too-cerebral process that stops short of meaningfully engaging participants. On a deeper (or heightened) level, the process of authentic dialogue enables individuals to experience that they are connected through common spirit, not only through common meaning in a cognitive sense.

Dialogue, as a concept, takes on a new and deeper meaning when it is perceived as a group's accessing a "larger pool of common spirit" through a distinctly spiritual connection between the members. True dialogue effectively acknowledges the spiritual part of our humanness.

That's why Viktor Frankl chose to call his particular system of psychotherapy, "Logotherapy." He believed the word *logos* had deep spiritual roots in addition to its more common translation and interpretation as "the meaning" by students and practitioners of dialogue. In my book, *Prisoners of Our Thoughts*, I mention that Dr. Frankl is often acknowledged as the founder of humanistic medicine and psychiatry, and he helped to "spiritualize" psychotherapy.

Dr. Frankl posits that "freedom and responsibility together make man a spiritual being." Moreover, he points out that the word *spiritual* does not have a religious connotation but refers specifically to the human dimension. In this context, the cry for freedom and responsibility can also be viewed as a call to be authentically human by manifesting our spiritual selves. And it is on this authentically and distinctly human plane where Frankl's notion of a "will to meaning" can be realized.

Juxtaposed against Sigmund Freud's will to pleasure and Alfred Adler's will to power, Viktor Frankl argues that it is the ability to realize our *will to meaning*—that is, our authentic commitment to *meaningful* values and goals that only we can actualize and fulfill—that guides us in the quest to tap into this uniquely *human* potential. Unlike either Freud or Adler, Frankl considers the main concern of human beings to be fulfilling a meaning and actualizing values, rather than simply the gratification and satisfaction of drives and instincts. And, in order to realize this will to meaning, both individually and collectively, we must, once again, hold ourselves and each other *responsible*.

In his bestselling book, *Man's Search for Meaning*, Viktor Frankl espouses: "Man's search for meaning is the primary motivation in his life." We are all responsible for discovering the meaning of everything that happens in our lives. And this responsibility "has two intentional referents. It refers to a meaning for whose fulfillment we are responsible, and also to a being before whom we are responsible. Therefore the sound spirit of democracy is but one-sidedly conceived of if understood as freedom without responsibleness."

Dr. Frankl also was critical of the popular understanding of the phrase "the pursuit of happiness" in the *Declaration of Independence*. He feels that it is wrong to be concerned only with pleasing oneself to the exclusion of others. Moreover, he views the pursuit of happiness as being misdirected and offers the pursuit of meaning as an alternative: "Don't aim at success. The more you aim at it and make it a target, the more you are going to miss it. For success, like happiness, cannot be pursued; it must ensue and it only does so as the unintended side-effect of one's dedication to a cause greater than oneself or as the by-product of one's surrender to a person other than oneself. Happiness must happen, and the same holds for success: You have to let it happen by not caring about it."

Life, Liberty and the pursuit of Meaning. To be sure, these words suggest more than "unalienable Rights." It's now time to listen to freedom's cry and assume the responsibilities that come with it.

Alex Pattakos, Ph.D., is founder of the Center for Meaning, based in Santa Fe, New Mexico, and author of Prisoners of Our Thoughts: Viktor Frankl's Principles for Discovering Meaning in Life and Work. *Call 505-988-5235; email: info@prisonersofourthoughts.com, or visit www.prisonersofourthoughts.com.*

17

Understanding Freedom and Responsibility

by Reese Haller

I began to better understand the meaning of freedom as I struggled with a homework assignment—a re-write project—when I was in fourth grade. I was nine years old at the time.

Our teacher had given the assignment of writing a paper about the *United States Constitution* and then presenting that paper to the class. For me presenting the paper was not the problem because I was already on a lecture circuit and was speaking at elementary schools around the country about writing. My problem was understanding what the *Constitution* was actually saying.

I read the *Constitution* over several times and found the wording confusing. So I decided to concentrate on just the *Amendments of the Constitution*. My history book had discussed the amendments, what their purpose was, and when and why they were adopted. That made easier for me to understand the point of each one.

As I sat and read them over, I thought it would be fun to just re-write them in my own words. I restated each amendment into the language my friends and I use. I briefly stated what I thought was the point of each amendment.

Here is how I interpret each Amendment in my own words:

The 1st Amendment is my favorite because I like to talk. It's about the freedom of speech.

The 2nd Amendment is about having a gun or other weapon. "We have the right to bear arms" is a funny way of saying we can own a gun.

The 3rd Amendment says that the army cannot take over my home. Good! I like knowing that my home is a safe place for me and my little brother.

The 4th Amendment says that no one can come in my home and look for stuff without my permission. I think this should also be about little brothers coming in your room and taking your stuff without permission.

The 5th Amendment talks about how a criminal trial should be run. I don't want to ever find out more about this, unless I become a lawyer or a judge.

The 6th Amendment says that a criminal trial should not take a long time. My mama was on a jury, I think it took a long time.

The 7th Amendment says that we have a right to a trial by people that are just like us. These people are called a jury.

The 8th Amendment says that people, no matter who they are, should not be treated in a cruel or mean way.

The 9th Amendment says that we cannot be denied our rights. I guess you could say, "We have the right to be right, and we have the right to be wrong."

The 10th Amendment says that the people in our country are the ones who should have the powers.

The 11th Amendment talks about how a person can't have a trial in a different state.

The 12th Amendment has to do with electing the President and Vice President.

The 13th, 14th, 15th Amendments are all about slavery and how it is just plain wrong. I'm glad our country figured this out before I was ever born.

The 16th Amendment is about creating state income tax. I guess we have to pay money to keep the state we live in the way we want it to be.

The 17th Amendment is about electing a person to speak for the people called a Senator. I met my senator at the state capitol. I think you should too.

The 18th Amendment says that making and selling alcohol is illegal. I don't think people should drink alcohol anyway.

The 19th Amendment is my mama's favorite. It gives her and other women the right to vote.

The 20th Amendment is about how long the President gets to be President. I think it's weird that they call it the "Lame Duck Amendment."

The 21st Amendment makes the 18th Amendment no longer valid. I think they should have just gotten rid of the 18th Amendment.

The 22nd Amendment says that the President can't be the President forever. He has to give someone else a turn. He can only have two turns, each one lasts four years. So every four years we vote for a new President.

The 23rd Amendment gives the people in the District of Columbia the right to vote for President.

The 24th Amendment did away with having to pay taxes to be able to vote.

The 25th Amendment says that if something happens to the President, like if he dies, then the Vice ßPresident becomes President.

The 26th Amendment lowered the voting age to 18. I think it should be lower, I know what kind of President I want, and I want a chance to vote too.

My dad checked on me to see how the writing was going, and I shared my version of them with him. He asked me to listen carefully to what I wrote as he read each Amendment back to me. I closed my eyes and thought about my words as I heard them.

When he finished I sat quietly for a moment. For some reason an idiom our 4th grade teacher taught us entered my thoughts. She was really into idioms and would teach us a new one every week. One of the idioms she taught us was, "You can lead a horse to water, but you can't make it drink." As I repeated that idiom in my mind, I heard myself say, "You can lead a person to freedom, but you can't make them free."

I said it again out loud, and my dad gave me a puzzled look. I answered his look by saying, "Freedom is a choice. What our Founding Fathers were doing in the *Constitution* was creating a country where people have a choice to live how they want to live and be who they want to be."

We can choose to live where we want, say what we want, eat what we want, go to school or work where we want, and go to church where we want.

What many don't realize is that with every choice comes a responsibility.

For example, the First Amendment states that we have the freedom to say whatever we want, but that does not mean we can call people names. We also have the freedom to live wherever we want, but being responsible with that choice means we don't become a space invader and live on other people's land. Adults can choose to drive a car, and their responsibility is to follow the rules of driving, like speed limits and stop lights.

The Statue of Responsibility is a reminder to all of us that an important part of having choices is being responsible with our choices. Freedom to "be" is complete when we are responsible with our "being."

The Statue of Liberty is a symbol to all that each and every one of us has the choice to be who we please to be. The Statue of Responsibility is a symbol calling on each and every one of us to be kind, gentle, and respectful with that choice. Together, the two statues represent what freedom really means—liberty and responsibility. With one statue on the East Coast and one on the West Coast, our country is wrapped in the full meaning of freedom.

As a country, we've been working hard to ensure we are free to live however we want. That is what makes our country what it is—free. Everyone has a right to be free, but not everyone in the world knows what that means. Not everyone in the world is ready to be free. We cannot make people free. You can lead a person to freedom, but you cannot make them free—the choice is theirs.

Remember: With every choice comes a responsibility. Use your freedom wisely. What is your choice, and what will you do with it? Live free!

At age 10, Reese Haller is the youngest published fiction author in America. Haller's book series, Fred the Mouse™ *includes book three:* Rescuing Freedom. *Visit www.reesehaller.com.*

18

Statue of Responsibility

by Denis Waitley

One of my dreams is to see that the flip side of freedom, responsibility, receives equal time in this land of the free. During the first half of my life, I assumed that responsibility was widely understood. But, my travels of the past 30 years have convinced me it is a vanishing concept. Responsibility is the forgotten side of freedom.

In Asia, I talked to thousands of young men and women, many desperate to seize educational and economic opportunities and to escape the oppression of their governments. They told me what they most wanted was what America represented to them—the freedom to be as uncommonly successful as they wanted to be. And they were willing to work to attain that. But when I interview immigrants who have spent some time in America, I find that their greatest cultural shock comes from discovering that many Americans are trying to escape to the very things they are escaping from. While the immigrants yearn to be free to work and grow according to their own visions, many Americans prefer being cared for by the government.

Responsibility is badly in need of redefinition. My friend Stephen R. Covey defines the word this way: *response-ability*—the ability to choose your response. In his bestselling book *The Seven Habits of Highly Effective People*, Covey states: "Proactive people recognize responsibility. They do not blame circumstances, conditions, or conditioning for their behavior. Their behavior is a product of their own conscious choice based on values, rather than a product of their conditions, based upon feeling."

Everyone likes to talk about freedom of choice. After all, that is one of the principles on which our nation was founded. But we tend to feel that much of what we do in life is forced on us. We really do not have to do much of anything. We choose to do the things we do because they are profitable to us and the best choices among the alternatives. People who feel they must do things usually forfeit many available options and alternatives, losing control of their lives in the bargain. But those who are aware that they have the power of decision—that they exert control over what happens to them—can choose more effective responses. Incidentally, these people are also generally happier.

Unfortunately we are living in an age of eroding responsibility. Although most people are willing to fight for the credit when good things happen, fewer people want to accept responsibility for their own actions. One way or another, our actions cause consequences. To every action, as Sir Isaac Newton observed, there's always an opposite and equal reaction. Good begets good, and evil leads to more evil. This is one of the universe's eternal, fundamental truths: the law of cause and effect.

Every cause (action) creates an effect (reaction) approximately equal in intensity. Making good use of our minds, skills, and talents will bring positive rewards in our lives. Assuming the personal responsibility to make the best use of our talents and time will result in an enormous gain in happiness, success, and wealth. This is true for everyone.

And yet, scarcely one person in a thousand puts his or her time to anywhere near its potential good use. Most of us fritter away much of our lives, watching the game from the sidelines. Nor is there any ultimate advantage in taking raises or rewards away from others. Every time we think we can cheat our boss, fellow workers, friends, family members, or peers, we hurt ourselves most of all. Every less-than-responsible act toward others slashes deeply into our own chances to grow and prosper.

Leaders who build financial empires or accomplish great deeds for society are those who take personal responsibility to heart and to soul. By being true to themselves and others, they achieve success, wealth, and inner happiness. In the end, we ourselves—far more than any outsider—are the people with the greatest ability to steal our own time, talents, and accomplishments.

I have long been a champion of equal rights and of equal responsibilities for all. Rich Meiss, an associate in Minneapolis, and I have formed a nonprofit foundation called The Center for Personal Responsibility. Our initial project is sponsoring an essay contest for primary and secondary school students to describe their ideas for a new monument called the Statue of Responsibility. As you might guess, it is meant to complement the Statue of Liberty.

For decades, the Statue of Responsibility has been a vision of mine. It symbolizes how we remember, in time, the obligations of freedom, rather than symbolizing, too late, the lessons from our ancestors that we forgot.

Inscribed on the Statue of Responsibility, I imagine these immortal words of John D. Rockefeller, Jr.: "I believe in the supreme worth of the individual and in his or her right to life, liberty and the pursuit of happiness. I believe that every right implies a responsibility; every opportunity an obligation; every possession a duty. I believe that the law was made for people and not people for the law; that government is the servant of the people and not their master. I believe in the dignity of labor, whether with hand or head; that the world owes no one a living but that it owes everyone an opportunity to make a living. I believe in the sacredness of a promise, that a person's word should be as good as his or her bond, that character—not wealth or power or position—is of supreme worth. I believe that rendering useful service is the common duty of humankind, and that only in the purifying fire of sacrifice is the dross of self-ishness consumed and the greatness of the human soul set free." This is the theme of the Statue of Responsibility.

Together with Viktor Frankl, who wrote *Man's Search for Meaning*, I have lectured about the need for such a symbol for years. The idea sounded frivolous to many in the 1970s, 1980s, and 1990s. But America's current condition has turned the seeming frivolity to somber concern, especially since 9/11.

Lately, I like to put myself in an imaginary time machine and arrive at the year 2020 with an unsettling premonition: "Together with my great-grandchildren, I am aboard a huge hydrofoil tour boat, taking off from San Francisco's Pier 39 for a 45-minute excursion around the new Statue of Responsibility on Alcatraz Island. Looking back at the city skyline, we see the Sumotomo and Hong Kong Bank centers, formerly the Transamerica and Bank of America buildings. Other landmarks have also changed. The Mark Hopkins, Sir Francis Drake, Fairmont, Hilton, and Mansion hotels are now called the Peninsula, Shangri La, Mandarin Oriental, Royal Garden, and Miyako hotels.

"In 1884, France gave us the Statue of Liberty as a gesture of friendship and a lasting reminder of the precious liberty that we citizens enjoy under a free form of government. In 2020, 136 years later, the Asian Common Market offered us a reminder of the investment in that liberty by giving us the Statue of Responsibility. It seems both ironic and entirely appropriate that this new monument was erected on Alcatraz Island, a rusting reminder of freedom forfeited by irresponsibility. At the base of the statue, I read a telling inscription: If you take good things for granted, you must earn them again. For every right you cherish, you have a duty to fulfill. For every hope you entertain, you have a task to perform. For every privilege you would preserve, you must sacrifice a comfort. You can take a quantum leap in your own quest for excellence, financial freedom and total fulfillment by embracing this critical concept of the Statue of Responsibility: Freedom will always carry the price of individual responsibility and the just rewards of your own choices."

I hope our generation understands this message. The statue can remind us of freedom's obligations before it becomes too late.

Denis Waitley is chairman of Waitley Direct International in Rancho Santa Fe, California, and author of Empires of the Mind. *Visit www.waitley.com or call 619-756-4201.*

19

Rights and Responsibilities

by Dallin H. Oaks

I'm concerned about the current overemphasis on rights and underemphasis on responsibilities. Where will this lead in our public life? No society can support continued increases in citizen rights while neglecting to foster comparable increases in citizen responsibilities. Yet, our legal system continues to recognize new rights even as we increasingly ignore old responsibilities. For example, so-called no-fault divorces—which give either spouse the right to dissolve a marriage at will—have obscured the vital importance of responsibilities in marriage. Similarly, I believe it is a delusion to think that we help children by defining and enforcing their *rights*. We do more for children by trying to reinforce the *responsibilities* of parents—natural and adoptive—even when those responsibilities are not legally enforceable.

The same principles apply in public life. We can't raise our public well-being by adding to our inventory of individual rights. Civic responsibilities—such as honesty, self-reliance, participation in the democratic process, and devotion to the common good—are essential to the governance of our country. Currently, we are increasing rights and weakening responsibilities, and it is leading our nation toward moral and civic bankruptcy. If we are to raise our general welfare, we must strengthen our sense of individual responsibility for the welfare of others and the good of society at large.

I believe that many in the legal profession have promoted societal goals through rights at the expense of voluntary fulfillment of responsibilities. In the vocabulary of the law, a *right* signifies a claim enforceable by law. This kind of right can't exist without law. In this sense, a person with a right can always compel action or inaction by someone. Lawyers thrive on rights. The enforcement of rights provides employment for the legal profession. In relation to rights, a lawyer functions as a popular champion—a gladiator or enforcer.

Responsibility connotes duty or obligation. In one sense, responsibility is just the duty side of someone else's right. That kind of responsibility is enforceable. I speak of a different kind. I refer to an obligation or duty that, as a practical matter, is not enforceable by legal processes. Such responsibilities include those that are owed to one's conscience and to one's God, and many that are owed to one's fellow beings, to one's community, and to a host of other groups. These responsibilities are "the rent we pay" for the privilege of living in a civilized society. They include such familiar virtues as tolerance, trustfulness, benevolence, patriotism, respect for human and civil rights, participation in the democratic process, and devotion to the common good.

There are important differences between rights and responsibilities. "Rights" is a lofty term, enshrined in the consciousness of Americans. The best-known and most highly revered portion of our *Constitution* is the *Bill of Rights*. A person who can put needs or desires in terms of rights captures the high ground of moral discourse.

Responsibilities are necessities we respect, but we rarely stand up and cheer for them. In contrast to rights, which can be enforced, responsibilities can only be encouraged. With the definition of new rights, we have tended to ignore old responsibilities. As a result, the responsibilities approach is now neglected and the rights approach is overburdened.

For example, modern legal discourse has much to say about the rights of children and little to say about the responsibilities of parents. I wonder how much we can really help children by defining and enforcing their rights. I think we may do more for children by trying to reinforce the responsibilities of parents, natural and adoptive, even when those responsibilities are not legally enforceable. We might start by reducing our enthusiasm for "no-fault" divorces in the case of marriage partners who are parents. In many such cases we should encourage the parents to keep their marriage together for the sake of interests larger than their own rights, convenience, and desires.

Another example concerns current laws against discrimination. I wonder whether we can accomplish much more effective enforcement by more extensive use of legal process. Instead of exploring new ways to reinforce non-discrimination *rights*, we might be more effective by exploring new ways to win hearts to the proposition that each of us has a *responsibility* to treat persons on their own merits as children of God, whatever their race, creed, color, sex or national origin.

I seek to promote responsibilities as a worthy alternative to efforts to promote social goals exclusively through the enforcement of rights. By this means, I seek to contribute to a better balance between what John A. Howard, in his address, "Education and Freedom," has called "the human impulse to pursue one's own course" and what he calls "the necessity to modify one's conduct according to the needs of the group."

Although lawyers relate more readily to rights than to responsibilities, there are at least two compelling reasons why the American Bar Association needs a Section that is actively involved with both. First, the enjoyment of rights cannot endure without the voluntary fulfillment of responsibilities. Morris Janowitz, in the *Reconstruction of Patriotism—Education for Civil Consciousness*, reminds us that a democracy needs patriotic citizens alive to their duties as well as to their rights. We need reminding. Our generation values the right to vote over the duty to vote, and the right to a trial by jury over the obligation to serve as a juror. No society is so secure that it can withstand continued demands for increases in citizen rights and decreases in citizen obligations.

Civic responsibilities, like honesty, self-reliance, participation in the democratic process, and devotion to the common good are basic to the governance and preservation of our country. Any person who is concerned with preserving the force of law and the enforceability of individual rights should be profoundly concerned about the civic responsibilities upon which the legal order is based.

Another reason for lawyer concern with responsibilities is that some of the goals we seek to achieve by the enforcement of rights may be achieved more effectively and at lower cost by the encouragement of responsibilities. Rights necessarily entail public enforcement. Responsibilities as defined here require only private persuasion and initiative. As a private remedy, responsibilities are subject to all of the limitations of voluntary action. But rights are also limited. The enforcement of rights is limited by the resources of government and by the will of government officials. The effectiveness of a rights approach therefore will ebb and flow with the fashions of different administrations and with the fortunes of the economy and its impact on public budgets.

The rights approach also has some side effects that should be counted among its costs. The subject of side effects reminds us of what has been called the first rule of modern packaging: One bag of groceries, when consumed, will produce two bags of trash. One side effect of the rights approach concerns the person who must act to achieve the goal. This approach uses compulsion, whereas the responsibilities approach uses persuasion. Using coercion to enforce rights may embitter the person who is compelled to act. In contrast, the use of persuasion to fulfill responsibilities may ennoble the actor, who sees himself as having responded to a higher impulse.

In a 1978 article in *The Public Interest*, Nathan Glazer has noted other effects of the judicial enforcement of rights, such as in welfare programs and in educational, penal, and mental institutions. A rights approach reduces the power, authority, and responsibilities of administrators. It gives primacy to the theoretical knowledge of the lawyer-enforcers over the practical or clinical knowledge of the defendant-administrators.

To cite another cost, the rights approach is subject to internal contradictions that may impair its utility. Individual rights and individual freedom are both worthy goals. Unfortunately, the more government seeks to enforce rights, the more it interferes with freedom. The more it assures one individual's freedom, the less it is able to enforce another individual's rights. This tendency

is all too apparent in the controversy over prayer in public schools and in circumstances involving laws against discrimination. The achievement of one
goal for one person often impairs the goal of another. The responsibilities
approach has no such contradiction, since it subjects freedom to persuasion
rather than coercion. Though less effective for achieving a goal in an individual case, the responsibilities approach imposes less cost on competing goals.

How can the legal profession and the law encourage the voluntary fulfillment of responsibilities? How can we strengthen the common sense of obligation, so that voluntary action will become a more effective means of attaining
worthy goals?

The most powerful instrument of conversion to any proposition is the
power of example. The legal profession's most powerful sermon on responsibilities is its voluntary compliance with obligations that are unenforceable,
especially when a lawyer's fulfillment of public responsibility is done at the
expense of his or her private interest. So it is with professional obligations to
work *pro bono publico* on matters such as legal services for the indigent, the
improvement of the profession, or the administration of justice. Many lawyers
fulfill such responsibilities admirably, but their example goes unheeded
because it is unnoticed. The profession should increase the power of its positive examples by making them more visible. And we should also recognize
that too many lawyers devote little time to their professional responsibilities.
The public influence and standing of lawyers would be enhanced if they were
seen as professionals who would prevent or mediate controversies rather than
concentrate on enforcing rights.

We can also encourage the responsibilities approach by strengthening the
position of institutions that promote moral development, including the content
and observance of responsibilities. I refer to family, church, educational institutions, community organizations, and educational media programs that are
concerned with moral development. If we can improve the performance of
these institutions, we will increase the extent to which worthy social goals can
be attained through voluntary action.

I illustrate this point by reference to the role of the family. Recent legal
and social developments have cast doubt on the value our society places on the
family. At the same time, the family is conceded to be our most effective
instrument for developing moral values. Hence, our laws and social priorities
should seek to strengthen families, instead of contributing to our acquiescing
in their decline.

Any forces that weaken the family or the practice of individual responsibility in family relations diminish the sense of responsibility and the vital work
ethic in our society as a whole. Conversely, by strengthening the family and its
role as a teacher of moral values, we encourage the fulfillment of responsibilities in society as a whole. The legal profession should be enlisted and the laws

should be shaped to strengthen the family. We should do the same for other institutions and efforts that strengthen our common sense or responsibility, such as the teaching of civic virtues in schools, community organizations, and the media.

We have tried throwing money and regulations at problems. We should now try throwing preachments at some problems. It may even be desirable to afflict responsible parties with the power of a good example. I suggest that it is time our leaders and our teachers turned down the volume on what we *deserve* and instead tuned us in to how we can *serve*. As President John F. Kennedy said in a line honored in memory but ignored in practice: "Ask not what your country can do for you. Ask what you can do for your country."

One of the glories of our free society is the way it protects the interests and worth of the individual against the overbearing preferences of the majority. None of us would have it otherwise. Yet there is truth in John Howard's observation that the "fixation in our thinking about the importance of rights, however well intentioned," is probably one of the reasons for the unsatisfactory performance of some organizations. Why? As Howard observes, "The very concept of rights inclines people to focus on their own well-being and to demand their due, instead of focusing on the well-being of all humanity."

Dr. Ben C. Fisher, in his lecture "The Challenge of Secularism to Christian Education," reminds us that our hope for a "unifying principle by which men might dwell together in peace" lies not in acts that affirm the autonomy of the individual but in acts that glorify the brotherhood of man. We cannot raise ourselves by adding to our inventory of individual rights. The fulfillment of individual rights depends on the fulfillment of individual and group responsibilities. If we are to raise ourselves and all mankind, we must strengthen our common commitment and service in the cause of responsibility for the welfare of others and the good of society at large.   ⸙

Dallin H. Oaks is a member of the Quorum of the Twelve Apostles of The Church of Jesus Christ of Latter-day Saints. This article is adapted from his article that originally appeared in the Mercer Law Review, *written when he was a sitting judge.*

20

Making a Better World

by Peter Senge

Every organization that aspires to learn has a sense of social responsibility and a mission to make a better world.

Our ideal of the learning organization comes from a different understanding of learning. Our culture uses the word *learning* in a way that equates it with taking in information: "I know a lot because I read a lot." This is a weak definition of learning. The expression for learning in Chinese is made up of two symbols: One stands for studying, the other for practicing constantly. In China, you can't think of learning without thinking of practicing constantly.

The central definition of learning is the enhancement of capacity to produce results that matter to you. We're all inquisitive about things we care about, and companies need to tap that intrinsic motivation. Because once you start doing your life's work, everything changes. When you connect what matters in your life and what you're doing professionally, work has a very different meaning.

People ask me, "How do you tap that motivation for production workers?" They imply that it's more difficult to find meaning if you're doing a job on the front line. Why would it be more difficult, unless these people are doing something they don't want to do or are treated as if they're only there to execute tasks and don't have brains.

The way jobs are defined by the system of management somewhat determines the opportunity people have to bring their whole selves to work. There's nothing wrong with hierarchy, but we might redefine it in a non-value-laden way, saying it exists because people at different levels deal with different time horizons. Some are focused on 20 years, some on 10 days. It's like somebody plays left field, and somebody pitches. It's a position. But we have tied positions with value, believing some people are more important because of their position.

Profit and Purpose

I question whether the purpose of any organization is to make a profit. I don't think that's descriptive of most successful companies. Russ Ackoff, at the Wharton School of Economics, says profit is like oxygen. If you don't have enough, you won't be around long; but if you think life is about breathing, you're missing something.

Obviously, profit is important. But it doesn't tell you about the purpose of the enterprise. The founders of such companies as Ford and AT&T believed that if you did something well, a natural by-product would be making a lot of money. That's not so radical. Maybe what's more radical is thinking about multiple dimensions of purpose, where one might be the continual growth of everyone in the enterprise. A social mission is the essence of a successful business: doing something that makes a difference to somebody. Otherwise, they wouldn't want to pay for it. The problem is that "social responsibility" has become a hackneyed phrase that sounds like do-goodism, and it doesn't get the right spirit of it. For organizations to prosper over the long term, they must contribute something. And the more they can contribute on multiple dimensions, the more they're likely to prosper. Those multiple dimensions include communities, customers, and employees. Yes, that amounts to a socially responsible view, but it also amounts to a systems view.

We tend to think in terms of dichotomies, of either/ors: Either it's good for society, or it's smart business. Might it be possible to have organizations that are both more consistent with our deeper values, and more effective?

We've bought into the idea that to be successful in business, you have to violate your values. The idea has been propagated using all these metaphors about the law of the jungle. But the root goes back to the industrial era, when we developed a set of practices which were not sustainable. Ideas that began with the Renaissance and the Scientific Revolution became crystallized in the attitude that we could control our world. We tried to set our own rules, with no appeal to the larger systems of which we are a part. It certainly accomplished a lot, but it's not sustainable over the long run.

The Vision of Learning

The learning organization is really a vision. We need to be weaned from the model of fostering innovation by watching companies that are doing it right and copying them. One illustration of how vision works comes from Allen Kay, who led the research at Xerox Park that produced the breakthroughs that led to the personal computer. He was responsible for the user interface. Their vision was of a "Dynabook." It would be like a book—something you could carry with you—but fully interactive. By Kay's assessment they failed, because the machine they created was not as portable as a book.

But that's the point. It wasn't whether they accomplished the vision; it was what the vision did. We're so hooked on getting it right that we miss the essence of the creative orientation, which is to aspire to something worth our effort. Maybe you never fully accomplish the vision.

Kay always thought of himself as a forcing function for change. And that's what the learning organization is about. The more progress that any organization makes, the more it will see its inadequacy.

The most radical aspect of the way we approach things is to focus on thinking. Most people believe you change organizations by rearranging external conditions such as the reward systems, the information technologies. Our premise is that organizations are the way they are because of how people think. Until we change how we think and interact, nothing really changes.

We're so hooked on getting it right that we miss the essence of the creative orientation, which is to aspire to something worth our effort. The idea of creative tension is important. When we have a vision of where we want to be and we tell the truth about where we are now, there's a natural tension between the two. Creative tension points us in two directions: Toward our aspiration, but also toward our ability to inquire into the current reality—not just the conditions, but the underlying causes of the conditions.

Now, as soon as you go in that direction, you realize there is no current reality, no absolute truth. There are only interpretations. And these reflect underlying assumptions. So that leads you into the discipline of surfacing the assumptions we bring to the table.

How do you have conversations that free up those assumptions so that we can come to a deeper shared sense of what's going on? For example, Royal Dutch Shell, the first company in the West to work with mental models, was at the bottom of the oil industry in the early seventies, and today it's at the top of the industry. A big part of that was a change in how they went about planning. At Shell, they talk about planning as learning. They see the purpose of planning as surfacing the underlying assumptions behind managers' plans.

Every strategy is an expression of a set of assumptions. Usually, business people argue about the right strategy, and that's pointless. The real conversation should be, what are our different assumptions, and how can we understand how each other's thinking?

Many leaders today are disoriented. They don't know what they're supposed to be doing. On the one hand, they may be pushing empowerment or breaking down traditional hierarchy. But, they're wondering: "What's my job? My job has always been making the key decisions, or having a key influence on how they get made. So what do I do now?"

We need to think of leaders as designers, stewards, and teachers, and not as the key decision-makers. I see many people leaning in that direction. It's not a matter of saying to someone, "Do it like they do it." You have to understand the direction of change underway in our time, and not just try to copy people.

The shared vision is an essential element to unite people, but it's just as important to develop a shared understanding of current reality. The Shell story illustrates the power of surfacing hidden assumptions and developing coherent shared images of reality. That's much harder than developing a shared vision.

How do you surface mental models? One key is the principle called "the ladder of abstraction," which has to do with developing awareness of how we move from direct observation to interpretation. It's like this: The meeting started at nine o'clock, and Joe walked in at 9:15. What goes off in everybody's head? "Joe's late; he's not committed; he can't organize time."

That's not data. The data is that Joe walked in at 9:15. The rest is an interpretation nobody bothers to test. The problem is not that we have these thoughts, but that we treat them as data. That's where the discipline of working with mental model starts. We have to become aware of our own thinking.

Maybe we need to pull back and say, "Let's look at the facts here," and try to separate the facts from the interpretation. But then you come to the next level of skills. If you go to Joe and say, "Joe, why did you come in at 9:15?" and try to be fact-based, very likely his first reaction will be defensiveness. We need to learn to talk to one another in ways that bring assumptions into the open without invoking defensiveness. It's not easy; there are no quick answers.

The world has changed profoundly, but we haven't changed with it. It's awesome the power we've acquired to shape the world. And yet our wisdom hasn't increased; in fact, it's diminished. It's like we're driving down a road at night and speeding up, and at the same time turning our headlights down.

All major crises today are systemic, and man-made. That's unique in history. All the major threats we used to face were short-term dramatic events, caused by something outside ourselves—whether a natural disaster or a sabertoothed tiger. But crises today are slow, gradual processes of our own making.

Our work is all about making a better world. You take any area of real concern—like long-term environmental issues—it's difficult to have improvement without a significant change in the way businesses operate. Businesses collectively are more important than government today. They have more global impact, and more ability to influence things.

We need to live our lives in the service of our highest aspirations. We can't afford to be paralyzed by fear or apprehension. We need a better sense of what the deeper issues are and what changes we are called upon to make.

Peter Senge is a faculty member of MIT, director of the Center for Organizational Learning at MIT's Sloan School of Management, founding partner of Innovation Associates, and author of The Fifth Discipline. *Visit www.solonline.org.*

21

Everybody Matters

by George W. Bush

Part of my vision for America is having a mosaic of people who provide love and comfort for people who need help. One of the great strengths of our country is that the social entrepreneurial spirit is strong. Our people don't wait for some law to be passed by Congress to ask, "What can I do to help a neighbor in need?" Thousands of people all across this country are making a singular difference in the lives of one person, one neighborhood, or one community.

I ask you to serve your community and to serve your country by finding a program that will make a difference in somebody's lives. It doesn't matter how big or how small the program is. What matters is your love and your energy and participation. Help somebody who is lonely. Mentor somebody who needs care and concern. Feed the hungry. Find shelter for the homeless. Please, answer my call to provide 4,000 hours, or two years, of volunteer service.

We started the USA Freedom Corps because we thought it was important for the federal government to lend a structure to the thousands who want to help, to provide an outlet for those who hear the call. And people are responding. There are over 60,000 opportunities for volunteer service that the USA Freedom Corps can steer people to. Thousands of people have asked, "How can I help?" They have said, "I want to help. Let me be a part of an optimistic future for America." And I thank those thousands who have signed up.

Corporate America also has a responsibility. It's important to make and sell a product. A lot of responsibility comes with running a company. Telling the truth is a responsibility that comes with running a country, by the way; being honest with your shareholder, if you're public company; being thoughtful to your employee. But I also believe there's a corporate responsibility to encourage employees to help in the community. Hundreds of companies have signed up to do this. I want to thank these companies for hearing and heeding the call. I encourage more companies to participate in this quest to make sure the American Dream extends into every neighborhood and every corner of this country.

AmeriCorps has thousands of people helping to inoculate children against disease, and thousands more people who are tutoring children. I support AmeriCorps. Another part of being a compassionate country is to be compassionate abroad. That's why I laid out a powerful AIDS initiative for the citizens in Africa who suffer from AIDS. It's an initiative that will lend the great heart of the American people to the salvation of many lives on that continent.

I'm pleased to see that Peace Corps applications are up by 30 percent. What I find even more interesting: 38 more countries have asked for Peace Corps volunteers to come into their land to help their country and to help their citizens realize their full potential. See, in this country, we say every life matters. Everybody is precious. Everybody counts.

I strongly believe in mentoring. I know we can change America one heart and one soul at a time. There's no doubt in my mind we can. So, I want to rally the compassion of this country to focus on junior and senior school high students who need a mentor.

You know why I say that? I say it because I've seen the benefits that come to both mentor and mentoree and heard their testimonies. For example, I heard about how the Best Friends Program in Washington, D.C., is changing lives. I met a young lady, a junior in college from Atlanta, Georgia, who responded to a call for volunteer mentors. When asked, "Can you help?" she said, "You bet, I can help." She is now mentoring a younger student, and I want to thank her. She is changing one life. Her love, compassion, and dedication to something greater than herself will give her the great satisfaction of knowing that she has made one life better. She may make a lot of other lives better, too. But right now, she can say, "I'm making one life better."

It's the cumulative effect of people making just one life better that will make the whole country better. I ask you to join many of your fellow citizens in loving somebody who needs help.

George W. Bush is President of the United States.

22

Pursuing Excellence

by Tom Peters

In an age when all value flows from creativity and initiative, we must imagine and embrace a model of leadership that is loose, open, and innovative.

We fall back, in these crazy and chaotic times, on the command-and-control model of leadership—a model that no longer accords with how dynamic leaders actually operate. We seek shelter in the fantasy of a leader who has the answers, who promises "change" or "success" or "profits" in exchange for patient "followership" or "obedience."

But in an age when all value flows from creativity and initiative, we must imagine and embrace a model of leadership that is loose, open, and innovative.

We ask leaders to be "good stewards" of the assets they inherit. But in an age when permanence is a dangerous delusion, we must instead ask leaders to challenge the legacies that they have inherited, to create entirely new value propositions—and then to get out before they get stale.

10 Enduring Traits

Here are 10 traits of leaders of excellence:

1. Leaders create opportunities. I was reading an article in a newsletter from an educational organization. The title sent me into a big rage. It suggested that excellent (educational) institutions "transform people." Nonsense! Nobody "transforms" anybody else! Instead, we create opportunities for people and then encourage them to apply their latent talents to grasp those opportunities. Leaders do not "transform people." Leaders instead construct a context in which Voyages of Mutual Discovery can take place. Leaders provide access to a portfolio of WOW Projects that challenge people to express their Innate Curiosity and to visit (or create) places that they (and their leaders) had never dreamed of. And when the voyage bears fruit, leaders applaud like hell, stage "photo ops," and ring the church bells 100 times to commemorate the bravery of their followers' explorations. As a leader, if you don't have the nerve to encourage people to redraw the map or to create a new map, you should not be leading anyone anywhere.

2. Leaders do! If you don't know what is going on, if you don't know the shape or even the location of the playing field, if you don't know the nature of the rule book or even if there is one, then in the immortal words of my Old Man, "Thomas, don't just stand there. Do something." It's a cute phrase. But it's far more profound than that. If you don't know what's going on, stop thinking. (It won't do you much good.) Try something. See what happens. That is, until you let fly the new system, new product, new procedure, or whatever, you have no idea what is going on.

3. Leaders re-do. If something goes awry, the typical big company shoots the messenger and aims to make sure this aberration never occurs again. In the process, the possibility of rapid progress is severely diminished. In short: "Do it right the first time" is stupid, a snare, a delusion, an abomination. Consider two superstars that don't give a second thought to what happens the first time (or the 21st). Namely, Sony and Microsoft. They "do" fast. And they re-do even faster. The Sony-Microsoft approach is remarkable—and an all-too-rare trait. Most either flog the tepid first version until they look like idiots. Or retreat—deciding that the failure means they weren't supposed to be in the market in the first place.

4. Leaders convey a grand design. A leader "sets the tone." That's obvious. The leader is also chief architect—not necessarily chief strategic planner. The architect model suits me better: She or he sets out the general design parameters, lets us know what she or he thinks about quality, about tolerating well-intended and energetically pursued failures, about innovation, about logistics performed to perfection. Call it core values. Call it essential philosophy or our charter or constitution. I call it the design specs. The essential stuff we care about, the way we intend to live and make our mark, and the stuff we won't compromise on. The stuff that is the essence of our character. Most conglomerates have proven unmanageable. But there's one that seems to work. That's the Virgin Group. Founder-CEO Richard Branson fits the Chief Architect model to a T. He says he won't launch a new product unless it's "cheeky." It also has to be of high quality and affordable. Branson sets the design specs. He embodies (lives) the design specs. So, too, Welch's performance fanaticism and talent obsession at GE. Iacocca's pugnaciousness, in a time of great darkness at Chrysler. Churchill's determination. Gandhi's persistence and unshakable philosophy of non-violence.

5. Leaders make mistakes. And they make no bones about it. Another thing that hangs on the wall of my Vermont writing studio is a quote by David Kelley, founder of IDEO Product Design: "Fail faster. Succeed sooner." Next to it hangs a saying by the extraordinary photographer Diane Argus, who told her students: "Learn not to be careful." In placid times, leaders may well have the answers. In turbulent times, leaders have the best questions that encourage (note the root word: "courage") others to undertake those voyages of mutual discovery. And the essence of process: allowing people to screw up. Screwing up is the essence of trying new stuff. If you try new stuff, you screw up. If you try a lot of new stuff, you screw up a lot.

6. Leaders nurture other leaders. The honors here go to leader-iconoclast-political-activist Ralph Nader. "I start with the premise," he said, "that the function of leadership is to produce more leaders, not more followers." I suspect that "the leader as strong man" times are past. That the technology is changing too fast. I talked to Bill McGowman, de facto founder of the telecom upstart MCI. "The 'chump-to-champ-to-chump' cycle," he lectured me "used to be three generations. Now it's about five years." Staying power, historically mostly fantasy, is now total fantasy. Therefore, I will offer a new guideline for leaders: Leaders don't create followers! They create energized, autonomous leaders. Leaders throughout the organization, starting with inspired youth at the bottom, help others discover new worlds. Encourage leaders who invent new worlds. Leaders who outstrip and dethrone their putative leaders. I mean that everyone is responsible for making/defining her own way. Everyone is charged with overturning today's beliefs. One can no longer depend on the big corporate fuzzball to nurture them for 30 or 40 years. Or even 5 or 10 years. Everyone is a renegade, innovator, and leader.

7. Leaders are great performers. FDR claimed, "It is necessary for the President to be the nation's No. 1 actor." Amen. Is this a plug for disingenuous behavior? No. If a leader attempts to induce risk taking, she or he must embody risk taking, even if she or he is a naturally reticent person. As one of my friends put it, bluntly, "Look, Tom, leaders aren't allowed to have bad days, especially on bad days. Leaders must exude the energy and confidence that will embolden others to act in the face of peril. It's that simple. And that hard." Every move by the 24-year-old supervisor, as well as the President of the United States, is scrutinized and dissected as to what it portends to the organization's (and individual's) future. Hence: Act accordingly!

8. Leaders accept responsibility. It's simple: Leaders take responsibility—visibly—for the decisions they make and the outcomes that ensue. (The spectacle of senior officers from giant, formerly high-flying companies "Taking the fifth" on national TV has not been inspiring.) At any level, at any age, in any position of responsibility: To play the "blame game" destroys the credibility of the blamer-leader faster than any other single act. Does this mean that retrospective analysis of things that go awry is inappropriate? Of course not. On the other hand, I've argued for 20 years that "a bias for action" is the single most significant positive attribute a successful enterprise—public or private—can have. A "bias for action" does not suggest thoughtlessness about the past. But it does suggest that there is a limit (relatively low) to the amount of introspection that might go on. Simple fact: Huge bureaucracies think too much and act too little. "Scapegoating" is a big part of this debilitating, paralytic process.

9. *Leaders take breaks.* The demands of leadership at any level could fill our waking hours thrice over, especially these days. And at times, 18-hour days are a must. But beware of burnout. Beware, in particular, of your unawareness of burnout and the unwillingness of those around you to point out that you are a zombie. This is not a homily about "work-life balance." I leave that to your spouse or preacher-priest-rabbi-shrink. This is a warning: Stress may kill. Literally. It surely kills effectiveness! Antidote? That's up to you. A few deep-breathing breaks, a two-minute-eyes-closed meditative stints, can be invaluable during the day. So, too, a long holiday—and the occasional four-day weekend. Such breaks are essential, and you probably need some active coaching-intervention to pull them off.

10. *Leaders do stuff that matters.* Sometimes I think that all "leadership literature" stinks—including much of the stuff I've written. Too much of the focus is on tactics and motivation (and, frankly, manipulation). All of that misses the point: Leadership for what? From King and Gandhi and Jefferson—to Bill Gates and Steve Jobs and Richard Branson—leaders lead because they want to get some particular thing done. They want to do stuff that matters.

Steve Jobs aimed to change the world with an "insanely great" (his term) idea about what a computer could be. Staying with the tech industry, you could say the same about Michael Dell. So, too, Larry Ellison (Oracle). Or, in the world of financial services, you could point to Charles Schwab and Ned Johnson (Fidelity). Those and other great leaders are not merely great at leading. They are great at inducing others to take novel journeys to places of surpassing importance.   ∽

Tom Peters is founder of tompeterscompany!, and has been hailed as the guru of gurus for management.
This article is adapted from his book, Re-Imagine! Business Excellence in a Disruptive Age. *Visit*
www.tompeterscompany.com.

Photographs: *Kenneth Linge Photography*
Architectural Renderings: *Kinateder & Associates*

3

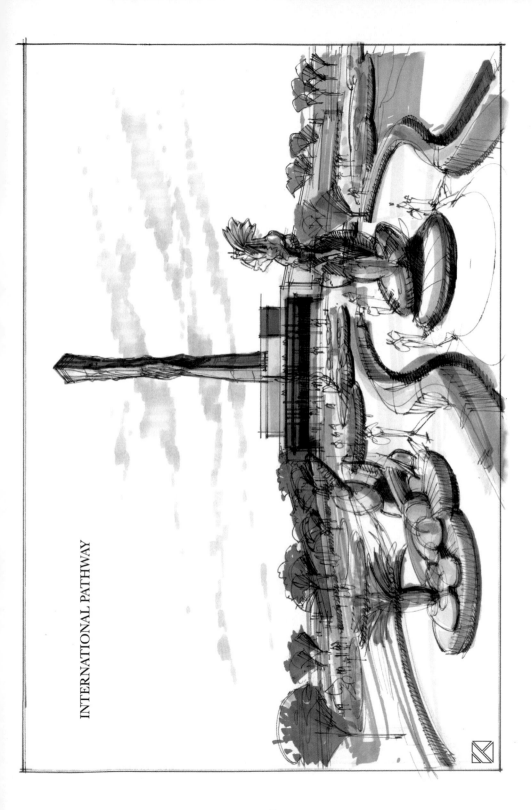

INTERNATIONAL PATHWAY

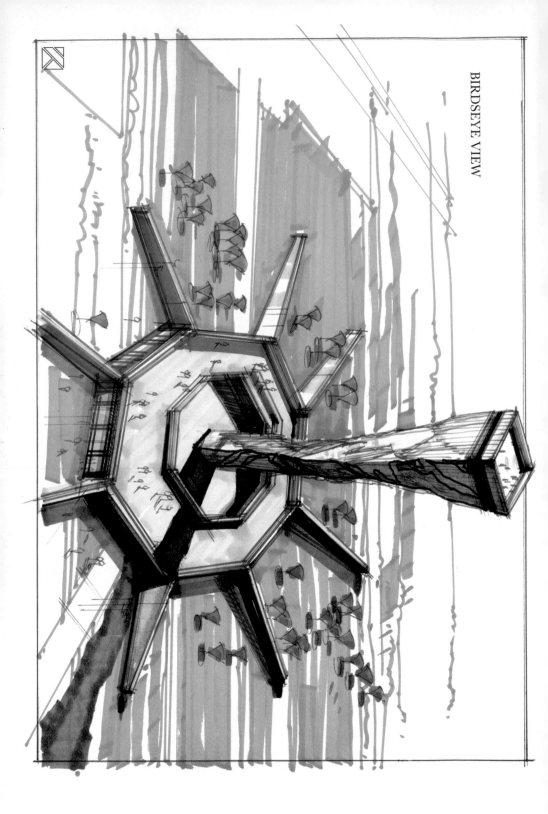

OPEN OBSERVATION DECK

INSIDE OBSERVATION

RESTAURANT I
RESTAURANT II

GIFT SHOP

2000 SQ FT/FLOOR

SKY VIEW

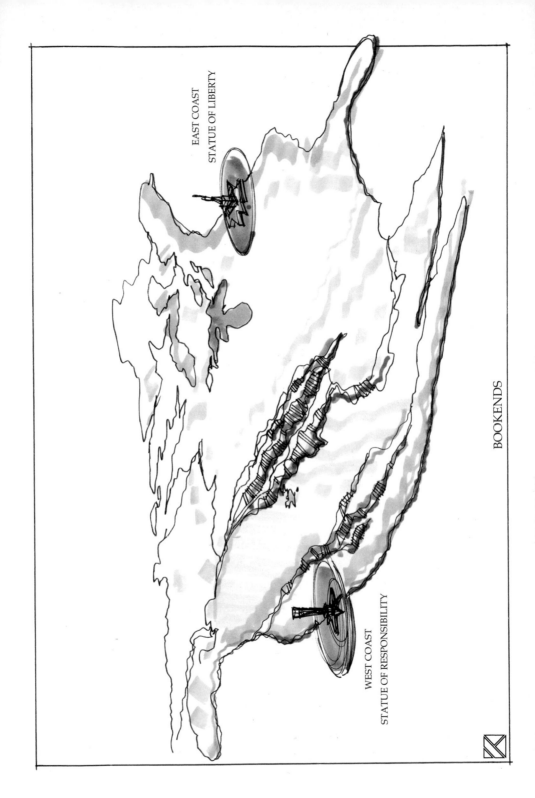

EAST COAST
STATUE OF LIBERTY

WEST COAST
STATUE OF RESPONSIBILITY

BOOKENDS

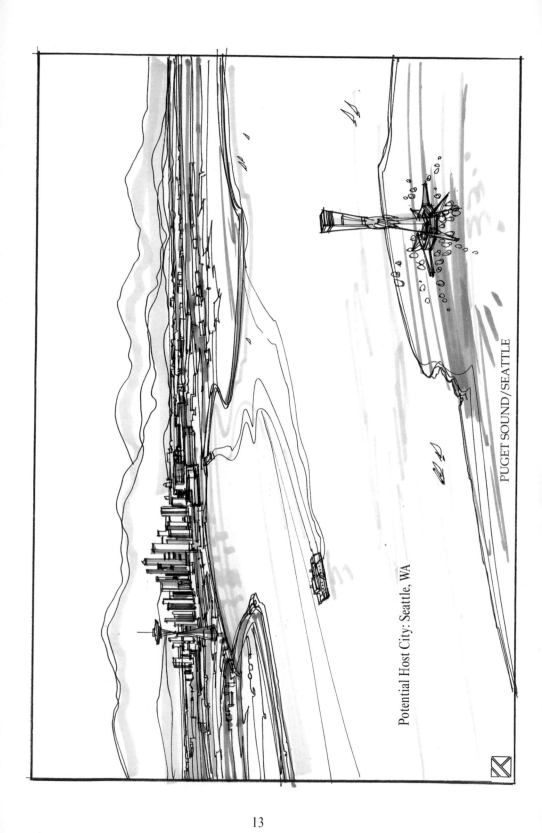

Potential Host City: Seattle, WA

PUGET SOUND/SEATTLE

Potential Host City: San Diego, CA

SAN DIEGO HARBOR

14

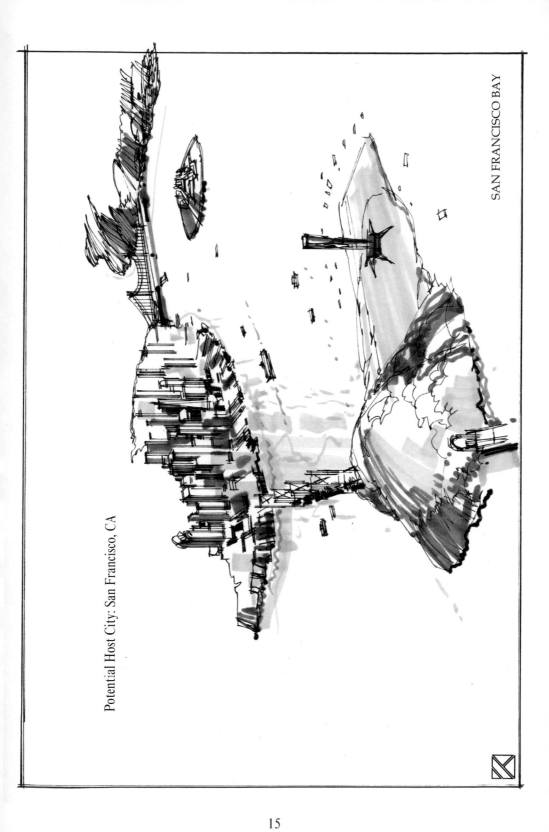

Potential Host City: San Francisco, CA

SAN FRANCISCO BAY

15

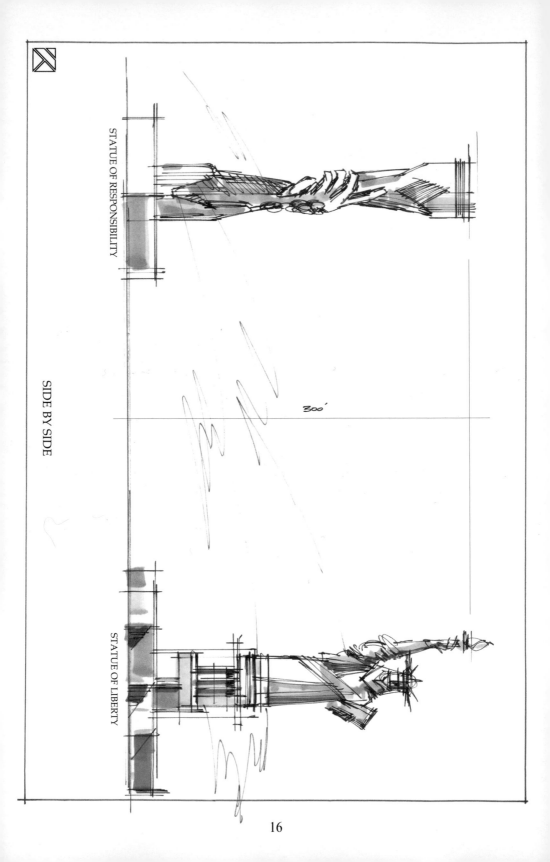

STATUE OF RESPONSIBILITY

SIDE BY SIDE

300'

STATUE OF LIBERTY

Moral Leadership

"The price of greatness is responsibility."

—Winston Churchill

Dynamics of Responsibility

by William O. Perry

Through all of recorded history, few of us have experienced the benefits of living in a free society. In fact, an objective observer might conclude from historical analysis that the natural state of human kind is not freedom, but tyranny.

Those of us who give our time and resources to Freedoms Foundation at Valley Forge understand that reality. We know that living in a tightly controlled state is tempting to those who are unwilling to bear the heavy responsibilities of freedom. We know that being told what to do and how to live daily removes the constant burden of freely making responsible decisions. We know that giving yourself to an ideology reduces the pressure to learn and grow and think responsibly.

Most importantly, those of us who support Freedoms Foundation know that each new generation must be taught not merely to appreciate freedom but to commit themselves to the responsibilities which freedom requires.

The two concepts—freedom and responsibility—are not simply complementary, they are integral, intertwined, inseparable.

You may be free to read from the best books, but that freedom is meaningless unless you actually read. As Mark Twain said: "A person who does not read is no better off than a person who cannot read."

This same truism runs through every freedom we enjoy. A citizen who does not vote is no better off than a citizen who can't vote. A worker who does not work is no better off than a worker who is denied work by a closed economic system. An individual who does not speak out about social injustice is no better off than an individual who is not allowed to speak out.

Too often, we think of responsibility and freedom in narrow terms, focusing on the responsibility of defending freedom on the battlefield. Certainly, military defense is a vital part of the responsibilities that come with freedom. But when one looks at history, it becomes apparent that relatively few of our nation's citizens have been called upon to bear the responsibility of military service in time of war. We honor every American who wears the uniform of the nation. We honor them not only as a responsibility but also out of sincere appreciation.

Nevertheless, over more than two centuries our nation and its people have learned that the responsibilities of freedom do not end when the conflict is over. Indeed, part of our responsibility as citizens is to minimize incidents of armed conflict. We do that by keeping the nation strong, by keeping our values intact, and by being the nation to which others look for an example. These, too, are responsibilities which come with freedom.

The genius of America is not simply that our Founding Fathers defined freedom for us: "We hold these truths to be self-evident . . ." Neither is it that they set clear examples of responsibility: "We mutually pledge to each other our Lives, our Fortunes and our sacred Honor."

The true genius of the nation is that each subsequent generation has built upon the example of America's first citizens. Each generation has accepted the definition of freedom provided by the *Declaration of Independence*. Each generation has added to the list of responsibilities which come with American freedom. And the nation has become greater because of it.

Young men and women tackle the issues of their times—not so much by changing the definition of freedom as by expanding the responsibilities which go with it. As each generation finds answers to the challenges which face it, our list of responsibilities grows . . . and our strength as a nation grows.

Albert Einstein said: "We cannot solve our problems with the same level of intellect we had when we created them." Neither can we meet the expectations of freedom with a concept of responsibility which does not improve from generation to generation.

For one generation, the challenge was to determine the responsibilities necessary to make a free enterprise economic system work—responsibilities of business, responsibilities of government, responsibilities of working people. For another generation, it was defining the responsibilities of citizenship and states' rights—a struggle which required a bloody civil war and a remarkable young statesman-president.

Several generations fought through economic turmoil to work out the proper balance of responsibilities between government regulation and business, especially banking. Two generations sent young citizens into worldwide conflicts to preserve freedom and help all nations, including our own, understand national responsibilities in an increasingly interdependent world. Recent generations sent their best and brightest to protect others from the dangers of totalitarianism.

One generation helped us find the way toward responsibilities we have to all citizens, regardless of race, creed, or color of skin. That generation added civil rights to the list of national, personal, and governmental responsibilities.

Today's generation struggles with helping us understand our responsibilities with regard to science, religion, and our position as the world's only superpower.

None of these many responsibilities is completely resolved. Each generation adds dimension, understanding, and meaning to our citizenship responsibilities. They are works in progress, just as our nation is a work in progress. Freedom, democracy, responsibilities, and life itself are all works in progress. They are processes, not conditions.

Freedom is a concept, a beacon, a torch atop the Statue of Liberty, lighting the way for those who wish to follow America's example.

Responsibility is a process—individuals reaching out to help others, generations from the past reaching across time to help generations of today, whole nations reaching across boundaries to help oppressed people find freedom.

Like the Statue of Liberty, the Statue of Responsibility will also be a beacon, illuminating the message that responsibility goes hand in hand with liberty, in maintaining freedom.

As long as we understand that liberty and responsibility are different but inseparable, then America will continue to be the great nation it is.

We must also accept our responsibility to make sure the next generation of young men and women truly appreciate the unbreakable connection between liberty and responsibility. History teaches the value of freedom. Experience teaches the necessity of responsibility.

The United States of America was founded on freedom. It survives—indeed, it thrives—through responsibility.

William O. Perry is chairman of the board, Freedoms Foundation at Valley Forge. Visit www.ffvf.org

24

Reframing Responsibility

by Nabyl Eddahar

Globalization, as a tendency to frame in a universal manner our ways of thinking, is changing our way of arguing about responsibility. Not long ago, discussion about responsibility and other themes related to it, used to take place in a "Westphalian" frame, distinguishing sharply "domestic" from "international" sphere.

Today, heightened awareness of globalization and geopolitical instabilities have caused this framework to lose its self-evidence and resulted in a new sense of vulnerability. The world, facing globalized dangers and challenges, needs a more comprehensive conception of responsibility that would introduce at the same time more meaning and more universality, by addressing the essence of the problem.

Under these changing conditions, the theory of responsibility is undergoing a paradigm shift. Globalization is problematizing and politicizing its multiple levels.

Islam, as a religion and as a theory for human behavior, is a balance principle that serves to measure, revise and change all human ventures. The theory of responsibility in Islam easily adheres to every case, be it personal or social. The moral and political foundations and limits of responsibility in Islam are clear enough not to allow any alterations to suit the latest fantasies or ambitions of men.

Contribution of Religion and Spirituality

Let's begin by replacing the problem in its broad dimension. It has become common to say that human societies have degenerated with the passage of time. But we must remember that they have, at the same time, accumulated many experiences in virtue of their old age. For example, we have a much broader view of the world than our ancestors; we see that our existence depends on the existence of others.

If we consider the most important religious and spiritual traditions, we could ascertain that "There is no traditional divergence as to what constitutes primordial man." There is a shared essence of man, although the imagery used to tell of the "fall" differs from religion to religion. But, in all cases, the "loss" incurred is always the same. We shall see that it is the loss of centrality.

In this context, the basic purpose of religion becomes the opening up for man of the way to return to his lost centrality. According to many philosophers and men of religion, "The outlook that governs the modern civilization represents no less than man's capitulation to the exact opposite of truth as regards what concerns him most—the nature and function of the human being."

The spiritual crisis of our times may be explained by the fact that "Instead of being bent on regaining what was lost, the loser has come to believe that he has suffered no loss whatsoever and that mankind, having evolved from next to nothing, is now better than it has ever been." This process of capitulation is unconscious.

We have been endowed with three main faculties: intelligence, will, and soul, corresponding to "the equally interdependent ternary of doctrine, method and morals; or to faith, practice and virtue; or again, on a different register, to comprehension, concentration and conformation." There can be no real comprehension without spirituality. And no spirituality can be achieved without wholeness, And there can be no wholeness without sincerity, which means the harmonious combination of the three faculties oriented towards the achievement of a common end.

Responsibility in Islamic Perspective

In Islam, the concept of responsibility derives from the phenomenon of Creation and is closely connected to the concept of manhood; it is intimately related to the doctrine of revelation and to the spiritual history of Man. It can't be completely understood unless conceived in that wholeness.

The concept of responsibility in Islam derives from the combination of two doctrines:

1. The doctrine of a Covenant: The *Holy Quran* is significant in this regard. "When thy Lord drew forth from the children of Adam—from their loins—their descendants, and made them testify concerning themselves, (saying): 'Am I not your Lord (Who cherishes and sustains you)?' They said: 'Yea! We do testify!' (This) lest ye should say on the Day of Judgment: 'Of this, we were never mindful.' "

Although this passage has led to different interpretations, it expresses the following ideas:

• A "Covenant" was taken from all of the children of Adam—from all humanity, born or unborn, without any limitations in time.

• The children of Adam, all humans, perpetuate the existence of Adam, and thus carry on his spiritual legacy.

• Humanity, in this perspective has a corporate perspective; God has given all nations and peoples certain powers and faculties to fulfill certain duties.

• Certain spiritual obligations, certain responsibilities, arise from this implied Covenant.

• All men should acknowledge that God is their Creator, Cherisher and Sustainer; they should also acknowledge their duties and obligations to Him, as these follow from their "first nature," when it is pure and uncorrupted. This first state of purity is that "small" voice in each one of us that acknowledges the Truth and leads us to awaken, see and face our responsibilities.

• Those special powers and faculties given to man should show him the distinctions between good and evil, licit and illicit, and warn him of all the dangers of going "astray" in this life.

2. The doctrine of a "Trust." The idea of a Trust derives from that of a Covenant. It is something given to us over which we have a power of disposition. It implies that God, the Giver, expects us, the trustees, to use it according to certain rules, not otherwise.

"We did indeed offer the Trust to the Heaven and the Earth and the mountains; but they refused to undertake it, being afraid thereof: But man undertook it; he was indeed unjust and foolish."

The symbols contained in this verse are intended to help us to reflect. The mountains stand for their firmness and stability, the Earth as a part of the solar system obeying the fixed laws of God, and the Heavens as celestial space, symbolical of the Angels, being also ruled by God's will. All these creatures have no will of their own.

Man, endowed with such a faculty, was too audacious and ignorant to realize the consequences of his acceptance; he can either betray the Trust and become a "hypocrite" or be "faithful" to it and receive God's mercy.

The main idea that stems out of this is that the Creator intended a high position and a high destiny for man, placing him in his pure state even above the Angels. He differentiated him when He breathed something of His own spirit into him.

Through the *Holy Quran*, many texts point to this idea: "But He fashioned him in due proportion, and breathed into him something of His spirit. And He gave you (the faculties of) hearing and sight and feeling (and understanding): Little thanks do ye give!" "When I have fashioned him (in due proportion) and breathed into him of My spirit, fall ye down in obeisance unto him."

These two doctrines of "Covenant" and "Trust" explain symbolically how we have undertaken this great Responsibility, and this is what made us the Vicegerent of God. But man fell from above, became corrupted, thus incurring the loss of this special position; this made him even lower than the beasts.

"Behold, thy Lord said to the Angels: 'I will create a Vicegerent on Earth.' They said: 'Wilt Thou place therein one who will make mischief and shed blood whilst we do celebrate Thy praises and glorify Thy Holy Name?' He said: 'I know what ye know not.' "

Men and women of all capabilities, talents and positions can have access to that spiritual insight, enabling them to understand their responsibilities. We will be held accountable for whatever we do. There will be no excuse for any of us. The *Quran* indicates both future penalties (if the warning is not heeded) and future privileges (for the righteous). A solemn promise to God can't be broken with impunity: "And yet they had already covenanted with God not to turn their backs, and a covenant with God must (surely) be answered for."

Acknowledging the Responsibility should lead us to follow certain behaviors: First, to see the modern world's spiritual corruption, political domination, economic inequality, social injustice, wars, and ecological threats as enormities. Second, to be actively opposed to theses enormities as a possible counterpower. Many people lack the sense of their own shortcoming because of their failure to understand their true nature.

Despite its many negative consequences on developing countries, cultures and economies, globalization uncovers many problems, raises ontological questions and introduces interactive processes bearing transformative approaches. It is an opportunity to reconstitute the "what" of responsibility. Responsibility has multiple dimensions and can be approached on multiple levels. Today, our globalized world needs to change the very grammar of conceptualizing it, thereby reconstructing its foundations.

One of the most urgent and crucial tasks today is to bring together women and men from all backgrounds, cultures, convictions and religions, in the name of the common principles of responsibility and of dignity. Overcoming the ideology of fear and loosening the grips of emotions when dealing with the great challenges of our era, requires the recovering of critical intelligence, spirituality and conscience as imperatives for our humanity.

The project of building a giant piece of art that would remind us of our duties as they follow from our position as accountable creatures is in fact an aim to democratize the process by which the framework should be redrawn and revised. It is also a means of establishing a transnational public sphere where all spiritual traditions can be represented and participate.

The project, adopting a democratic approach, shows also that the question of responsibility needs a collective decision-making.

Nabyl Eddahar, Ph.D., is a professor of social sciences at the University Hassan II, Casablanca, Fulbright Visiting Scholar at the Institute....and Fulbright Visiting Specialist at Utah Valley University.

25

Real Courage

by Johnny C. Taylor, Jr.

Today, all decisions aren't made with formulas or complicated matrices. Every answer can't be found in a book or an MBA curriculum—or even at a leadership seminar. Some decisions must be made from the heart.

When most of us think of "courage," names like Abraham Lincoln, Muhammad Ali, or, perhaps Anne Frank, come to mind. These were extraordinary individuals in extraordinary circumstances. And then there are the individuals—many of them "ordinary" in the sense that they aren't well-known—whose stories of resolve and heroism are told in John F. Kennedy's widely read *Profiles in Courage*.

When I think of courage, the first person that comes to mind is a seemingly ordinary African-American lady in an ordinary place, who, in an act of moral courage, changed the world. Although she wasn't a business leader or a politician, her courageous example of leadership galvanized a movement. It was over 50 years ago that Rosa Parks boarded a city bus in Montgomery, Alabama. She sat where she always sat—at the back. But on that afternoon, the bus was crowded and a white man couldn't find a seat. So, the bus driver ordered Ms. Parks to give up hers. Rosa Parks didn't create a scene; she quietly refused. She did a remarkable thing, at great personal risk. She was arrested, but in that time and place, she also could have lost her job, been beaten, or even killed for her actions.

Her courage that day started ripples that eventually became a powerful wave. The rest of Ms. Parks's story is American history: Her trial, the year-long Montgomery bus boycott, and the Supreme Court's ruling in November 1956 that found segregation in public transportation unconstitutional.

Years later, when asked about her decision to refuse to move that day, Mrs. Parks said, "People always say I didn't give up my seat because I was tired. That isn't true. No. The only tired I was tired of—was giving in."

This is a quintessential example of moral courage. Sometime in our careers, each of us will face a moment where we must make a choice that will test our character and our inner strength. It may not seem as dramatic as the choice faced by Rosa Parks; still, doing the right thing may require us to summon *our* moral courage.

Examples of courageous leaders are all about us. Major General John Hawkins is one such model. As Assistant Deputy Chief of Staff for Personnel, he's responsible for human resources across the entire United States Army. Many HR professionals consider recruiting to be one of their main challenges. They should try lining up 80,000 men and women each year for a job that may involve miserable living conditions, months at a time away from home and family, and being on the receiving end of live ammunition—now this is a tough HR assignment. And here's another.

Not long after the September 11 terrorist attacks, General Hawkins was asked to take on a special mission—one that would test his physical courage as never before. He became Director of the Coalition Information Service for "Operation Enduring Freedom," and was assigned to Afghanistan to lead an international team during the war. The General spent 143 days, 8 hours, and 13 minutes in Afghanistan; but those last 13 minutes make quite a story.

The day General Hawkins left Kabul, the Afghan capital, the airport had just reopened, and the airport road was crowded with pilgrims and military traffic. Suddenly a car came up from behind. It was filled with terrorists—and General Hawkins was the apparent target. His driver sped for the international security forces checkpoint a few miles ahead. French and British troops raced with him to the airport, where he jumped out, crawled under barbed wire, and sprinted to the plane just in time.

Not many of us will have our courage tested like General Hawkins—or like Alayne Gentul, who performed an unforgettable act of physical *and* moral courage. Alayne was the HR Director for the Fiduciary Trust Company, and she was working at Fiduciary's offices on the 90th floor of World Trade Center Tower 2 on the morning of September 11, 2001.

When the plane hit, there was panic and confusion. One of Alayne's co-workers said that everyone was screaming—that it was chaos. But Alayne Gentul was not screaming—she was working, with courage and purpose, to help others. Her co-worker Nora Haldon remembers: "I looked at Alayne and said, 'What do you want us to do?' She was so calm. She looked at me and said, 'Nora, everyone should go downstairs in an orderly way—you go now.' " But Alayne didn't go downstairs—she went *up*, to the 97th floor, to make sure all of Fiduciary's people—her people—got out. It was from there, as smoke filled the offices, that she called her husband for the last time. Moments later the tower collapsed, and she was lost. Through her courage and sacrifice, Alayne Gentul is credited with saving the lives of 40 Fiduciary employees.

Earlier this year, I spoke about courage at a conference of HR leaders. Afterward, one of the conference attendees pointed out that being courageous isn't always easy. She said, "It's fine for you to talk about being courageous, but I've got a child in college, a mortgage to pay, and a car note. I'm a single mom. I can't afford to lose my job." She went on to describe a situation where she was forced to choose between pleasing her CEO and breaking the law.

After hearing her story, I acknowledged that there was no easy answer for the dilemma she faced. In the end, I told her that it boiled down to a personal question that she needed to ask herself: "Am I brave enough to do the right thing?" She looked at me for a long moment and said, "Am I brave enough to do the right thing? Yes. I believe I am." And she walked away. That was a test, a defining moment, for that woman in her career and, perhaps, in her life. And while I do not know what she did, I'd like to think she did what she believed was right.

Few of us will have to defy oppression like Rosa Parks; or dodge terrorist attacks like General John Hawkins; or give our lives, like Alayne Gentul, to help save others. But most of us, like the single mom who confronted me, will at some point have our integrity tested and our beliefs challenged. At those moments, we can choose what kind of leaders we want to be—passive, submissive or courageous. It's up to each of us.

Johnny C. Taylor Jr., J.D., SPHR, is the president of McGuire Woods HR Strategies, LLC, a human resource consulting firm, and chair of the board of the Society for Human Resource Management (SHRM), the world's largest association devoted to HR management. Visit www.shrm.org.

26

Moral Courage

by John McCain

Life is full of promise, at least so it seems when a passage of life is marked by accomplishment. On such days, it may seem as if the world attends you.

But if tomorrow the world seems indifferent as it awaits new achievements from you, your families will likely be your most unstinting source of encouragement, counsel, and support. So, thank those who have attended you and whose pride in your accomplishments is even greater than your own—your parents. When the world looks elsewhere, your parents' attention is one of life's certainties. Thank them for the sacrifices they make for you, for their confidence in you, and their love for you.

I'm not clairvoyant, and so I don't know what you'll become. But I know what you *could* become. What you *should* become. Today you may not know precisely how you will lead an accomplished life or use your talents in a cause greater than your self-interest. You have choices to make and challenges to confront. Usually such choices reveal themselves over time. They seldom arrive just once, are resolved at one time, and permanently fix the course of your life. Many important choices emerge slowly, sometimes obscurely. Often, they are choices you must make again and again.

Once in a while you are confronted with a choice, the implications of which are so profound that its resolution affects your life forever. But that happens seldom. For most people, life is long and varied enough to overcome occasional mistakes and failures.

Still, I can attest, speaking from experience, that failure stinks. So, be afraid of failure—just don't be undone by it. Move on. Failure is no more a permanent condition than is success. "Defeat is never fatal," Winston Churchill observed. "Victory is never final. It's courage that counts." That's my advice: *Be brave. Have courage.* I assure you, no one ever gave me more important counsel.

You may not have plotted your life in detail or even defined your ambitions, but hopefully you have developed within you the wherewithal to make the race; to choose well; to confront your challenges intelligently and forth-

108

rightly; to overcome mistakes and failures in a way that diminishes the likelihood of your repeating them. All who care about you hope they have helped you build the one thing you must possess—courage.

Again, Churchill makes my point: "Courage is the first of all human qualities because it is the quality that guarantees all others." Without courage, we can possess no other virtue securely. Without courage, honesty, compassion, justice, happiness, and love are fragile qualities—admired, sought, professed, perhaps, but held cheaply and surrendered easily without a fight. That's what we mean when we claim "the courage of our convictions." Our convictions possess no innate courage, but if we lack the courage to hold them, not just when they accord with the convictions of others but against threatening opposition, in the moment of their testing, they are superficial, vain things that add nothing to our self-respect. We can admire virtue and abhor corruption sincerely, but without courage we are corruptible.

Patrick Moynihan coined the phrase "defining deviancy down" to criticize how we have embraced situational morality rather than insist on moral absolutes. Similarly, over the last 30 years we have defined courage down. We attribute courage to all manner of actions that may be admirable, but they hardly compare to the self-sacrifice on behalf of something greater than self-interest that once defined courage. We now accept one attribute of courage—fortitude, discipline, or daring, for example—as the entire virtue. Sharing your secret fears with others is considered courage. We say it takes courage to be different from the mainstream in our preferences in fashion, music, or hairstyle.

What does real courage look like? Pat Tillman gave up a professional football career to enlist in the Army. He served one combat tour in Iraq and another in Afghanistan where he was killed in action. He was, by all accounts, a hell of a guy—a good son, brother, husband, friend, student, and athlete—a decent, considerate man, a solid citizen in every respect. Obviously, he had been raised to be an honorable man, and to possess the virtues that make an honorable life. He had skill, fortitude, and daring. But it was his unexpected choice of duty to his country over the riches and comforts of celebrity that proved his courage.

He loved his country, and he worried that he had "never done a damn thing" to serve her. Love and honor oblige us to pay our debts to those who sacrificed to secure our blessings. Pat Tillman felt that debt, and he did not consider it an unwanted burden. He knew that the recompense of such debts earns us happiness. His loss grieves us. I mourn his death. But I will not dwell on it when I remember him. Many men live a longer life than Pat, but few ever live a better one. It is far better, and more respectful to his memory, that we celebrate his brief, brave and happy life.

Few of us will need the physical courage of Pat Tillman, nor must we serve in the military to prove real courage. But we all need and can possess moral courage. For courage to be authentic, it must encounter fear and prove itself superior to it. A sense of honor and duty, a regard for the dignity of others as well as our own, and the shame we feel when we neglect them motivate both moral and physical courage. By *fear* I mean fear of harm to your well-being—physical, emotional or material—that wars with your need to take action but is overcome because you value something or someone more.

Moral courage will sometimes require physical courage. Martin Luther King had the moral courage to struggle non-violently for justice, and it gave him the physical courage to persevere not only in the face of political opposition, social alienation, slurs and insults, but when suffering threats of physical injury and death. "If a man hasn't discovered something that he will die for," he declared, "he isn't fit to live."

You will need moral courage to remain virtuous, and you will need physical courage, strength, and skill to act. Fortunately, moral courage, unlike physical courage, is seldom exhausted. For a time I lived in a prison cell in Vietnam next to a senior officer, a fierce resister, maybe the bravest of us all. The stories of what he would do to resist our enemies strengthened our morale and courage. Many times when I was brought back to my cell after a physically challenging interrogation, I would communicate with my neighbor by tapping on the wall that separated us. I wanted to tell him what had happened and how well or poorly I had endured it, even though I risked punishment.

Once, when my neighbor had been hauled back into his cell after a rough interrogation, I waited for him to tap me up on the wall so I could learn what had happened and offer him some encouragement, as he had so often given me. The tap never came. So I tried tapping him up, again and again. No reply ever came. He was as brave as they come, a good and great man. But sometimes you just get tired; your physical courage just fails you. No one can ever be entirely certain of it.

But moral courage is more certain and can be summoned more readily. And it grows stronger with exercise. You can have moral courage when you need it. How? As Eleanor Roosevelt, a woman plagued by feelings of insecurity, put it: "Do the thing you think you cannot do, and you will gain strength, courage, and confidence by every experience." We all have to face fear and make choices to act or not, to love well or not, to be brave or not. The quality of our lives depends on the choices we make.

So, use your education and other advantages to become valued contributors to your chosen professions, your communities, your country, to the progress of humanity. I wish that of you because I wish you happiness. Your happiness, however, requires you to choose well, despite your fears. It requires your courage. And how well you choose in the tests that come to you will affect the happiness of others as well.

If you do the things you think you cannot do, you'll feel your hope, your dignity and your courage grow stronger every time you prove it. You will face

harder choices someday that may well require greater courage. You're preparing for them now. And when those moments come, and you choose well, your
courage will be recognized by those who matter most to you. When your children see you choose to value virtue more than security, to love more than you
fear, they will learn what courage looks like, what love it serves, what happiness it earns, and they will dread its absence.

We are all afraid of something. Some have more fears than others. The one
we must all guard against is the fear of ourselves. Don't let the sensation of
fear convince you that you're too weak for courage. Fear is the opportunity for
courage, not proof of cowardice. No one is born a coward. We were meant to
love. And we were meant to have the courage for it. So be brave. The rest is
easy.

*John McCain is a U.S. Senator and candidate for President. He is also the bestselling author of
the book,* Why Courage Matters, *a naval aviator, and Vietnam veteran. This article is adapted from
his speech at the University of Southern California Class of 2004 commencement, where he was
awarded an honorary doctorate.*

27

Leadership

by Norman Schwarzkopf

You can divide man's work into a calling, like a priest, or a profession, like a doctor. It's either a career, where you go from step to step, moving up a ladder of progression, or just a job, where you walk in every day and punch a ticket. Nobody stays in the military—or in any position—and makes a success of it, unless they feel called to do so.

The military is someplace between the calling and the profession. It's something you're identified with; you have a title, and everybody calls you that. And yet, you also have to have this inner drive of service. West Point gave me a creed to live by: "Duty, Honor, Country." I have tried to live by that creed. It became a way of life for me. I enjoy the sense of service. You know that you're serving something beyond yourself. You derive the reward from the fact that you are dedicating your life to serving your country.

My experience in Vietnam was one of the most self-fulfilling experiences I've ever had, because there was no gain in it for me at all. I was making a tremendous sacrifice for no personal gain.

The troops make it all worthwhile. It's great to be with them. Many times, it wasn't fun, but we experienced more peaks than valleys, and I came to know people of many different nationalities, cultures, and ethnic backgrounds. Meeting all of these people was a wonderful education for me. It taught me that there is more than one way to look at a problem—and they all may be right. It gave me a deep appreciation for people—to enjoy them as you find them and not prejudge anybody. I learned to be flexible to get along with people of different nationalities.

Love your troops, the people you lead. Any general who is worth his salt cares very much for his troops and knows that war is not fought by robots but by soldiers, by people. That liberty is bought by the blood of soldiers, and the sacrifices of these people. I don't know any modern U.S. generals who are war-mongers. They will go to extreme steps to avoid war, because they know just how bad it is. They all went through the Vietnam experience. They know the horrors of war, and they are greater pacifists than most people.

Also love the duty that you're performing. Duty is one of the most powerful motivators. The sense of duty keeps you going when things get very rough. In war, you have this sense of duty. When you must go to war, you want to get it over with as quickly as possible. To bring all of your power to bear and get the darn thing over. If you have to fight it, then the smart way to fight it is to use everything you have and get it over with. That's the way you save lives. If you lead men in battle, they're your people.

I still grieve for the loss of every single person who was ever under my command—and I show it. I inspire morale among the troops because I show emotion. If you believe something, you should believe it passionately. To be a good leader, you have to lead passionately. I'm a passionate person, and I feel strongly about things. I'm an emotional person. The tragedy of losing young men and women is tough to swallow.

I did not come into the Army to be a lieutenant, or a captain, or a major. I always intended to be a general. If I started pumping gas at a Shell service station, I would want to be the CEO of Shell Oil. I always aim high and dream high. It leads to heroism. Nobody says on the battlefield, "I think I will be a hero today, and do a heroic act." It's people doing their duty. Somebody else sees them and says, "Wow, isn't that heroic!" But the people who are doing it don't think at the time or after the fact that they're being heroes. They say, "I'm was just doing my duty."

Anybody who says they're not afraid of war is either a liar or crazy. There is nothing wrong with fear. Fear will keep you alive in a war—and in business. Fear tends to cause you to focus and see things in much sharper perspective. What is bad is when you allow that fear to turn into panic and paralyze you to the point that you can't perform your duty. True courage is being afraid, and going ahead and doing your job anyhow.

Leadership is not managing an organization. Leadership is all about motivating people. You have to have competence to be a leader, but you also have to have character.

The secret to modern leadership is two rules:

Rule 1: When placed in command, take charge. The leader is the person who takes the responsibility. There are many other people who are willing to do the job, but they don't want to get hung with the loss when it happens. As a leader, you have to take the responsibility and take charge. When you are placed in command, you must take charge. Have confidence in yourself and in your training. Work smart so that when you've got to make the tough decision, you can make the decision. Nothing is more debilitating to an organization than a leader who won't make a decision. The whole organization just stops and waits, and nothing happens. If you're not confident in yourself, how can you expect others to have confidence in you?

Rule 2: Once in command, do what's right. All of us know, when placed in those circumstances, what the moral, what the ethical, what the correct thing to do is. We all know it. So, the true leader takes charge and does what's right. You've got to believe in what you're doing. If you don't believe in what you're doing, you're not going to do it well. You truly have to believe that you're doing what's right. I don't think I could go to war if I thought we were doing something wrong. I think I would get out. You don't have to stay—you have an alternative. You can't justify what you do by saying, "I was only doing my duty." That's not right, because you have a higher duty to your moral code. You've got to do what's right.

Leadership is an art, not a science. A lot of gut instinct comes into everything you do. It can't be reduced to a piece of paper and a few simple mechanical equations that you apply to, out drops the answer, and you just go out and do that. Much of leadership is gut feeling and risk-taking. You don't take risks with your troops' lives, though. You've got to have your priorities and know what you believe in. You learn more from negative leadership than you do from positive leadership.

In the Gulf war, I was determined that if we were going to war, we were going to use our full military might. Our President allowed us to do it that way. He did exactly what a President should do. He told us what to do, he gave us our orders, and then he stayed informed all along the way, in great detail, as to what we were doing. But he did not interfere and decide that he was going to play general. There is a right way to fight a war. That's the way that will minimize your casualties, save the lives of the people who are fighting. Get it over with as fast as you can. In the Gulf, the young troops there were not afraid of the enemy. They were afraid they were going to get involved in another war that the American people weren't going to support.

I never underestimate the strength of an adversary. My job is to have doubts and think of everything that could possibly go wrong, and then try and fix it. I knew that I would be ordering many thousands of men and women into battle, and if I didn't have it right, I could be responsible for the deaths of thousands of people. That's a heavy burden to carry, so you don't carry that burden lightly. If you have any conscience at all, you have doubts, but you work your way through those doubts in such a way that you're satisfied that you've done everything you can possibly do to have a favorable outcome.

I adopted a campaign plan that capitalized on using our strengths against their weaknesses. I avoided their strengths and our weaknesses. That's a good strategy for any business. You know your strengths and weaknesses, and then use your strengths against their weaknesses. You don't rush into things without thinking. You learn to work with all constituents to build a coalition with a common goal so you all know exactly what you want to do. It is then easier to get people to focus on the goal. When things come up that are not part of the goal, you put them aside. You stay focused on the goal.

What makes for a great leader? Character, competence, selfless service, caring about people, and caring passionately about your cause. You're not doing it for yourself; you're not doing it to stroke your ego; in fact, you're doing it in spite of yourself. When you serve in the military, you serve something other than yourself. You get a great sense of satisfaction whenever you serve something greater than yourself.

Great leaders are also self-critical. I'm my own strongest critic. I am much tougher on myself than anybody I know, consistently. People who think they are right all the time scare me. None of us are infallible. We all make mistakes. That's okay. What's important is to learn from those mistakes.

To leaders, I say, how many of you learned something about how to do your present job by screwing it up the first time? How can you not allow yourself mistakes? You're not giving yourself the freedom to fail, and the latitude to learn. I've learned most things I now do well by screwing up the first time.

When I graduated from West Point, I saw things in black and white. And I demanded a great deal of myself then, in black and white. I had to do everything right; I couldn't do anything wrong. But I learned that's not what life is about. Self-fulfillment is the most important thing—being happy and feeling good about what you do and how you do it. You don't measure your success by what you take out of life; you measure your success by what you leave behind.

You can have all the money, power, and prestige in the world, but none of that is important. What's important is what you do with it when you have it. Dare to be what you want to be. Don't do something just because it may bring you fame or fortune. Do it because it will make you happy. So, dare to be yourself. Take your God-given talent and use it the way you feel you should use it. Don't let anybody steer you down the path of money or prestige or success. I've seen so many people in my lifetime who burn out. They get all of these things and then see that there isn't anything else. So, they ask, "What do I do now?" It's not in their heart. They don't feel good about themselves. They don't feel satisfied, because they measure their lives in terms of the next promotion, award, or pay raise. And one of these days, all that's over with.

My most fulfilling times were times when I was doing my duty, with no personal gain for myself. I got nothing tangible from it, and yet I got everything from it. If I were to write mine my own epitaph, it would say: He loved his family, and he loved his troops, and they loved him—period.

H. Norman Schwarzkopf is a five-star general (retired) in the U.S. Army. This article is adapted from an interview from the Academy of Achievement: Visit www.achievement.org.

Lessons for Leaders

by Arnold Schwarzenegger

To think that a once-scrawny boy from Austria could become Governor of the state of California and then speak on behalf of the President of the United States—that is an immigrant's dream. It is the American dream. For me, it's like winning an Oscar—as if I would know about that. One gentleman came up to me and said, "Governor, you are as good a politician as you were an actor." What a cheap shot!

I was born in Europe, but I've traveled all over the world. And I can tell you that there is no place, no country, more compassionate, more generous, more accepting and more welcoming than the United States of America. As long as I live, I will never forget that day 21 years ago when I raised my right hand and took the oath of citizenship. I was so proud that I walked around with an American flag around my shoulders all day long.

I'm even more proud today to be an American. And I'm proud of our leaders. Here are seven lessons I've learned about leadership:

1. Leadership means confronting evil and overcoming fear. When I was a boy, the Soviets occupied part of Austria. I saw their tanks in the streets. I saw Communism with my own eyes. I remember the fear we had when we had to cross into the Soviet sector. We were told, "Don't look the soldiers in the eye. Just look straight ahead."

It was a common belief that Soviet soldiers could take a man out of his own car and ship him back to the Soviet Union as slave labor. Now, my family didn't have a car. But one day we were in my uncle's car. It was near dark as we came to the Soviet checkpoint. I was a little boy. I was not an action hero back then. I remember how scared I was that the soldiers would pull my father or my uncle out of the car and I would never see them again. My family and so many others lived in fear of the Soviet boot. Today, the world no longer fears the Soviet Union, and it is because of the United States of America.

2. Leadership is all about dreams, determination, and desire. As a kid I saw the socialist country that Austria became after the Soviets left. Now, I love

116

Austria, and I love the Austrian people. But I always knew America was the place for me. In school, when the teacher would talk about America, I would daydream about coming here and living here. I would sit there and watch American movies for hours, transfixed by my heroes like John Wayne. Everything about America seemed so big to me, so open, so possible. I finally arrived here in 1968. What a special day it was. I remember I arrived here with empty pockets but full of dreams, full of determination, full of desire.

I want my fellow immigrants to know how welcome you are in this country. We admire your ambition. We encourage your dreams. We believe in your future. One thing I learned about America is that if you work hard and if you play by the rules, this country is truly open to you. You can achieve anything.

3. Leadership is about vision and passion, power and influence. I was motivated early in life to set goals. I grew up in a harsh life in Austria, but I had my dreams of grandeur. Some people might label me *delusional*, except that I have achieved most of those dreams. As a youngster, I was impressed by stories of greatness and power. I really don't like the word *power* because sometimes it has the wrong connotation. Power is basically *influence*. That's the way I see it. Power is having the influence to make changes to improve things. Power requires a clear vision. No one will back me off my vision. I will go over burning coals for that.

I know about visioning from my bodybuilding. I can see my goals very clearly. Beyond vision, leadership takes passion. It also takes the confidence to ignore critics and naysayers. It takes the ability to command lots of attention and then to use that attention to persuade people to adopt your position.

4. Leadership is about seizing opportunity. The "discipline" I got growing up would now be called child abuse. My hair was pulled. I was hit with belts. But so was the kid next door. It was just the way it was. Many of the children I've seen were "broken" by their parents. It was the German-Austrian mentality: Break the will of the child. They didn't want to create an individual—it was all about conforming. I saw one who did not conform and whose will could not be broken

So, I became a rebel. Every time I got hit and every time someone said, "You can't do this," I said, "This is not gong to be this way for much longer because I'm going to move out of here and become rich and become somebody."

Everything I have—my career, my success, my family—I owe to America. In this country, it doesn't make any difference where you were born. It doesn't make any difference who your parents were. It doesn't make any difference if you, like me, could not even speak English until you were in your 20s. America gave me opportunities, and my immigrant dreams came true.

5. Leadership is about keeping people focused on what unites us—on common goals, like growth—not on differences that divide us. You and I are probably much alike in our hearts and in our beliefs. But we don't agree on every single issue. I believe that's not only okay, but that's what's great about this country. Here we can respectfully disagree and still be patriotic—still be American.

As Governor of California, I often tell people, "Don't get stuck on the Mickey Mouse things." In other words, don't get hung up on the minutia. Let's keep focused on the real business of growing again. Every one can play an important role. I want to declare victory together. That's my ultimate goal.

To grow, you must have faith in free enterprise, faith in the resourcefulness of the American people, and faith in the economy. And to those critics who are so pessimistic about our economy, I say: "Don't be economic girliemen. Let's move prosperity ahead. Let's move freedom ahead. And let's move people ahead."

6. Leadership is about making decisions you think are right, and then standing behind those decisions. It isn't about taking polls and then doing what's popular. We want leaders who don't flinch, who don't waiver, and who don't back down. Terrorism is more insidious than Communism, because it yearns to destroy not just the individual, but international order. You can't reason with terrorists. You can't reason with people who are blinded by hate—you must defeat them.

7. Leadership is also about sacrifice and commitment. Let me tell you about the sacrifice and the commitment that I have seen first-hand. In one military hospital I visited, I met a young guy who was in bad shape. He'd lost a leg, he had a hole through his stomach, and his shoulder had been shot through. I could tell that there was no way he could ever return to combat. But when I asked him, "When do you think you'll get out of the hospital?" He said, "Sir, in three weeks." He said he was going to get a new leg, and then get some therapy, and then go back to Iraq and fight alongside his buddies. He said, "Arnold, I'll be back."

Well, America is back—back from the attack on our homeland, back from the attack on our economy, and back from the attack on our way of life. We're back because of our perseverance, character, and leadership.   ❧

Arnold Schwarzenegger is the Governor of California. This article is adapted from his speech at the 2004 Republican National Convention.

29

Why Lead?

by Phil Swift

For the past 22 years, I have worked in the energy business, but here I share a few aspects of my personal leadership journey over the past six years and how that journey has changed my outlook on life.

You are leaders with your own roles and responsibilities. Your journey will be unique; however, I believe that we share many concerns in common. At times leadership can feel overwhelming. There are so many practical issues— how to communicate, coach, and develop strategy. But there are other, more fundamental questions—like "Why lead?" or "Why continue leading?" or "Am I doing the right thing?" or "How do I find meaning, purpose, and joy in my leadership?" These are the bigger questions we all have to answer for ourselves, and I'd like to share with you the answers I have discovered.

Leadership can be very rewarding—personally, professionally, and financially—but it can also be very challenging. Nothing is ever quite right. There are many setbacks and sacrifices. We often get caught up in the struggle without taking time to reflect on the greater meaning of our journey.

Even after becoming a successful entrepreneur, I wrestled with "why?" questions. In fact, they seemed even more pressing. When you don't have to work anymore, you can get very honest with yourself. The questions are still there—no matter how far along the leadership path you go. But the further you go, the better the answers have to get. Beyond words that sound right, the answers have to be deeply meaningful to sustain you.

I set many business goals, and experienced much satisfaction from our achievements. But "more of the same" didn't seem like enough. I was seeking more important insights. Our lives and businesses are very complex. But I came to feel that the real answers should be simple. Truth, I believe, is simple.

Simple Truth

One catalyst in this process was my attendance at the Global Institute of Leadership Development conference five years ago. Warren Bennis was a co-host, and I was impressed with his wonderful example of leadership and inspired by his ideas. The theme that had the greatest impact on me was "find your leadership voice and passion." His message spoke to me. I asked myself, "Have I ever really done that?" It seemed to hint at something deeper that required using more parts of myself. The more aligned we are with our unique abilities and talents, the better everything seems to work. And fully expressing ourselves suggests values and beliefs—even spiritual qualities.

At that time, another story line developed that became the source of many new insights that helped change my life and my leadership. It started with plans for the new Millennium in 1999. I initially had a fun idea to charter a yacht in the Caribbean, but it became something much more meaningful. My family planned to contribute to the building of a 150-bed hospital in southern India. Over the last six years, this has led to involvement in building a school, a seva hall to feed the poor, and a spiritual park to nourish peoples' souls—among other projects.

Four Leadership Lessons

Through my experience in India, I learned four leadership lessons:

1. Joy. As the locals, as well as people from around the world, came to help us with our projects in India, they worked long and hard, but with joy and passion. Now, I'm familiar with the "24/7" thing from the investment banking world; however, these people also seemed to find meaning and joy. Their mode of operating seemed to be a more enlightened way to live, and pointed to a more effective form of leadership.

Happiness is good, but it's fleeting. It may be the feeling you get from buying a new car, or house, or getting a new job or promotion. The feeling lasts for awhile, and then passes. You then need a new acquisition or achievement. It's externally bound.

Joy is deeper, fuller, more sustaining. It's a feeling you would have about your children, something special you did for someone, or something you received. It's a feeling you can always revisit with joy. It's internally connected.

How do you move from happiness to joy, and how can you create more joy in your life regularly? Joy isn't something you can buy (a thing), or something you can do for yourself. You can't create joy for yourself directly—it is only through others. You can't operate in that joyful realm in a sustained way until you get outside yourself, because it's not about you. Churchill said, "You make a living by what you earn, but you make a life by what you give." Helping and serving others is what all great leaders do.

In his book, *The Spirit of Leadership*, Bob Spitzer describes four levels of happiness: Physical gratification, ego gratification, service to others, and service to others in pursuit of a greater cause. The last two are in the realm of joy, as they take you from selfish to selfless, from conditional to unconditional.

2. Enough. Early in my career, I set some ambitious goals for myself, including financial ones. People suggested that once I achieved these goals, I would keep moving the goal posts. I didn't believe them then, but they were right. What I achieved went far beyond my expectations, but I still found myself reframing my goals.

This isn't necessarily a bad thing, except for one aspect. It wasn't making me any happier; in fact, it started to take a toll on my life—stress, pressure, obligations. When is enough, enough? There is no absolute point. Deciding is difficult. We are naturally attracted to *more*. Most people think if they reach their next destination or goal, they will finally have enough. But once they arrive, they discover another level of desire.

"More of the same" will not help us attain what we ultimately seek. In fact, "more" implies we're incomplete. We think that we'll finally arrive when we achieve the next goal. Of course, the horizon moves out. After a certain level, it's a choice. When you reach the point where you can honestly say, "That's it—I have enough right now," something remarkable happens. It's no longer just about you. It's a transformational awareness. It moves you from your own self-interest to other-interest, from conditional to unconditional, and from happiness to joy.

So what about work? What about those goals that are so motivating? They are still there, but they take on more importance—because now they're for a greater purpose. I continue to work as Co-Chairman at ARC Financial Corporation, but I contribute all the growth in value to others. It's turned my business work into something with more purpose—and it's more sustaining. How you share your talents and gifts will be unique. But I can attest that when you start operating on this basis, more incredible things happen *to* you and *for* you than ever could have happened when your own needs were paramount. That's the paradox of opening yourself to joy.

3. Wealth. This is an interesting topic for someone like me who has devoted much of his career to finance, investment, and wealth. I could talk all day about maximizing shareholder value or about making investments in energy markets. Instead I want to talk about wealth in a different way and offer a new perspective. Wealth is generally thought of as assets, and if you were truly wealthy, then you would think that your financial wealth would provide "enough." But if you ask many people with wealth, you find that they generally have both a need and a plan for more.

In India, we see a lot of poverty and hardship, but we also see a lot of joy. What we all need to realize is that real wealth is in the heart, and it is experienced when you have peace and joy—that is when you finally have "enough."

As I struggled to integrate my future business life with my philanthropy, I asked Linkage founder Phil Harkins to work with me—on the condition that he come to India. He was skeptical, but he joined our family there in 2004. We talked about the challenges facing leaders. One morning, he said he had been up all night writing the outline for a book. "We need to explore some key insights here that could be important to leaders," he said. "But there's one condition—you need to help me write it."

Part of the book involved interviewing 25 successful leaders to understand how they answered those questions. What qualities, intentions and aspirations did they have that made them so successful? To what extent did those insights from India about wealth and joy play out? That brings me to my fourth lesson.

4. Unconditional leadership. What draws us to leadership will not sustain us. For us to grow and evolve so must our leadership. If we are aligned with our purpose and what we find meaningful, then our leadership is more successful and sustainable.

Each leader in our study found meaning and created more impact through an orientation towards serving others. They commented: "Personal reasons will only take you so far" and "In building a company, ultimately you are serving others." "Leadership will challenge you in ways you couldn't imagine."

Warren Bennis describes the process of becoming a leader as much the same as the process of becoming an integrated human being. Leaders evolve through both failures and successes to their mature style. One aspect of that style is moving from leading for oneself, to leading with others, to leading for others. I describe this last stage as unconditional leadership.

When I visited an orphanage with over 100 children in India last year with my family, the experience evoked many emotions and much anxiety. These children have so little. When we arrived, the kids came out to greet us, and our anxiety disappeared as we were swept up in the experience of being with them. We brought ice cream and cookies, but the kids wouldn't eat any until we had some of their treat for us first. They performed songs and dances, and they embraced us. Even though they had so little, they still had joy and laughter and shared it with us. I think children have an innate way of seeing the truth in things, and my children saw abundance in a whole new way—a way that did not relate to the material world but to the heart. Despite their hardships, we felt that abundance and love, which is ultimately more meaningful and joyful.

You are all leaders with drive and ambition. You have an incredible opportunity to make a difference. If you want to change the world, first you have to change yourself. If you change yourself, if you change your heart, it will change the world."

Phil Swift is co-chairman of ARC Financial Corporation, co-author of Why Lead?, *and recipient of the 2005 Warren Bennis Leadership Award. This article is adapted with permission from his acceptance speech.*

30

Never Retreat

by Rudolph Giuliani

You must stand on the front lines of freedom in the challenging years ahead. Seven years ago, your aspirations were limited only by your imagination. Then on a beautiful, clear September morning, your innocence was shattered, and the life of your generation, and the life of our nation were changed forever. You are the 9-11 generation.

You no doubt remember where you were on the morning of September 11, 2001. As do I. Let's make a pledge to each other: Never to forget it and to make sure we do everything we can to prevent it from happening again. Chose to become a leader of the 9-11 generation. You're being called upon to face head-on the conflict that we face, which is one not of our making but one that we are not going to shrink from.

This is a time for leaders. Before September 11, some people questioned whether this generation of Americans had the strength of our forebearers. In America's pioneering past, courage and honor were the true measures of an individual, but in recent decades, faith in these common values has diminished. The virtue of moral and physical courage was cast aside and replaced by a moral relativism, which claims that there are no causes or principles worth defending, worth dying for, that comfort and convenience take precedence over honor, courage, and sacrifice. But on September 11, we saw firefighters, police officers, rescue workers and civilians running into the flames as other people were running away. They were motivated by a sense of duty, love for their fellow citizens, and a determination to defend our liberty. Confronted with an unexpected act of war, our national character revealed itself in an instant as strong as ever.

In the days after those attacks, our nation was united in grief, anger, and resolve. We put patriotism ahead of partisan politics. Two-thirds of Americans gave money for the benefit of the families of the victims. Public approval for government service and the military soared. As the leaders of the 9-11 generation, you have now acquired the insight, training, skills, courage, and dedication to prevail over the terrorists and create a more peaceful world. You are facing head-on a major threat. Some don't see it. Some are in denial. Some just hope it will go away. It won't. You get it. You see it clearly, and I know that you'll face it and prevail.

It's hard to face evil. America is a good country of wonderful motivations. Of course, we're not perfect—we're human, we make mistakes, but we have a good heart. We hate war. We love peace. It's difficult for us to believe that there are people who have evil intentions. But our leaders need to recognize it and face it, because if we don't, we'll be in even greater danger. In this world today, there are radical terrorists who are planning to kill us. Here, overseas, they've succeeded in the past in killing Americans. And they've even done the unthinkable here at home. Your leadership provides a lesson to us about the way to fight and to win this war. We need to be on offense.

You know that the only good defense is a strong offense. Those who counsel that we share with our enemy a timetable of our troop withdrawal don't lack patriotism or love of this country. What they lack is a clear vision of what we're facing to keep us safe. And you need that clear vision in order to guide us safely through the risks that exist. That's why you're the leaders of the 9-11 generation.

Never ever retreat in the face of terrorists, dictators and bullies. Never retreat. Never ever wave the white flag of defeat in front of those who want to come here and kill you and take away your way of life. Never! America doesn't retreat. America advances. America is not about defeat, America is about victory.

Your service is based on the idea that you are men and women that see victory in a world that gains realistic peace through the strength of the best prepared, the best trained, the most inspired, and the most talented military in the history of the world. You've channeled your emotions into constructive action. And there are few causes more noble or more enduring than the defense of liberty. But you can't do it alone. We all need to do this. You need our support, and we need your support. It will take more troops and more training to meet the great challenges of our time to win this war of terrorism.

Americans love peace, and we hate war. That honorable instinct has meant that sometimes in our history, we wait too long to mobilize our armed forces to face the world's dangers. We tend to demobilize too rapidly once we think we've achieved victory and the danger is gone—the pattern repeats itself again. History has shown that this pattern is a mistake. We can't slash our military and intelligence budgets as radical terrorists are committing acts of war against us.

Bin Laden even declared war on us in 1996. We didn't hear it. And all through this time of acts of war against America—of coming here and killing Americans, of killing Americans overseas, all through this time—we ignored the wise advice of Ronald Reagan who reminded us that the surest way to achieve peace is by maintaining strength. And what did we do? We cut, we cut, and we cut some more.

You're now asked to do much more in many different places and in much more complex situations. If we're going to ask our military to do more, we need to give them the resources and the support to get the job done—that's our responsibility.

At one time, there was a romantic thought that America could be isolated. Isolation is no longer an option in the age of globalization. Isolation is no longer an option when there are people in various parts of the world planning to harm you. Conditions for our fighting men and women have improved in recent years. President Bush has increased our military strength and further increases are planned. But we need to do more. We need a force that can both deter aggression and meet many challenges that might come our way. America must increase the size of our armed forces, starting with the Army. America needs at least 10 new combat brigades. This commitment would offer rein- forcements where they're needed most—deter others from calculation that America may be stretched too thin. Let's increase the size of our force and allow the United States greater flexibility to win the wider war of the terrorists against us.

In the past when America's population was ten of millions smaller than we are now, we easily maintained a larger Army and a larger armed forces than we have now. A volunteer professional army of citizens is our greatest source of strength. And I believe that the 9-11 generation will step forward to meet this challenge. We must also look at the level of expansion that's necessary for our Navy, Marines, Coast Guard, and Air Force. They have to have the support, and they have to be at the levels necessary to deal with the challenges that we have today, and they need to be modernized, and they need training to accept our new responsibilities while we increase the size of our armed forces.

We also have to think about the constructive role that America plays in combat zones when the fighting is over. The reality is that America is some- times faced with a difficult choice. After defeating the enemy as we did in Iraq, after deposing Saddam Hussein, we have a choice. We win the classic tradi- tional military victory faster and better than it's ever been done before, and then we have to decide: Do we leave the combat zone? Do we leave it in anar- chy? Do we leave it in chaos? Do we leave it so, after we've deposed the dicta- tor, the tyrant or the terrorist, it'll just be recaptured by our enemy? Or do we stay behind and help people build a functioning civil society with accountable governments that meet their needs and serve as bulwarks against terrorism?

The choice is clear. In the world we live in, with the enemy that we face, we need to not only win the war, we have to win the peace as well. That means we have to reorganize the military and related aspects of government to provide a great deal more support and focus and education on post-conflict operations such as stabilization, policing and rebuilding. It can be difficult. It's going to require a new orientation. It's going to require some reorganization of our military and our civilian components that are needed to do this—some kind of hybrid that we're going to have to create. That's difficult, that's hard, but here's the good news: Our American military, of which many of you are a part now, is by far the best educated, the best motivated, the best trained, the best it's ever been and the best in the world, and I believe it can do anything that it's asked to do.

When the history of the 9-11 generation is written, and it's going to be written by you, it will say that you built a better America by strengthening the sense of dignity and deep purpose attached to national service. Your education has emphasized integrity and honor amid a culture that can sometimes celebrate the opposite.

The world needs more men who do not have a price at which they can be bought, who do not borrow from integrity to pay for expediency, whose handshake is an ironclad contract, who are not afraid of risks.

We best honor the memory of those who have paid the greatest sacrifice and lost their lives in this effort to protect us against terrorism by being inspired by their service, holding their families close in our prayers, fighting for what we believe in, and refusing to live in fear. I believe that the 9-11 generation will see an end to the terrorist war against us. I have no doubt that we'll prevail. It'll be difficult at times. It'll require sacrifice. There'll be mistakes made, and we're going to have pick ourselves up from those mistakes and figure out how to do it better. That happens in all wars. You know that. Final victory will take time, but we will prevail. And on that day, because you're going to achieve it, your generation will take its place beside the greatest generations in our nation's history. Our ideas of freedom, democracy, respect for human rights, respect for human life, and the rule of law—these are the principles that the human heart and the human soul yearns for. These are gifts that are given to us, not by government, not by men or women. These are gifts that are given to us by God. They're the principles along with the strength and skill and valor that make me confident that we'll win the terrorist war on us. We will prevail.

The terrorists who attacked us on September 11 misjudged the character of the United States of America. They thought that freedom makes us weak, that democracy makes us decadent, that our diversity made us easy to divide and conquer. It's a mistake that tyrants have made in the past about America. All of these principles make us stronger. You are the leaders of the 9-11 generation, and I believe that you and I have learned the same lessons from our history. Never retreat. Never wave the white flag of defeat. America doesn't retreat. America advances.

Remember the now famous photograph showing three firefighters covered in ash, raising the American flag over the rubble of Ground Zero. There were fires below their feet of 2,000 degrees or more. Their actions echoed the photograph of the flag being raised over Iwo Jima a half century before. In America, the heroic example of past generations are carried on and built upon by the next generation. When I saw those firefighters, I saw in their eyes, and I saw in their action the same thing that their fathers or grandfathers would have done in the same situation. In the face of being attacked, in the face of having their lives in jeopardy, in the face of watching their brothers and comrades die in front of them, what they said was, "We don't retreat. We stand for something bigger than us—for democracy, for liberty, for freedom, for peace. And we're going to put up our flag, and hold it there, and it is going to prevail, and it is going to wave as a symbol of freedom and democracy for us. And we don't want to impose it on anyone else. We want to give it to them. Share it with them as a gift that isn't ours alone, but a gift that comes from God."

You've learned this lesson and put it in your hearts. Now we're counting on you to be the leaders of the 9-11 generation.

Rudolph Giuliani is former mayor of New York City. This article is adapted from his commencement address at The Citadel.

31

You Have a Role to Play

by Barack Obama

America is an unlikely place—a country built on defiance of the odds; on a belief in the impossible. It's now your turn to keep this daringly radical notion of America alive: No matter where you're born or how much your parents have; no matter what you look like or what you believe in, you can still rise to become whatever you want; still go on to achieve great things; still pursue the happiness you hope for.

We have made progress, but progress isn't good enough. There is more work to be done, more justice to be had, more barriers to break. We still face poverty, violence, joblessness, and hopelessness What role will you play in meeting these challenges? Each of you will have to discover your own answer. But I can offer a few suggestions that may be useful.

1. Take risks. When I was graduating from college, I had this crazy idea that I wanted to be a community organizer and work in low-income neighborhoods. My mother and grandparents thought I should go to law school, and my friends were all applying for jobs on Wall Street. But I went to work for a small group of churches on the south side of Chicago, helping them deal with the consequences of unemployment. The churches offered me $12,000 a year plus $1,000 to buy a car. So I bought a beat-up old car, packed up my belongings, got out a map, and started driving west to Chicago—a place I had never been and where I didn't know a living soul. I could've taken my family's advice and could've taken the path my friends traveled. But I knew there was something in me that wanted to try for something bigger. So don't let people talk you into doing the safe thing. Listen to what's in you and decide what it is that you care so much about that you're willing to take a chance.

2. Stay global. As we become more connected to each other, globalization will bring both benefits and disruptions to our lives. Either way, it's here, and it's not going away. We can try to build walls around us, and we can look inward, and we can respond by being frightened and angry. But that's not what we're about. We are a confident country, not a fearful one. We can meet these challenges. Every one of us needs to learn more so we can compete more. It means we need an energy policy that will create new jobs in this country and end our dependence on oil from the Middle East. And it means we need to update our social contract to make sure that people have health care and pensions and training no matter where they work or how many times they switch jobs. But it doesn't mean we should ever withdrawal. We are better than that.

3. Cultivate a sense of empathy to put yourself in other people's shoes and to see the world from their eyes. Empathy is a quality of character that can change the world—one that makes you understand that your obligations to others extend beyond people who look like you and act like you and live in your neighborhood. I know that many of you have served at homeless shelters and high schools and youth centers and job placement organizations, and I hope this spirit of service lives on. But as you continue in life, it's not always easy. In the years to come, you will encounter many obstacles in the way of empathy. You will find people who, out of fear or need for power, try to divide us and deny what we have in common. You'll hear that the Americans who sleep in the streets and beg for food got there because they're all lazy or weak of spirit. That the immigrants who risk their lives to cross a desert have nothing to contribute to this country. That the inner-city children who are trapped in the nation's most dilapidated schools can't learn and won't learn and so we should just give up on them entirely. That the innocent people being slaughtered and expelled from their homes half a world away are somebody else's problem. You'll hear all of this, and you'll have to decide where your obligations lie. The easiest thing is to do nothing at all. To go about your busy life, expecting someone else to deal with these problems. To remain detached; to remain indifferent; to remain safe. But I hope you don't do what's easy. I hope you do what's hard and exercise in the words of Robert F. Kennedy "courage over timidity, adventure over the love of ease."

4. Stay amazed—remain in wonder at this unlikely place we call America. I think it's easy to look at all the challenges we face—poverty, war, racism, inequality, hatred, helplessness—and to get down and think that there's little hope to make things better. If you ever feel like that, I ask you to remember all the amazing things that have happened in this country. This is America— a place where millions of restless adventurers from all over the world, still weary of their lot in life, still hoping for something better, have traveled great distances and taken great risks for a chance to arrive on our shores.

My father was one of them. Born and raised in Kenya, he grew up herding his father's goats. But he wanted more. He dreamed of coming to America so he could further his education, improve his skills, and return to help lead the next generation of newly independent Kenyans. He wrote more than 30 letters to colleges and universities all across America, asking for a chance to come and live his dream. It is because someone answered that dream that I stand before you, hopeful for our collective future, excited for your individual prospects, and eager for you to keep the legacy of this country alive.

You will be tested. You won't always succeed. But you have it within your power to try. There is no community service requirement in the real world; no one's forcing you to care. You can go chasing after all the things that money can buy. But I hope you don't. Focusing your life solely on making a buck shows a poverty of ambition. It asks too little of yourself. You need to take up the challenges that we face as a nation and make them your own, not because you have an obligation to those who are less fortunate, although you do have that obligation. Not because you have a debt to all of those who helped you get to where you are, although you do have that debt. Not because you have an obligation to those who are less fortunate, although you do have that obligation. You need to take on the challenge because you have an obligation to yourself. Because our individual salvation depends on collective salvation. Because it's only when you connect to something larger than yourself that you realize your true potential.

Keep these principles alive in your own life.

Barack Obama is a U.S. Senator and candidate for President. This article is adapted from his commencement addresses at the University of Massachusetts at Boston in June 2006 and at Knox College in June 2005.

32

Leadership and Responsibility: One Frankl's Perspective

by Elliott Frankl

When the idea to construct a Statue of Responsibility was first brought to my attention in the 1980s after reading Dr. Viktor Frankl's book, *Man's Search for Meaning*, questions came to mind: What does this statue represent? Do we need a Statue of Responsibility? What does responsibility mean to me?

Growing up in Toronto, Canada, in the 1970s, I have been fortunate to have lived in an era where all we have experienced is liberty and freedom. We have experienced liberty and freedom for many decades now and have been fortunate to have never gone through the experience of having it taken from us. I think it has come to a point that it is easy for us to take freedom for granted. This is where responsibility comes into play; it is our responsibility to ensure liberty and freedom are maintained. Sometimes I think we as a society are in danger of forgetting how much our ancestors have suffered, fought for, and in many cases died for the cause of freedom.

What Does This Statue Represent?

Former U.S. President Woodrow Wilson once said, "Liberty has never come from government. Liberty has always come from the subjects of it. The history of liberty is a history of resistance."

People fight for freedom; we then begin to establish government to put order to it. To maintain our freedom, we must safeguard it, even for those we disagree with. If we don't, we then establish a precedent that will eventually come back to us. The only way to preserve our rights is to preserve the rights of our opponents, too. We also should remember that the right to be heard does not necessarily mean the right to be taken seriously. If we don't believe in freedom for the people we despise, then we don't believe in freedom at all. Freedom is not about doing as one pleases—it's about the opportunity to choose.

Over the years, I have worked with many politicians, developing government policies working on many government initiatives and consulting with tax-paying constituents. I find it concerning that sometimes decisions are made by politicians and government for the wrong reasons, just to push a political agenda. I think politicians need to be reminded at times about the need to act responsibly, to be fair and accountable for their actions.

A problem I have noticed in recent years is that some laws and policies established by various levels of government are not enforced fairly. In order to maintain our freedom we must ensure that our laws and policies are equally enforced to everyone and not fall into a selective enforcement form of governance. It is sometimes said, The true mark of any civilized society is how its government treats its most vulnerable citizens, such as seniors, the disabled, children and the poor. To me, the Statue of Responsibility represents how we, as citizens, can preserve freedom.

Do We Need a Statue of Responsibility?

I truly believe the time has come to erect a Statue of Responsibility, to remind us all to take our part to maintain our liberty and freedom. Responsibility comes in many forms and means different things to different people. We need to build this monument now, so that the discussion on how we can preserve freedom will begin.

What Does Responsibility Mean to Me?

The statue will remind politicians to operate a responsible and accountable government, to remind them that they are servants of the public. They must confront tough problems, not avoid them and leave them for others. Just as it takes dedicated people to run a government, it also takes money. The Statue will remind politicians that every dollar spent by government is the taxpayer's money. We work hard to earn it, and the government should show responsibility by spending it wisely.

The statue reminds me about human responsibility: being responsible to your fellow neighbor, for your actions, and for the actions that affect all of us; to treat people the way you would like them to treat you and your children.

The statue reminds me about environmental responsibility: to do our part in preserving our planet; the need to find alternative environmentally friendly ways of living our everyday lives.

The statue will help remind companies about social and corporate responsibility: to hold organizations and corporations accountable for its effect on the people around them; to maintain accountability to it's employees, customers, shareholders and communities.

The statue will remind the media to operate in a responsible manner. It will also remind the many lawyers we have in Canada, the USA, and around the world to be professionally responsible—to conduct business in a professional manner, avoiding conflicts of interest, obeying the laws and putting the interests of their clients ahead of their own personal interests.

The statue will visually represent responsibility. It will stand as a counterpart to the Statue of Liberty, that visually represents liberty. I find the project to erect the 300-foot statue on the West Coast of the United States and to erect smaller 30-foot replicas of the statue in many countries around the world will bring together many people, communities, and countries around the world. Where freedom exists, peace follows. We need to work in harmony for a single goal—the preservation of freedom. If we are not part of the solution, then we are part of the problem. No single voter ever feels responsible for the election of a politician. I feel it is my obligation to do my part in succeeding to build the Statue of Responsibility

Dr. Viktor Frankl, in my eyes, was one of the world's great leaders. I am confident that his vision of building the Statue of Responsibly will be completed with the participation of thousands of people from many countries around the world. Being a leader is not about accumulating followers; it's about inspiring more leaders. If your actions inspire people to dream, to learn, to do and accomplish more, then you are a leader. Do your part in participating in building the Statue of Responsibility—be a leader *for* freedom.

Elliott Frankl is president of a Canadian sports marketing firm, community activist, and government policy advisor. According to research and conversations between his immediate family and Dr. Viktor Frankl in the 1970s, they may be related. Visit www.sportsrepmarketing.com and www.elliottfrankl.com.

Accountability vs. Entitlement

"Man must cease attributing his problems to his environment, and learn again to exercise his will—his personal responsibility."

—*Albert Einstein*

33

Just Another Statue? No Way!

by Joseph Thannickal

In this reflection, I look at the Statue of Responsibility project from my side of the globe. I love this project. The main reason is my beliefs about the meaning and the demands of freedom. Great men and women in history have fought and died for liberty. Liberty was but an opportunity to become free. Freedom is a task that remains, not for them, but for us. I also believe that America is a good place for truth to be spoken and heard the world over: about life, love, freedom, and responsibility. When this monument is built, it will hold meaning not only for Americans, but for all of humanity.

Focus on Freedom

A focus on freedom seems appropriate today more than ever. I love to wish freedom as my best gift for those I love. When called back to India to serve in the training of clergy, my heart grew heavy at having to take leave of my parish in the U.S. I searched long and hard for some appropriate words that would express my feelings for a people I loved, words that would show me and them how to keep on going in our life journies, words that would once and for all cement our relationship on a solid, mature, and lasting base. After days of soul-searching, I decided on the following lines. They were from the Nobel Laureate Rabindranath Tagore of Bengal, India. He wrote:

> *Where the mind is without fear, and the head is held high,*
> *Where knowledge is free,*
> *Where the world has not been broken up into fragments*
> *by narrow domestic walls,*
> *Where words come out from the depth of truth…*
> *Where the mind is led forward by Thee*
> *into ever-widening thought and action—*
> *Into that heaven of freedom, my Father,*
> *let my country awake.*

Both Tagore and Frankl seem to believe that our nations need to wake to the demands of freedom.

Tom Polackal, a colleague of mine and an ardent believer in God, sees the message of freedom in the familiar phrase "In God we trust." He thinks that God entrusted us with the gift of free choice in all its awesome ramifications. "God respects this gift in us even when it goes 'against' 'His' interests and 'our' best interests. He respects the way we use this gift, even when it breaks His heart," says Tom. The Indian Philosopher Swami Vivekananda, likewise, sees freedom as the first condition of human growth; and, freedom implies freedom even to commit mistakes. Yes, freedom has its risks, but the attendant responsibility goes a long way to ensure its benefits.

For some, freedom looks like the goal of human life. Indian Catholic priest and world-renowned spiritual guru, Anthony D'Mello is reported to have said: "In the first part of my spiritual journey, my longing was to become a holy man. Later, when I understood this better, I wanted to become a truly loving man. Now what I most want is to be a free man."

Freedom and Boundaries

Freedom needs the boundaries of responsibility, just as love and law need each other, although both may at times try to wish the other away. Yet, can anything about love be loving, if it does not obey the laws that upkeep the interests of the beloved? Can law bring us any good, if love does not temper it? Freedom, likewise, is tempered by responsibility. The boundaries of responsibility make freedom that much more focused and efficacious.

Freedom is sweet, especially if won through pain. A sense of relief overwhelms a people who are thus delivered from bondages. But only in course of time does freedom begin to weigh on our shoulders. To make choices that do not undermine the cause of freedom itself places a heavy responsibility on us. How right Frankl was when he said: "Freedom threatens to degenerate into mere arbitrariness unless it is lived in terms of responsibleness."

Or as Swami Vivekananda said: "From the freedom of individuality, he (*man*) must grow into the freedom and responsibility of personality."

Freedom and Inner Liberation

Dr. Kumplankal, a scholar in Buddhism, tells me that Buddhist philosophy considers true freedom as deliverance from the need to circumscribe realities according to our own limitations. Labeling, identifications, and the refusal to consider the fullness of things are some of the ways we act out our limiting ways. Interior freedom that lets realities be what they are, making ourselves big enough for them rather than making them small, to fit our boundaries, is the one process that can ensure freedom for us and others.

Freedom gives life. But life can achieve more than itself. Our body can output more than what it needs for itself. Our energy continues to flow, spreading its impact on reality beyond us. It is as if somewhere on our genetic codes is written that we were meant for a purpose greater than our own selves. To discover that purpose, we need to leave our shores and walk unfamiliar terrain, in freedom. Freedom and choice make life into an adventure that builds up not just ourselves, but the world out there.

Responsibility for the World

We need to assume responsibility for our own lives. Trouble comes when we imagine that we can actually be free without others. The belief that we can live a life just for ourselves, and any effort to do so, are often thwarted by life demands that force us open to other people and events. The mystery of life seems to be that we can reach out to happiness only when we also do it for others. In being responsible for oneself, responsibility for others seems inbuilt.

Responsibility for others is manifest in service; and service to others builds freedom. Gandhi exemplified this. In his book on Gandhi, Eknath Easwaran writes:

> *The ideal of selfless service had taken hold of Gandhi and caused rapid changes in every aspect of his life. The financial returns of a successful law career, the European style of living, the complicated household—all these fell away when they became obstacles in his path of community service. Each simplification freed new resources of time, energy, and ability. Often, especially at first, it was painful to give up his time or pleasure for the sake of others' needs. But the freedom that followed was exhilarating. Gandhi's joy knew no bounds...*

That responsible service builds freedom was proclaimed loud and clear in the way Mother Teresa, that modern icon of selfless service, was laid to rest here in India in 1997. She was accorded the highest honor: a state and military funeral. The decision to do so came from the state government of West Bengal, as well as the federal government in Delhi. The same gun carriage used to carry the body of Mahatma Gandhi was used to carry Mother Teresa's remains, with the added exception that the military commanders wanted a cross bearer and candles to accompany the gun carriage. They thought this would signify peace, as opposed to the image of the carriage as an instrument of war. This was done, and the team of four boys that included a Chinese, an Anglo-Indian, and two others drawn from the local population were seated next to the body. According to the then Archbishop of Calcutta, Dr.Henry D'Souza, the country wanted to recognize the significance of Mother Teresa's selfless service as of the highest order in the building up of free India.

When we extend our worlds beyond the limitations of our own horizons, then we are privileged to be in others' space, which calls for responsibility. And then we see that the space we called our own, really never was. That, however, reduces nothing from our claim on it. Responsibility becomes mutual all at once. When we are truly free, then what we do for others becomes our own, and what we do for ourselves becomes others' too.

When Maximilian Kolbe, the Saint from Auschwitz, steps forward in the concentration camp to die in the place of another prisoner—this is freedom at its most beautiful height. He chose love over fear, and refined the meaning of being alive. "Freedom finds its finest expression when it is self-directed on the path of love. This is what responsibility—the ability and the decision to respond in love—is all about," says Dr. Joe Mannath, another of my esteemed colleagues.

With such thoughts in our hearts, about freedom, about responsibility, about love and service, it seems possible to conclude that Viktor Frankl's suggestion to have a Statue of Responsibility as a counterpoint to the Statue of Liberty would be met with thumping approval this side of the globe. There would be many here who would be grateful if America could provide the world with a symbol such as this that can enrich the cultures of the world. Anything that invites people to become more responsible for themselves and the world around them can only provide unqualified benefit for humankind. May this project see the light of day, and may it stand as an eloquent witness to the universal values of freedom and responsibility for all time to come.   ✎

Rev. Joseph Thannickal, Ph.D., is a Catholic priest, an associate in Logotherapy from the Viktor Frankl Institute, and lecturer at Don Bosco Renewal Center in India.

34

Accountability for Results

by Peter Block

Every manager and leader wants people to feel responsible and be more accountable for achieving desired results. The popular version of accountability is that we are all self-employed and must act like owners. But accountability doesn't just mean you are simply on your own—Me, Inc.—because you can be on your own and still not feel accountable or behave accountably.

Accountability is a point of view that says, "I'm a cause and a creator of the life I am leading and of the work I'm doing. I'm not just an effect, and not a victim." Just because an organization no longer commands my loyalty or buys my time does not make me less accountable. My mindset may be stuck in the employee mode, in the "they own me" mentality, regardless of my external circumstance. Besides, the notion that we are all free agents is just a way of trying to make palatable the fact that organizations no longer care about their people.

Why is that? I think that organizations are becoming so dominant, so powerful, that they feel they don't have to build loyalty or be committed to people over the long term. Employees are seen as commodities or economic assets. And so the question becomes, "What is the most economically beneficial or sensible way to deal with our people?" If we can outsource work to save benefit costs, or if we can lay off older workers and hire younger ones to lower costs, we do it.

The notion that leaders and managers are accountable to various stakeholders and that they have a social responsibility beyond making a profit is certainly out there, but I think we're at a low point in the attention leaders give to both employees and communities. We are at a high point of giving priority to economic stakeholders. That's why many non-profit organizations are under such economic constraints right now. All the attention is going to the money and away from service. Technology, with its economic value, is taking the place of the employee.

I realize that I'm painting a rather bleak picture of financial responsibility taking priority over social accountability, but at times it seems all that matters is winning market share. Every business has to be economically accountable— I have no argument with that. But you do have a choice as to how much focus and attention you give to financial matters—and right now it seems all that matters is winning market share and creating shareholder value, because the rewards are enormous for those in leadership and ownership positions. I don't blame the leaders. The rest of us are passive in the face of this. Instead of confronting the leaders, we want to be like them and get what they have. We are lost in our own entitlement.

Many responsible people are trying to do the right thing. I think the people who run businesses are every bit as ethical, compassionate, and caring as the people who buy the products. Most leaders who get caught and become media celebrities only did blatantly what others did quietly. Materialism and economic growth have become a religion for this culture.

To develop a culture that has a sense of shared responsibility you have to change your mind about accountability. As long as you think accountability can be purchased, mandated, or motivated, you are trapped in trying to create high accountability in a low-accountability culture. Accountability has to be chosen by people.

Gratefully, many people, perhaps most, actually choose accountability and responsibility. Why would they choose that option? Because what they are offered in return is their freedom and the chance to find purpose and meaning in life and work. Purpose and meaning come with responsibility and accountability. I will be most accountable for the things I have chosen or created or identified with. And my freedom is expressed by the fact that I have made a choice and a commitment—that this is my life, my company, my city, my country.

True, some people seek a false freedom because they confuse freedom with license (liberty) and entitlement. Freedom is false if it comes with a sense of entitlement. "I want mine, and I want it now" is not freedom. That's just wanting to be decorated more attractively. You haven't gotten out of the jail of entitlement. You're still captive to your wants. "What's in it for me?" is the most oppressive question of our culture.

We hear managers wailing that their employees are not responsible and accountable for results. Is that the fault of managers, employees, or both?

It's our fault. The employees are every bit in charge of the organization. We can't place blame, find fault, and render judgment only with managers and owners. I think we've gone too far in holding managers responsible. I'd like to put the spotlight more on employees and tell them to stop asking questions and waiting for answers. Managers need to say, "We have no fundamental answers to your questions. We have to find or create the answers together." I think we've gone soft on employees.

Some managers work this way. One good example is Dennis Bakke, CEO of AES, a company that builds and manages power-generating plants. Dennis understands that people have the power within them to make most of the decisions related to their work. He's paid a price for that. For example, they experienced some quality and safety problems, and he had to wrestle with what to do about that—whether to go back to a more controlling environment.

How did he work through those quality and safety problems? He decided not to back away from participative management. He faced the problem by saying, "We're in trouble. How are we going to deal with it?" It was a test of faith on his part. He decided to sustain the culture he had created rather than impose a short-term solution.

Richard Teerlink, former CEO of Harley-Davidson, was another leader who respected people's ability to self-govern. Of course, no person or organization is perfect, but there are people who operate on the basis of principles. The disappointments, in my mind, are those who have a participative or self-accountability philosophy, but who don't have the will or courage to practice it. And so it becomes a kind of benevolent authoritarianism or paternalism. They talk about self-responsibility and accountability, but in fact have little faith in people.

The culture in those organizations becomes too permissive. Accountability is the opposite of permissiveness. Holding people accountable is really about the distribution of power and choice. When people have more choice, they are more responsible.

Are there cultural nuances to accountability? There are some cultural differences. Socialistic cultures and countries think differently about accountability. In Amsterdam, for example, we see massive permissiveness mistaken for openness. It's not freedom. Freedom is accepting that what you see around you is in part your creation. It is not saying, "Let's not have any rules or regulations."

How do you establish a relationship of accountability? First, you stop doing certain things, such as annual performance reviews, that undermine accountability—stop overseeing and legislating. You also need to realize the power in questions, conversations, and collaborations. It stuns me to see managers try to convince people of something. Accountability and change come through a new conversation.

Are knowledge workers often treated with condescension? Yes, many of them feel patronized, as do most staff members and factory workers. I recently did a one-day workshop at a university. Managers kept cautioning me that the workers would not understand empowerment—having choice in your hands concerning how best to serve the organization, and being willing to cooperate. In fact, the workers understood immediately. It was the administrators who were struggling. Workers know they need to be making more decisions. Managers are more concerned about boundaries than empowerment.

The difference in performance between accountable organizations and those that are not accountable is night and day. All high-performing organizations are moving toward more empowerment, enlightenment, and accountability.

You can't have a deep sense of accountability without a deep sense of ownership. You have to be an owner to be accountable, but an emotional owner, not an economic owner. I don't see signs that ESOPs lead to big changes in accountability. I like the idea of having an economic stake, but it has to be real. People intuitively know that if their company isn't financially successful, they can't expect to get more money. If people want more money, they need to create more wealth. The ultimate consequence is that you lose your job and your company. I believe in ultimate accountability. Poorly managed and poorly led companies deserve to die.

Some groups believe that we have to protect people from failure. Why? Maybe we don't wake up until we fail. I like this statement: "Compassion always begins with a broken heart." Until you've been wounded, you haven't experienced your humanity. We are too afraid of failure. I would rather see failure as a necessary condition of accountability. Remember the flip side of failure is the possibility of success.

Because we can't guarantee success, we need to stop being paternalistic caretakers and start engaging our employees with difficult questions that carry with them the complexities, ironies, and paradoxes of life. That type of confrontation is a deep form of caring.

Peter Block is a partner in Designed Learning. He is the author of The Empowered Manager *and other books. Visit www.peterblock.com and www.designedlearning.com.*

35

Create a Culture of Accountability

by Roger Connors and Tom Smith

How do you feel when someone holds you accountable? You likely feel that you are in trouble, let your team down, or missed an important item on the balance sheet. Most people view accountability as something that belittles them or happens only when performance wanes, problems develop, results suffer, something goes wrong, or someone seeks to identify the cause of the problem, all for the sake of pinning blame and pointing the finger. When things sail along smoothly, people rarely ask, "Who is accountable for this success?" Only when the ship begins to sink do they search for the responsible party.

Most dictionaries define *accountability* in a negative view. Consider *Webster's* definition: "Subject to having to report, explain, or justify; being answerable and responsible." The words "subject to" imply little choice in the matter. This confession-oriented and powerless definition suggests that accountability is a consequence for poor performance, something you should fear or avoid because it can only end up hurting you. When people experience accountability this way, they shun it and justify poor results.

A more positive and powerful definition of accountability can do more to achieve outstanding results than all the finger pointing and blaming. Consider our new definition of accountability: "A personal choice to rise above your circumstances and demonstrate the ownership necessary to achieve desired results—to *See It, Own It, Solve It,* and *Do It*.

This definition includes a mindset or attitude of asking, "What else can I do to rise above my circumstances and achieve the results I desire?" It involves a process of seeing it, owning it, solving it, and doing it, and requires a level of ownership that includes making, keeping, and answering for personal commitments. Such a perspective embraces both current and future efforts rather than reactive and historical explanations. Armed with this new definition of accountability, you can help yourself and others do everything possible to both overcome difficult circumstances and achieve desired results.

Accountability in Action

As hard as he tried, Dave Schlotterbeck, CEO of ALARIS Medical Systems, could not get his 2,900 employees to perform. The $500 million company had resulted from a merger of two medical device companies, IVAC and Imed. While the merger should have produced strength, debt and under-performance stalled all efforts. ALARIS had missed performance numbers for three years. Nothing Dave did made any difference. He said, "I was giving these problems a lot of attention, but still I saw no improvement."

The breakthrough at ALARIS was the result of focused effort at every level. Through a series of cross-functional feedback sessions between operations, sales, quality, customer care and service, individuals were confronted with hard facts. These sessions helped everyone to "see it" and build greater cooperation. People could see the problem and how they could personally change it. They overcame the barriers of functional expertise and preferences and aligned themselves for the common good. Powerful forces went to work—forces that improved performance in dramatic ways. The common goal of getting "above the line" to capture these advantages preoccupied every leader and team.

When ALARIS started exceeding their quarterly numbers for the first time since the merger, Wall Street rewarded this impressive turnaround with an equally impressive increase in stock price—a whopping 900 percent. In May, 2003, *Money* magazine listed ALARIS as the top-performing stock for the last 12 months. ALARIS had attained a culture of accountability in which everyone wanted to do and achieve more.

Four Steps

Here are four steps to take in creating a culture of accountability

1. Know what result you need to reach. Whether you have a sales goal, a delivery date for your product, or a minimum ROI to achieve, know what result you need to reach. Once you set the goal, make it clear to all managers and employees. Everyone must know what they are working for and how their job moves the company forward.

2. Generate joint accountability for results. This occurs when everyone assumes accountability for the result. In a culture of joint accountability, no one can even think, let alone say, that he has done his job if the team has not achieved its targeted result. In fact, no one can think or say that she has achieved her individual result if the company has not achieved its result. Leaders can create joint accountability by targeting a clear result, driving the result though the company, and holding everyone accountable for achieving the result—not just doing his or her job. Joint accountability demands that everyone become accountable for producing the results the company must achieve.

3. Keep people focused on achieving the result, not just putting in time and doing tasks. Often, job descriptions push people into boxes. They give people the idea that they are getting paid and using their skills to perform a defined function or task. The task mindset leads people to believe that if they perform their functions, they've done what they're supposed to do, whether or not the result was achieved. Effective leaders lead people beyond the boundaries of their jobs and inspire them to relentlessly pursue results by creating a culture that motivates them to ask, "What else can I do?" until the results are achieved. They help people see that their "job" is to achieve the results. The daily activities that comprise people's jobs must be aligned with the targeted results. This mindset can become part of the culture only if people understand the results they are asked to achieve in the jobs they perform.

4. Direct your own destiny. Only when you assume full accountability for your thoughts, feelings, actions and results can you direct your own destiny; otherwise, someone or something else will. Accountability enables you to influence events and outcomes before they happen. You will gain much more from a proactive posture than from a reactive one.

This view of accountability can help revitalize your business character, strengthen the competitiveness of your organization, heighten innovation, improve the quality of your products and services, and increase your responsiveness to the needs and wants of your customers and constituents. When you *create a culture of accountability*, you will achieve the results you want, and everyone will help you along the way.   ✍

Roger Connors and Tom Smith are principals of Partners in Leadership, Inc. an international management consulting and training company, and authors of The OZ Principle: Getting Results Through Individual and Organizational Accountability. *Visit www.partnersinleadership.com.*

36

Moral Laryngitis

by Laura P. Hartman

W e need to believe that we can make a difference, or we will make no difference at all. Any business ethics worthy of the name should be an ethics of practice. The great challenge of ethics, therefore, is to be relevant to management. Are we relevant? Is our concept of ethics one of practice and application? And, if so, are we accountable to our constituents and ourselves for the practical impact that we have?

Accountability

We must have accountability for the impact of our decisions on all stakeholders. But do we? Who are our stakeholders? Don't we have some obligation of accountability for our impact on them? Aren't we responsible in part if one of our people acts in an unethical manner? If we are not responsible for the impact that we have on our people, then what is our purpose? Doesn't each of us seek to leave an imprint on others? And if that imprint is irrelevant to their later decisions, what is our value?

I am not claiming that we are responsible for every decision by people in our employ. However, if we did not believe we could impact their decisions, perhaps we should not be doing what we do. If we do believe we can have an impact, are we not responsible somewhat for the nature of that impact?

Under what circumstances, then, does "can" give rise to "ought"? Obligation arises when you have met four requirements: Where there is need, proximity, capability, and where it serves as a last resort. Obligation also arises when the potential actor is the first resort. If an accountant reviews financial statements, as a first resort, he or she has the obligation to report fraud if found. Similarly, if we, as advocates of business ethics, are the first resort—we are the people to whom others first turn for answers for ethical challenges. We have chosen to serve people, and we have the obligation to guide them, to try to prevent harm and even to do good. If we try to make a difference, we are far more likely to do so. What should be the nature of the impact that we seek?

Do we simply teach valid precepts, principles, and processes, and hope that they are followed?

People often move through the world unchallenged—they are not asked questions that help to illuminate for themselves exactly who they are, what they care about, and what they feel passionately for or against. We need to ask people the questions that they have not asked themselves. What "wrongs" would cause them to quit their jobs? We need to flex their gut instincts so that they can trust them—so that they have integrity consistent with their values.

They need to work at defining their value systems, drawing lines, at determining their personal priorities so that, if they choose to cross a line, they are completely aware, and hopefully accountable, when they do so.

Action

A culture derives from the tone at the top, and one means for setting that tone at the top is through action more than words. How do we identify an ethical leader? She or he exhibits ethical behaviors. We observe these behaviors and understand that this is the way to progress.

We are all role models, but what are we modeling? A virtual epidemic of unethical behavior has caused an unprecedented shattering of investor confidence that has caused a $4 trillion meltdown of U.S. market value. Our lack of vigilance in communicating to our stakeholders may have impacted this consequence. We must strive to serve as a vaccine against further epidemics. Our ability creates that responsibility.

I implore us to consider our roles, to consider what we can do. Ability creates social responsibility. We need to act; we need to serve as leaders in our communities; we need make our voices heard. We need to act in ways of which we can be proud to share with others.

What will it take to encourage us to take a stand; to play a role; to speak up when wrongs are committed; to serve as change agents? Laryngitis is characterized by a cough and a hoarse voice. I think our voices are not heard, and we're now too ill to carry on normal activities. We need to believe that we can make a difference, or we will make no difference at all.

Amplification

Now, our actions, without a voice—without amplification—are almost irrelevant. We need to be the ones to communicate, to spread the word. Once we have created in ourselves the effective model, we need also to amplify our actions to inspire a passion in our people to become their ultimate. Our job is to encourage people to see challenges as critical, as if they demanded answers and could not be resolved without their impassioned action.

I propose that we embark on self-review that results in an action plan for our future. Let's install more effective prevention measures to forestall as much as possible further ethical misconduct. Let's gather around common goals. Yes, we have a mission statement, but we need to put that mission into action.

How can we best answer the needs of our stakeholders? What do we do well? What do we add to the mix? How can we capitalize on our core competencies to best serve our mission? How can we position ourselves to serve the objectives? By what measures should we judge ourselves? How can we proactively meet our objectives?

If we have met our goals, our mission, we need to amplify that action to our stakeholders. We need to find our voice and use it. I ask each of you to find your own voice and then to make it heard so you can amplify your actions to your stakeholders.   ✎

Laura P. Hartman is president of the Society of Business Ethics. This article is adapted from her speech to Society for Business Ethics and used with permission of Vital Speeches *of the Day.*

37

Entitlement

by Daniel F. Prosser

If you have ever managed or owned a business, you've thought about the impact of entitlement on your company and wondered what to do about it. It's an issue that drives every CEO right up a wall.

Entitlement is most noticeable in companies where leadership seems to give everything they can think of to keep their employees satisfied and remain with the company, while employees expect more from the employment relationship and withhold their commitment and performance if they don't get it.

Like a growing tree that uproots the adjacent sidewalk, entitlement is a virus growing beneath the organization that has definite roots and can undermine your best intentions and vision for the future. Entitlement keeps you, your employees, and your company weak and unable to meet the challenges of competition and growth. You need to know what's at the source of the entitlement mentality and what you can do to transform it. Your future depends on it.

Employees who have an entitlement mentality consider themselves victims of management. But while entitlement is a real problem, it's not the real issue. Entitlement mentality is merely the symptom of a greater and more dangerous underlying condition. Entitlement can result in covert acts of revenge.

Patriarchy Is the Root

Entitlement is the result of a patriarchal belief system designed around control and a clear line of authority. It says that if you're the boss, you are endowed with special privilege that others don't have. It usually gets set up when management is trying to avoid being seen by employees as taking advantage of the system themselves. It's a symptom of management's belief they are entitled to special privileges that others are not entitled to due to their rank.

In his book, *Stewardship*, Peter Block states, "At the heart of entitlement is the belief that employee needs are more important than the business." Who believes this way? Managers who are trying to avoid the manipulation of employees who know they're attached to not losing business, employees, clients, or even losing face. This is the pretense that keeps organizations from operating with integrity. When managers are so focused on not losing or not failing, they can't be focused on winning or holding people accountable, or creating alignment, or building a healthy culture through communication.

Having observed cynical employees for 30 years, I see two root causes of the entitlement virus: 1) the fear of losing, thus making clients, employees and others more important than the business; and, 2) an inauthentic pretense of management that says employees are more important than management, when in fact management believes chiefly in its own entitlement. When management believes its own sacrifices entitle them to special benefits of their privileged class, there will be feelings of entitlement among the rank and file.

Only management can transform entitlement into empowerment.

Attacking the Virus

To attack the virus of entitlement, take these five steps:

1. Eliminate the conversation that "we're like family around here." Sure, it might seem like the desirable thing to create close familial relationships because they feel good to everyone, but the fact remains, most families are dysfunctional. Families tend to be either patriarchal or matriarchal by nature. So, even with the best of intentions, trying to be a family breeds resentments and undermines accountability. When employees become familiar with each other, they tend to stop holding each other accountable because nobody wants to step on friends' toes or upset them.

Start relating to each other's accountability instead of their personality. Ask employees to make promises and then measure the results of those promises. When an employee doesn't keep a promise, rather than getting into an upset with them for not doing their job, simply ask, "What's missing that prevented you from keeping your word?" Then, close the gap.

2. Create a structure for fulfilling on promises. When employees know the vision of the company and how they contribute to the fulfillment of that vision, they can make promises to accomplish those things that will make a difference to the bottom line. That requires a different conversation. Stop talking about your great ideas, about what "you're going to do," and start making promises for what specific measurable actions you'll take. Managers often confuse *talking* about taking action with actually *taking* action. They hold a meeting to talk about a problem, and a week later they have the same problem because no action has been taken to resolve it. It's because no one is managing and measuring the promises for action—they're simply managing talking about it. Stop talking. Start making promises. Get into action and hold employees accountable. Those are the only things that matter.

3. Communicate fully. If you have secrets and aren't telling the truth in your company, you will surely build resentment—and feelings of entitlement will emerge. Without information, employees can't be expected to act in ways that support your vision. When you withhold, you teach your people that withholding is a value. Withholding is not a value you want in your company. What's the alternative to fully communicating? The alternative is not trusting anyone with important information. And if you don't trust your employees, then your employees will question their trust of you.

4. Alignment is a leader's work of art. My own coach taught me this many years ago. It was then I realized that alignment is my principal job as CEO. Nothing moves unless there is alignment with the vision and mission. Without alignment, there is no accountability. No accountability—no alignment. They go hand in hand.

5. If I can't count on you doing what you said you'd do, then why do I need you? We hold on to employees who have no intention of keeping their word longer than we should. But if employees aren't keeping their word, the first place we need to look is at our relationship to our own word. If what we say and what we do don't match, people begin to believe it's not important. You'll know you have a problem in this area when you notice employees breaking agreements with clients. When we think we don't have to keep our word because of our position or rank, we breed the strain of entitlement virus that spreads internally and is hard to knock out even with our best strategies.

The entitlement mentality exists, to some degree, in every organization. To neutralize it requires that people be put in charge of themselves and be allowed to choose how they will perform. With those privileges come responsibility, accountability, and a purposeful alignment with the mission. That presumes that the purpose is well communicated and well understood. With choice, employees are empowered to be responsible for their own future. The choices are to take responsibility for performing and continue to enjoy the benefits of behaving like an owner. Or, choose not to perform as promised and accept the consequences of that choice.

When given choice, some people choose wisely and contribute purposefully. Those few who won't commit tend to self-select out when it's clear they aren't on the same path. It becomes too uncomfortable to stay. The best antidote for entitlement is a well-conceived structure for holding employees accountable and measuring promised results.

The virus of entitlement can prevent any organization from reaching its objectives. When leaders see they are squarely at the source of this issue, they can effectively open up the conversations for alignment and accountability. ✎

Daniel Prosser is the CEO of Conversint and creator of The CEO Toolbox. Call 713-706-6355 or email dprosser@conversint.com.

38

Real Accountability

by Carolyn B. Thompson and James W. Ware

Holding employees accountable for performance contributes greatly to performance. The best way to get results is to hold people accountable. When people know that they are accountable, they produce results.

If we had to select just one motto for the leadership style of President George W. Bush, it might well be "Results." Bush makes it clear that he is interested only in results, not excuses or grand schemes.

Bush helps his team produce results by giving them clear performance goals. Leaders who are indecisive about goals, or who micromanage goal achievement, damage the creativity and morale of their people. Bush motivates people by showing them the target and then getting out of their way.

The principle of accountability and results is a timeless principle of leadership! Do leaders have to hold their people accountable to pave the way for excellent results? Yes. Holding employees accountable for performance—by rewarding them for outstanding results and terminating chronic nonperformers—contributes even more to performance than hiring excellent people. One study showed a 16.5 percent increase in the stock price of companies with leaders who reward people for good work, refuse to accept sub-par performance, offer excellent pay and benefits, link pay to performance, promote competent people, help poor performers, and terminate nonperformers.

How to Get Results

Do you want to be known as a leader who is known for results? With a side benefit of building trust? Read and heed nine principles:

1. Have a clearly articulated strategic direction that enables you to succeed against competitors. In business, a clear strategy is important. Your people should never be in the dark about the direction. Tip: Ask, "Where are we going?" to help craft a compelling vision.

2. Help followers focus on a few key priorities and clearly stated goals. Keep it simple. Zero in on key objectives. Articulate the outputs you expect

152

from your business and people. Then, trust your people to find a way to make those targets. Tip: Prioritize goals and focus only on the top two or three.

3. Recognize and reward successes and take action on employee problems. Pay for performance, and cut your losses. Reward people appropriately. This is crucial to results. Tip: Be specific when you praise employees; tell them exactly what they did to merit the recognition.

4. Gain agreement on necessary roles and accountabilities. Some leaders never get clarity and buy-in about roles and responsibilities. Results come much easier when roles are clear. Tip: Take the time necessary with the entire team to discuss, negotiate, and agree on roles and responsibilities. Write down the final agreements and send copies to all team members.

5. Hold people accountable to the highest standards of performance. Use "stretch" goals and reward people for great performance. Stretch goals are a way of life at the best firms. Tip: Set the example for the team. Let them know your stretch goal to signal that you'll be stretching along with them.

6. Create a sense of urgency and a drive to succeed. Bush can make decisions fast when he has the information he needs. His ability to move quickly and decisively contributes to the sense of urgency. His natural drive to succeed also contributes to a clear sense of "Let's get it done!" Tip: Along with stretch goals, set clear deadlines and hold people to them.

7. Make decisions on tough issues in a timely manner. No single act is more damaging than delaying a decision. It frustrates followers. Bush notes: "I am a decisive person. I get the facts, weigh them carefully, and decide." Bush likes to move on decisions. Tip: Encourage collaboration and involve stakeholders in the decision. Decide and move on!

8. Give people the resources and autonomy they need to be successful. Bush is known for his hands-off management style. One fast way to kill motivation and creativity in people is to micromanage their projects. Hire smart people, trust them, and leave them alone. Tip: Ask your people, "Do you have the resources and freedom you need to do the job?" Ensure that they get both.

9. Invest in and support the development and education of employees. Your people need to continually develop their skills and abilities. If employees sense that their leader won't support them in this way, they will likely move on. Tip: Find excellent articles that relate to the team's work and circulate them to everyone to stimulate discussion and create new approaches.

President Bush employs these "timeless principles" of leadership. Start putting these timeless principles to work for you.   ᔕ

Carolyn B. Thompson is president of Training Systems, Inc., and James W. Ware is a partner of the Focus Consulting Group, Inc. This article is adapted from their book, The Leadership Genius of George W. Bush. *Visit www.trainingsys.com.*

39

Being Accountable

by Paul G. Stoltz

Accountability is the way we demonstrate responsibility. And adversity is the true test for both. What are our loved ones, colleagues and customers more interested in: A) how we behave when everything is going smoothly, or B) what we say and do when something goes *wrong*? It is B, what we do in the moments of truth that reveal the truth. And it is in these moments that the greatest opportunity for accountability and responsibility arise. This is true at all levels—individual, relational, professional, even societal.

Adversity has the power to test accountability, and accountability has the power to help you harness adversity. Accountability implies taking ownership for doing something to improve the situation. It is an internal call to arms, a noble request for doing what is right, especially when things go wrong. It is about taking responsibility for the issues others may hesitate to take on. Accountability strengthens resilience, resolve, traction, and momentum. It is what separates the best from the rest.

Accountability Pitfalls

Twenty years of accountability research reveals that most people show suboptimal levels of accountability. This sends leaders into some avoidable pitfalls.

Taking on the entire problem is a classic pitfall. Many resilient leaders are at their best when things go wrong. So, they naturally step into the storm, and shoulder the entire problem, not realizing they may be weakening the accountability muscles of others who were denied the responsibility to step up.

Stepping up when you need to step up and not letting others take accountability for resolving a situation is another way leaders can weaken their people. It takes tremendous discipline and trust to let others attempt to resolve a situation you already know how to deal with. But, that is how leaders grow their people.

Using the job description to define the parameters of accountability can induce helplessness in one's self and infuriate others. True accountability is demonstrated by stepping up to do one's part to make things better, regardless of the job description, or "formal" responsibility.

Accountability Builders

Your goal is to get yourself and others to demonstrate accountability when it really counts. Among the approaches that have proven effective with more than 500,000 people across all job levels, worldwide are these.

Focus the accountability by asking, "Given the whole situation, what is the one small facet of it you care about most?"

Engage possibilities by asking, "What could you do to at least increase the chances that this situation improves?" And from that list of possible actions, which you write down without judging, discussing, or commenting, you need to hone things down with the next step.

Funnel the actions into a plan and motion by asking, "Of all the ideas you've listed, which one do you want to commit to doing first? By when do you want to begin or do this? And, how are you going to go about doing this action?"

Shift accountability to others in the right way by only asking questions, and not giving any answers. If you have advice, put it in the form of a question, like, "Would it help if you asked someone besides just your boss about this situation? Who else might have some wisdom on this issue?"

Provide a compelling "why" others should take action by asking, "What is the most important reason why you want to improve this situation?" This way the other person taps a deep, inner spring of energy and resilience. It is the why that fuels us through the potential unpleasantness of the "how."

Adversity fuels greatness. It is the great mentor. We can't achieve greatness without its tests and lessons. The greater the challenges we face, the more compelling the case for accountability becomes. By demonstrating accountability and responsibility in moments of truth, we can forge greatness.

Paul G. Stoltz, Ph.D., is chairman and CEO of PEAK learning, Inc. and director of The Global Resilience Project. This article was adapted from his book Adversity Quotient @ Work, *and used with permission. Visit www.peaklearning.com to learn more about AQ, or Adversity Quotient—the most widely adopted method in the world for measuring and strengthening human resilience.*

40

Ecology of Success

by Gifford Pinchot

To be successful in the new era of the environment, executives must make both preventive and corrective actions. The effective management of ecological issues is critical to the success of businesses as well as to the survival of ecosystems and people. The pressures for environmental responsibility are growing. Global warming and the ozone hole are deadly serious issues. The rate of species extinction is rising exponentially, and there is no end in sight.

People are beginning to note that the current course is not sustainable. Since most people already consider themselves to be environmentalists, and most consumers prefer environmentally safe products, the challenge a business faces is not just how to bring the desired product or service to customers at a price they are willing to pay, but how to do so without creating waste and environmental degradation.

Wise business leaders will adopt the principles of ecological management: Think in terms of whole systems; carefully monitor and measure results; anticipate issues by knowing and caring about the biosphere; set clear long- and short-term environmental goals; build an intelligent organization to manage ecological issues; avoid expensive retrofits by designing in ecological friendliness; prevent pollution at the source rather than cleaning up later; lead, rather than resist change; and stay well ahead of the current environmental standards.

War Stories

IBM achieved its goal "to eliminate ozone depleting chemicals from all products and processes" six years ahead of the date mandated by the Montreal Protocol. Already, IBM's CFC emissions are down 63 percent. Their San Jose facility, which was the number one CFC-113 emitter in the United States, has reduced emissions 96 percent.

Du Pont was the first major CFC producer to listen to its own scientists' concerns and change sides in the battle over ozone depletion. Rather than continuing to fight for more studies, Du Pont lobbied the government to mandate a faster phase out of ozone-depleting CFC production. By accepting the inevitable before their competitors, they got the jump on developing replacements for ozone killers. They also developed a highly profitable recycling business that keeps existing CFCs out of the atmosphere and reuses them to keep old refrigeration plants running. These strategies were motivated by genuine concern for the environment, which lead to far more profitable strategies than selfishly fighting against what was best for everyone.

American automobile makers tried the other approach. When the government mandated tough emission and fuel economy standards, they devoted too much energy to fighting the standards and not enough to meeting them. For years, American cars coughed and wheezed to meet the standards while Japanese cars purred smoothly through their pollution tests. As much as any other factor, U.S. automakers' half-hearted adaptation to environmental demands gave American cars the feel of low quality. Failure to do anticipatory environmental design was a major cause of the catastrophic decline in the U.S. automakers' market share.

Environmental side-effects can be prohibitively expensive to control as the last step in the process. Interestingly, they can be controlled easily if this goal is integrated in the process design from the outset. Anticipatory environmental design can't be pasted on by adding new staff groups. Nor can it be faked to mollify environmentalists or government regulators. Effective whole system solutions will elude people trying to get around the scores of regulators, each concerned with preventing a different set of environmental tragedies. Satisfying environmental standards imposed by others, while necessary, is not enough.

Wise and Foolish Executives

Wise executives value the environment for its own sake as well as for its impact on the bottom line. Foolish managers avoid finding out about environmental problems rather than facing and managing them honestly.

It pays to take major steps to align yourself and your business with sustainable systems. If you choose to rely on non-sustainable systems, you take an unacceptable risk of business failure when environmental turmoil shakes some larger system of which you are a part. Even if you take that risk, your customers or your bankers may not go along with it. Just as they demand radon tests before issuing a mortgage, banks are beginning to demand environmental assessments before making loans. Serious environmental problems can destroy the balance sheet and income statement of a company.

Foolish executives ignore the environment and hope that they can quickly adopt ecological ways when outside pressures force them to change; but environmental pressures build suddenly, and an environmentally sensitive organization takes years to build. Those who study complexity and chaos theory believe that the timing of the ecological shocks to a specific business or industry is inherently unpredictable. This suggests that a safe environmental strategy is based on doing what is ecologically correct, not on guessing how long until some currently unregulated form of environmental abuse will take to create a crisis. In complex systems, we can't know when sudden breakdowns will occur. We know the stresses, but we can't know when triggering events will crack through system resilience and set off a chain of catastrophes large and small.

When under attack by the forces that will destroy it, a living system absorbs the early assaults. This creates an illusion of invulnerability and vitality in reserve. However, when the links in the chain of systems begin to break, each element that was doing heroic acts to keep the system going begins to get less than the support it needs. In a chain reaction, the heroic elements burn out with increasing frequency and the strength of the overall system drops catastrophically. We are beginning to see signs of system breakdown in a variety of areas.

Six Ways to Be Wise

The trend toward greater citizen concern with the environment is driven by increasingly obvious signs of environmental decline and the continual growth of scientific evidence supporting environmental concerns. As more people understand what the scientists are pointing out, more will take powerfully ecological stands. Governments will increase the sophistication of their environmental standards. Customers will demand environmentally correct products. Magazines with names like "The Ecological Consumer" will provide customers with the information needed to make informed ecological decisions. Wise executives will note the trends and take action.

1. Avoid doing business with suppliers who take ecological shortcuts. Wise executives will refuse to work with such suppliers, both to keep their people inspired and for fear of getting their own environmental rating downgraded. They know that investment money will flow toward ecologically astute practices, and so they will strive on a personal and a corporate level to become ecologically wise.

2. Hasten the end of bureaucracy. The arrival of ecology on center stage requires executives to deal with so many complex dilemmas that bureaucracy cannot cope. Bureaucracy worked in the industrial era, when the primary scientific model was physics, and linear cause and effect. Managing the environment forces us to deal with biology and ecology, where the most fundamental law is "everything connects to everything else." The segmented thinking of bureaucratic functions cannot deal with rich interrelationships of the biological world. The new systems that will replace bureaucracy remain effective when dealing with many complex dilemmas, none of which permit simple or universal solutions. Such complexity requires the intelligence of every member. This, in turn, requires great freedom, but also strong discipline to work together for the long-term good of the system.

Ecological issues demand a distributed intelligence incompatible with the system of bureaucracy. New issues to manage create new entities whose approval is then required. Ways to say "no" proliferate. The changes that survive an approval chain of fourteen signatures will not be the bold experiments or quick responses needed simultaneously to deal with environmental concerns and to satisfy customers. Waiting for the bureaucracy to make up its mind can be as bad as making the wrong decision.

3. Make every individual an ecological champion. Environmental responsibility can't be tucked away in a staff group; for peak performance, nearly everyone must feel the urge to serve both the customers and the environment. The primary job of leaders is lighting the fire that drives people to make the right decisions on their own and keeping the system from putting that fire out. Good leaders are making bold statements of ecological concern that would have been unthinkable just a few years ago.

For example, Stephen M. Wolfe, chairman of United Airlines, writes, "Whether one is a conservationist or not, it cannot be denied that the specter hovering over endangered wildlife casts a shadow on the earth and ultimately threatens the existence of all species, including mankind." Wolfe is lighting an environmental fire in the hearts of employees and giving big-picture thinking legitimacy.

4. Take preventive and corrective environmental action. The defenders of the environment within the company and without will assume roles beyond that of the regulators. They will appear as educators, coaches, teammates, and leaders. One major role is making it easier for others to prevent pollution.

In 1975, 3M created the 3P program (Pollution Prevention Pays) which has conducted over 3,400 pollution prevention programs and eliminated more than 1.2 billion pounds of pollution to air, land, and water. Part of the secret of 3P's success is that it is not a bureaucratic overlay aimed at stopping what is wrong; rather it creates another alternative source of approval and funding for those who would make things better. Over the last decade, 3P has saved 3M over half a billion dollars. More importantly, 3M has developed the systems, attitudes, and human processes to stop pollution at the source, a cultural resource that will be of ever-increasing value in the years to come.

5. Measure for environmental impact. Since you get what you measure for, smart executives will get better at measuring ecologically significant variables. Rather than wait to react to pressures, IBM executives use self-assessment, peer reviews, and a rigorous five-week corporate environmental audit. No major company today is close to perfect, but IBM, 3M, and other intelligent firms are trying to tap into the genuine desire on the part of every employee to do right by the ecosystem.

6. Promote self-organizing systems. Wise leaders will move their organization from a group of lightly connected feudal fiefdoms to a highly interconnected self-organizing system. Only self-organizing systems, whose members have both the freedom and the intention to seek solutions that work for the greatest number, will flourish in the environmental era. These systems need freedom, but that freedom will work only if the organization is full of ethically and biologically wise members and if the system has structural practices to discipline those who cannot discipline themselves.

As we enter the era of environmental challenges, the leading companies will develop local and global systems that anticipate environmental problems and empower people to act to prevent them. They will move beyond bureaucracy to create intelligent, or better yet, wise organizations. The challenge is educational, structural, moral, visionary, and practical.

Gifford Pinchot is chairman of Pinchot & Company in Bainbridge Island, Washington. Visit www.pinchot.com.

41

Action This Day

by Ross Perot

If we hope to reform education, we must do more than public relations and planning—deeds and action must win the day.

I remember when our public schools were the envy of the world. Today we rank at the bottom of the industrialized world in academic achievement. We have the largest number of functional illiterates in the industrialized world.

I once went around the world with a bunch of sailors raised in the Depression. When we hit the Orient, you could buy anything you wanted. You name the drug, and it was there. We were there a year, and nobody touched drugs. Sailors didn't use drugs. U.S. citizens didn't use drugs. Today we have 5 percent of the world's population, and 50 percent of the world's cocaine use.

So we have the dumbest, most drug-laden work force in the industrialized world. You can't plan and PR around that. Our great country is the most litigious nation in the industrialized world. A recent *Time* magazine cover put it all in perspective. It's a picture of George Washington with a tear in his eye, and it asks, "Is government dead?"

I suggest to you that on education and other domestic issues, for all practical purposes, our government has died—and I question that it went to heaven. Just look at conditions in our cities. If you compare New York, Philadelphia or Detroit with Toronto, you can see the difference. Now doesn't that make you mad? Go to the great cities of Europe, that are much older that our oldest cities. Why can't we keep our cities clean? Why can't we keep our infrastructure up to date? Why have we let services to our people deteriorate? Why have we abandoned entire sections of our cities to crime? And why can't we make our schools work?

Go to Asia. Look at Tokyo. Look at Hong Kong. Look at Singapore. Are they tomorrow? Are we yesterday? Now that is absolutely unthinkable and inexcusable. But if all we do is hold press conferences about these problems, as opposed to go to work on them, the way you are used to going to work on problems in business; we are yesterday, and they are tomorrow. And while we are creating images, courageous Eastern Europeans are making permanent, revolutionary change. Lech Walesa of Poland, the President of Lithuania, the President of Czechoslovakia, and yes, Gorbachev, put their lives squarely on the line for what they believe in. In contrast, our leaders won't even put their images on the line. When Lech Walesa spoke to a joint session of Congress, he said, "Words are plentiful, but deeds are precious." We need more deeds.

We once had a senior man in the White House who says he doesn't care if we sell potato chips or computer chips. Well, I would suggest to you that that man needs a bit more practical education. If we lose our ability to manufacture, we also lose the ability to defend our country. There is a vast difference between potato chips and computer chips. Japan produces more engineers than we do with half our population, and they file more patents with our country each year than we do.

Let's take a quick look at our public education system. We're at the bottom of the industrialized world in academic achievement. In New York City, 85 percent of our high school graduates, before they can take simple clerical jobs with a public utility, must be trained in basic literacy. You know, if our high school graduates can't read and write well enough to do a clerical job with a public utility—when you think what education costs per student in New York City public schools—we've got a real problem.

In a world where everyone has a credit card, only 6 percent of our 11th graders can calculate a simple interest problem. Our 13-year-olds participated in a worldwide math test, and they were asked, "Who are the greatest mathematicians in the world." They said "We are." They finished last. Koreans didn't think they were very good, but they won. If you were in the Koreas as a young man, as I was, you wouldn't think it possible that the country could go from where it was to where it is today. That those children could go from where they were to where they are today. And that we could go from where we were to where we are today. And yet here we are. Forty percent of the Japanese and German students graduate with degrees in science and engineering—less than 10 percent do so in our country. Their best and brightest are creating new and better manufacturing products; our best and brightest are going to Wall Street to sell junk bonds, do program trading, or becoming lawyers.

And what is our solution? A two-day education summit. Great photo opportunity—get all the governors together and have everyone say something sincere. And I rest my case on "sound bites" and "spin control."

The international trade war begins by having the best educated work force, not the dumbest. We are dreaming of the past while the rest of the world builds for its future. We, too, must build for our future in a tough hard world that's in front of us.

In Washington, D.C., 43 percent of sixth-grade children have witnessed a murder, 67 percent have been present at a drug transaction, and 75 percent have witnessed an arrest. Now that describes a city in ruins, and nobody does anything about it.

The family unit is deteriorating. Only 50 percent of marriages last seven years; 48 percent of the children in the Texas schools come from a single-parent family, with mother devoting her full time to the child. In contrast, the Japanese mother is the Japanese secret weapon in education. Nothing has been developed to replace the strong family unit. And we must address this problem if we hope to tap the potential of our children.

In a free society we've got to have a raging debate about how to solve our education problems. Our best and brightest need to develop detailed and long-term strategic plans to solve these problems and strengthen our country.

We must select leaders who will focus on results and not images. And we have not even taken the first step in that direction so far. It's a massive undertaking. It must be done. If we don't do it, the businesses you work for will suffer mightily, the people who work in those companies will suffer, and the tax base will suffer at a time when we must build and strengthen the tax base because we are in debt. The sooner we start, the sooner we will finish.

Churchill's dictum in World War II, "Action this day," should apply to education and all other domestic problems. In business, where we can control a little bit of what's going on, our first priority is to make the finest products or service in the world. This protects our people while we work on these other things.

H. Ross Perot is chairman of Perot Systems, Inc., 214 788-3001. This article is edited from his speech at the Planning Forum "Challenging Conventional Wisdom" and used with permission.

42

Accountability at Enron

by Peter Koestenbaum

A free market economy is not for soft and dependent souls, nor for those who seek security above risk.

Executives are expected to manage issues of depth, character, and morality, just as much as balance sheets and stock prices. Superficial answers to life's problems are no longer possible. At one time, conversations on freedom and courage, evil and death, anxiety and guilt, meaning and responsibility may have seemed boring. No longer. Today you can't manage a business without having meaningful dialogues and intelligent answers on these themes.

Our national priority has swiftly shifted from terrorism to the economy, and the focal point is Enron. The question is: How can your organization achieve better results through in-depth reflection on today's big news stories? Every big news item can be seen from different subjective perspectives.

There are many points of view from which the Enron catastrophe can be perceived. You may see the Enron case as cause for alarm, proof of corporate corruption, or simply entertainment.

What is your point of view? Are you open to the attitudes of others? What does this story teach you about managing your own business?

I will restrict my comments to two viewpoints: 1) executives who stand accused, and 2) retirees and other investors who feel betrayed. In each case we ask: What do the people see and feel? How do they cope? What can and should they do? What can we learn?

The Accused

The accused executives must be in despair. In fact, former Vice Chairman, J. Clifford Baxter, 41, committed suicide, the most dramatic expression yet of how they feel. Arthur Andersen's regional partner, David B. Duncan, refused answering a Congressional Committee, his televised face revealing intense internal struggles. These executives see before them the specter of dropping from corporate apogee to the penitentiary. The underlying question is always: Are we prepared for the harsher realities of life, unexpected, and hidden in happier times? Do we believe that terrible things happen only to others, never to us? Why are we always ill-prepared for life in the raw? Are we not stronger to create good times if we are armed for the bad times?

It is the mark of a leader to be ready for defeat, if it comes. For then you have the strength to do the right thing in the first place. Are you ready? For Arthur Andersen, this is also a time to practice recovering from defeat.

What can these executives do? I see four things:

Hire a lawyer for the best deal you can negotiate and hire a strategist to find your best political survival plan. This requires a sharp intelligence, a primitive survival instinct, a fighter's raw determination, a calculating mind, and a cool distant, detached, and unemotional attitude. Remember that no matter how generously Enron money for political contributions was distributed, when push came to shove everyone bailed out, jumped ship. It was a strategy that failed massively, even backfired. Morality is still the best policy, albeit temptations to cut corners are always beckoning. It is wise to be cynical about the power of immorality.

Acknowledge what you have done and experience the pain fully. We tend to repress these feelings, for we know little how to manage them. They do not respond well to repression and denial. They do respond to self-discovery and self-disclosure. We change who we are and how we look at life—from frivolous to serious, from entertaining to accountable, from a victim mentality to total personal responsibility.

Examine your feelings. Do you feel that you have made a horrible mistake? Did you know you should not do it? Did your conscience bother you? Did you succumb to greed? Were you tied up in a web of entanglements and thought that cutting corners was the way out? These are all terrible feelings.

Summon the courage to come clean and take the consequences. Your life may be shattered. You must work for restitution, but trust that you can reclaim your name. How many have the strength for such a personal transformation? We all need social approval. Are you strong enough to become your own source of energy and affirmation? Make the transformation of coming clean before external forces do it for you. Let your conscience run your life. Do not wait until others become your conscience. Done belatedly, the price is high—even higher if never done.

The real lessons then are these: You have a conscience. It is real and makes powerful moral demands on you that you can't escape. Make every effort to be morally clean at all times. Don't cut corners. Learn a lesson from the suffering of others and spare it yourself. Pay attention to the truth that you are born with free will. You are free to choose morally or not. Your character is determined by these choices. More than anything, you are your character.

Managing your ethics can be saturated with anxiety. Anxiety is normal and leads to health, rather than medication. Guilt is not to be dismissed.

These insights are always true. If we do not think in these terms, we fail when summoned to be mature leaders. When we go astray, it feels really bad. The rewards for cutting ethical corners are not nearly as good as the failures are painful. You restore your honor with the help of someone you trust and who cares for you: a relative, minister, friend, coach, or therapist.

The Victims

These people feel equally defeated, except they may feel not culpable, as may be the case with the executives. The media supports them in believing they were not at fault. But they must acknowledge the reality: They have been defeated. Their life's dreams, based on what was tempting but turned out to be spurious hope, have now collapsed. Retirement, and all its glorious fantasies, their ultimate aspiration, has now disappeared.

So, they now ask, "How do I manage disasters, well or poorly? What can I salvage from this? What did I do wrong, knowing what I was risking? What can I learn? How can others protect themselves? And how can I protect myself from other disasters, such as illness and accidents?"

Disaster is always a wake-up call. We must resolve not to collapse but act as leaders, keeping up our energy, good spirits, hope, and imagination.

The answer to loss of retirement is the decision to fight and to adapt—redefining life from relaxation and fun to intensity and rigor. Had we done this from the beginning, today we would not be victims. That is the lesson to learn. With new resolve we redefine our lives. We experiment with the thought that the end of retirement is a blessing in disguise: We will likely live longer and be more productive and happier. We will not envy those who fared differently. We will greet life as a journey and its vicissitudes as lessons to be learned. Learning, we are better off, for meaningful labor gives life its worth. We thank God for having taught us this lesson while we can still fix it.

A free market economy is not for soft and dependent souls, nor for those who seek security above adventure, and peace of mind above risk. These are decisions about who we are and what kind of societies we choose to create. We need education about these decisions, how they are taken, and how, having made them, we can prosper. Self-reliance is the key to success in business. Self-reliance quickly drops to the bottom line. Kierkegaard said, "To dare is to lose one's footing momentarily. To not dare is to lose oneself."   ✺

Peter Koestenbaum is the founder and chairman of PiB and the Koesterbaum Institute. 310-315-9700.
Visit www.pib.net.

43

A Vision of Life

by Oprah Winfrey

Even as a young child, I had a vision, not of what I wanted to accomplish, but I knew that my life would be different and better than what my circumstances suggested. I was raised on a farm with my grandmother for the first six years of my life. When I was just four years old, I remember standing on the back porch and watching my grandmother boil clothes in a big iron pot (no washing machines), and I remember thinking, "My life won't be like this. My life will be better." And it wasn't coming from a place of arrogance. I just knew that things could be different for me somehow.

I was born at home in rural Mississippi in 1954. My Aunt Ida had chosen my name from the Bible, but nobody knew how to spell it. It went down as "Orpah" on my birth certificate, but people didn't know how to pronounce it, so they put the "P" before the "R" and it got translated to Oprah.

I came to live with my grandmother because I was a child born out of wedlock, and my mother moved to the North in the late 1950s, and I was left with my grandmother, like so many other black youngsters. It actually saved my life. It is the reason why I am where I am today. My grandmother gave me the foundation for success. She taught me to read, and that opened the door to all kinds of possibilities. Had I not been with my grandmother, and had been with my mother struggling in the North, moving from apartment to apartment, I would not have had the foundation that I had.

So I grew up in Mississippi for the first six years of my life and felt somewhat special because I was a precocious child. I could read at an early age. By the time I was three and a half, I was reciting speeches in the church. And they would put me up on the program and say, "And now Little Mistress Winfrey will render a recitation," and I would do "Jesus rose on Easter Day, Hallelujah, Hallelujah, all the angels did proclaim." And all the sisters sitting in the front row would fan themselves and turn to my grandmother and say, "Ida Mae, this child is gifted." And I heard that enough that I started to believe it. Maybe I am. I didn't even know what "gifted" meant. I just thought it meant I was special.

167

Anytime people came over, I'd recite Bible verses and poetry. Since I was four, I've been coming up in the church speaking. I did all seven of James Weldon Johnson's sermons for churches all over Nashville. I've spoken at every church in Nashville at some point in my life. By the time I was seven, I was doing "Invictus" by William Ernest Henley: "Out of the night that covers me, black as a pit from pole to pole. I thank whatever gods there be for my unconquerable soul." At the time I was saying it, I didn't know what I was talking about, but I'd do all the motions, "O-u-t of the night that covers me," and people would say, "Wow, that child can speak." Whenever you do something a lot, you get good at doing it. And that's how this broadcasting career started for me.

We often hear about child prodigies in music, but I was a prodigy in speaking. I've been an orator all of my life. Other people were known for singing; I was known for talking. For most of my life, I wanted to be an actress. My father didn't want me to be an actress, because his idea of "an actress" was a "lewd woman."

So, I had to take a roundabout way to get there.

For a while, I wanted to be a school teacher. In the fourth grade, my teacher, Mrs. Duncan, was my greatest inspiration. It was then that I first began to believe in myself. I believed I could do almost anything. I felt I was the queen bee. I felt I could control the world. I was going to be a missionary. I used to collect money from all the other kids on the playground to take to church on Sundays. In school we had devotions, and I would sit and listen to everything the preacher said. Then in school on Monday morning, I would beg Mrs. Duncan to let me do devotions and sort of repeat the sermon. So, in the fourth grade, I was called "preacher."

The kids used to poke fun at me all the time. It didn't bother me because I was so inspired. And a lot of it was because of Mrs. Duncan. We once did a show on favorite teachers, and I just broke down and bawled when Mrs. Duncan came on. It was the first time that I realized that Mrs. Duncan had a name. I said, sobbing, "Her name's Mary!" I couldn't believe it.

By the time I entered college, what I really wanted to do was be an actress, but I got hired in television, and so I was never able to make any of the play rehearsals. Story of my life.

Oprah Winfrey is host of her own television show, magazine publisher, and president of Harpo Entertainment. Visit www.Oprah.com.

44

Accountability

by Lois J. Zachary

A re you tired of the same old story?

> *There was an important job to be done. Everybody was sure that Somebody would do it. Anybody could have done it, but Nobody did because it was Everybody's job. Everybody thought Anybody could do it, but Nobody realized that Everybody wouldn't do it.*

Accountability requires shared intention, responsibility, ownership, and commitment to action. Without these, we succumb to *shoulda-coulda-woulda*.

Accountability is serious business. Board members exact added accountability. Stakeholders want more information. Association boards are asking more of each other. The current approach to accountability encompasses effort, energy, and efficiency; it has become the key driver for learning, performance, design, and behavior. Everyone needs to embrace the same definition of accountability to assure results.

Seven Elements

Here are seven key ingredients of accountability:

1. Setting goals. Goals drive success. Without them, projects, initiatives and relationships are prone to drift and become rudderless. As a result of lack of direction, it becomes difficult to make real headway, because there is nothing in place to keep on course. Goals set the parameters that circumscribe the effort. They frame, define, and focus the work to be done, eliminate ambiguity, provide a framework for gauging progress and measuring success, and set a context for the work to be done. They also increase motivation, because they harness and focus energy and action.

The initial goal setting must be implemented on the macro level. This activity focuses on the entire business or on all teams. There must be alignment between organizational goals and individual goals. As needs change, goals may need to be revisited and adapted. Publishing goals clarifies intent and affirms commitment.

2. *Clarifying expectations.* Expectations are the assumptions we hold about others' intentions and behaviors. They impact our interactions and behaviors. The act of articulating expectations promotes self-accountability. It is tempting to assume that everyone is on the same page and knows what is expected once goals have been set. Whenever individuals, teams, and organizations move too quickly from goal to task without first clarifying expectations, they're usually disappointed in the outcome, be it performance or results.

We can't hope for accountability unless we clarify expectations. Too often we think that laying out or discussing expectations will have a negative impact on others. We fear that we might undermine trust, create suspicion about intention, or be too structured.

Clarifying expectations promotes accountability and focuses individual and collective energy and effort. When individuals know what is required, they can self-manage better and feel a sense of ownership in meeting desired results or performance objectives. Clarifying expectations need not be heavy-handed and excessively structured; rather, it should provide the scaffolding for focused action.

Promoting shared accountability for expectations requires adherence to a process to ensure that expectations are both met as well as individually and collectively owned.

3. *Defining roles and responsibilities.* Defining roles and responsibilities provides a mechanism to clearly assign accountability to those responsible for carrying out a task.

When roles and responsibilities remain unclear, multiple untested assumptions often supplant them. The ambiguity that results leads to unintended consequences: Individuals do the minimum required; attempts to get work done using a scattershot approach forces others to pick up the slack; long hours and extra work are exacted that are not essential to obtaining the result; resentment and frustration block productivity; work gets completed but not as efficiently and effectively as it could have been otherwise; and the lines of accountability become blurred.

Clear definition of roles and responsibilities promotes autonomy, ownership, and self-accountability. When individuals are confident about what it is in their control, they can accept responsibility with full knowledge of what is expected from them. Roles and responsibilities exercised out of a sense of ownership inspire commitment. Defining roles and responsibilities identifies specific benchmarks for performance and creates boundaries around the work to be done, both of which foster self-accountability.

4. *Monitoring progress and measuring results.* It is not easy to monitor progress or measure results without having something against which to evaluate them. Setting goals, clarifying expectations, and defining roles and responsibilities provide that frame or standard for evaluation. Monitoring progress and measuring results go hand in hand. Monitoring progress allows us to understand what is happening as learning unfolds. Measuring results provides data points to compare against a standard and each other. Both monitoring progress and measuring results can yield formative and summative data that promote process improvement and development. Monitoring progress and measuring results is an essential accountability process for individuals, teams, and organizations that want to build their capacity to grow and improve. Monitoring progress should take place on all levels. When progress is monitored personally, day to day, by the individual, it is a powerful tool for promoting learning insights and self-accountability.

What gets measured gets done. When there is no advance planning, it doesn't get measured. Measurement is a long-term commitment that requires adequate preparation. Failure to continuously measure results detracts from the value initially created and limits ability to achieve sustainable results.

Success factors, like goals, become important in deciding what to measure. Together with the goals, they frame the measurement and evaluation process. There are many ways to measure success, from questionnaires to performance assessments to focus groups to key informants. Some organizations are survey-averse. You need to know what works in the culture if you are to get accurate data. Think about data already available that you can access before you collect your data.

Monitoring progress and measuring progress create value only when they are done deliberately and are carefully planned and continuously embraced Spending adequate time to plan reaps dividends for years to come.

5. Gathering feedback. Feedback encourages accountability in subtle and not-so-subtle ways. It, too, fosters ownership, nurtures commitment, and creates ongoing value for individuals, teams, groups, and organizations. The feedback process builds relationships, opens lines of communication, encourages participation, drums out resistance, engages people, and creates continuing interest and awareness. Information, insights, and learning gathered through the feedback process have immediate application. And regular feedback fosters a culture of continuous improvement and learning.

Gathering feedback can be a means to an end—a data-gathering tool for monitoring progress and measuring results. Or, it can be an intrinsic part of the accountability process. To reap its full benefit, feedback must be embraced proactively. Gathering feedback is not just about amassing data but using data for improvement and change. It is a looping process: Learning from the feedback and integrating what is learned so that the return on the investment is clear and commitment is consolidated.

Asking for feedback, providing it, receiving it, accepting it, and acting on it are all part of the gathering process. This can happen as informally as asking an open-ended question such as, "How are we doing?" The idea here is not to wait until something goes amiss but to ask the question regularly.

6. Formulating action goals. When we don't act on what we learn, we block process improvement. When program champions sit on a task force, their sense of ownership, enthusiasm, and investment is high. Their rose-colored glasses often prevent them from asking for and accepting feedback. After spending months planning and implementing a program, few of us want to hear that we've missed the mark. But the lessons learned from such a circumstance are often more powerful than lessons learned from successes. Failure cannot be seen as an end; it must be embraced as a beginning.

Often, however, the feedback may not point to total success or complete failure. Rather than try to claim success, we need to reflect on what we learn so that we can take action by formulating appropriate action goals and integrating process improvement.

7. Integrating process improvements. Accountability is the portal to process improvement. It opens doors to action by requiring that goals are set, expectations are clarified, roles and responsibilities are defined, progress is monitored, results are measured, and feedback is gathered and acted on. However, it is a demanding master.

Without accountability doors remain shut to individual and organizational learning.

Too often accountability is used as a synonym for blame. For many, the fact that it was "everybody's job" is enough; hold everybody accountable. Accountability should be a positive part of a culture. The failure wasn't everybody's alone; the entire organization failed everybody and itself. The fact is everybody, somebody, anybody, and nobody could have become a remarkable team if only they had embraced the seven key processes needed to ensure that they achieved accountability.   ✎

Lois J. Zachary, Ed.D., is president of Leadership Development Services, in Phoenix, Arizona. Call 602-954-9934.

Corporate Responsibility & Ethics

"Liberty means Responsibility—that is why most men dread it..."

—*George Bernard Shaw*

45

The Point of Corporate Purpose

by Christine Arena

Besides making money, what in the world is a business here to do? What makes a company invaluable to people and *worthy* of succeeding? Questions like these test the traditional capitalist mindset, and yet they are ever more integral to the fabric of corporate America.

A steady pressure is building inside the hearts and minds of many of today's corporate leaders. Even within the most relentless capitalist institutions—from Wal-Mart to DuPont, General Electric, Ford and Microsoft—there is an impetus: a budding desire to stand for something greater than the sum of products sold or wealth generated for shareholders; an urge to respond to humanity's most pressing needs.

Changes in the global climactic system, the increasing scarcity of natural resources like water, our continued reliance on foreign sources of energy and the widening gap between the rich and the poor are just some of the problems that have come to epitomize both the downside of a particular brand of commerce and the failings of our past. But equally, these issues represent great future opportunities for companies with the will and wherewithal to seize them.

At DuPont, for instance, a clear motive steers the company's profits and impact on the world at large. DuPont's higher purpose is "to create sustainable solutions essential to a better, safer, healthier life for people everywhere." The concepts "better, safer, healthier" manifest on a deeper level than just corporate communications. They invade every corner of DuPont's business, changing the way the company operates, what it makes, and how.

DuPont's higher purpose, for instance, guides the company's "zero injuries, illnesses, and incidents" approach to safety, for which it has won countless industry awards. It also influences the company's "zero waste and emissions" commitment to operating in an environmentally sound manner, which since 1999 has resulted in a 65 percent reduction of greenhouse gas emissions and saved over $2 billion in overhead costs. Most significantly, though, DuPont's higher purpose gives rise to the technological breakthroughs that enrich communities and hurl the company forward towards its goals.

Dawn Rittenhouse, director of sustainable development, says that DuPont's most prized developments—such as Sonora, a resilient and eco-friendly fabric made from corn; Avaunt, a low-toxicity insecticide designed to meet the needs of poor farmers in developing nations; and Tyvek, an innovative roofing system that saves energy while cutting pollution and carbon emissions—characterize the company's commitment to corporate responsibility.

"We determine: What do our customers need? What does society need?" says Rittenhouse. "Then, knowing where our core competencies lie, we combine these factors in order to draw the next generation of research and development." DuPont's long-term performance, she explains, hinges on its ability to use its greatest strengths in order to solve society's ills. So while DuPont is not a perfect company, it is highly responsive to the challenges its stakeholders face.

The same can be said for Patagonia, a California-based retailer of outdoor apparel and gear. As all high-purpose companies do, Patagonia makes its intentions known: "We exist as a business to inspire and implement solutions to the environmental crisis." Patagonia's higher purpose serves as an organizational catalyst, bringing all within the company together under one central goal and infusing the corporate culture with meaning and substance. "The people who work here get to live out their deepest values," explains Eve Bould, director of communications. "The company encourages people to do their part to make a difference."

Indeed, making a difference is what Patagonia does best. The company was the first major retailer to switch all its cotton clothing over to 100 percent organic, the first to make its fabrics from recycled plastic soda bottles and scrap fiber, and the first to pledge one percent of its annual sales to organizations that promote environmental preservation. It is also one of the few companies that relies on renewable sources of energy like wind for power, builds its buildings using the latest in green technologies, and uses its marketing muscle to spread the word about issues like deforestation and polluted costal waters. It even pays employees for their volunteer work and gives out a $2,000 bonus for buying hybrid cars. And yet, despite all this, Patagonia concedes: "We are a long way from calling ourselves an 'environmentally friendly' business."

DuPont and Patagonia are vastly different entities. One makes industry-grade chemicals, the other fleece jackets. One targets bullish Wall Street investors, the other diehard tree-huggers. But both companies own up to their imperfections and share a distinct formula for success. The more ingeniously they help to solve world problems, the more prosperous they become. And the more prosperous they grow, the more stakeholders their solutions benefit.

DuPont and Patagonia endure because, without them, society would be worse off—just as without their higher purpose, each would have difficulty sustaining forward momentum and optimal financial performance. Of this, DuPont CEO Charles Holliday says: "We are on a journey to transform DuPont into a more sustainable company…not only because it is the right thing to do, but also because it is our core strategy to grow the company."

High-purpose companies like DuPont, Patagonia—and a critical mass of others including GE, which aims to "provide imaginative solutions to the mounting challenges to our ecosystem;" Jet Blue, which exists to "bring humanity back to air travel," and Toyota, which means to "make sustainable mobility a reality"—aren't necessarily widely regarded as the world's most "responsible" corporate citizens. Many are often overlooked for industry awards. But these companies deserve a closer look because, through the pursuit of purpose, they make a tremendous difference to their shareholders and stakeholders.

High-purpose companies are the world's most *responsive* corporate citizens. They answer to the changing demands of the market and to the tribulations that plague our society. Often the reality or net impact they create trumps commonly held perceptions about what it means to be a good corporate citizen in the 21st century. Each one stands for a cause that is vital to human kind. Each is driven by something larger and more significant than that which is conveyed on a one-dimensional balance sheet. Moreover, each one should inspire us to re-evaluate our performance, to think and act in a new way.

Making money is undoubtedly a rule of the game of business, but to ensure our survival we need to answer the question: "What's the point?"

Christine Arena is the award-winning author of The High-Purpose Company *and* Cause for Success, *two books that define the business case for corporate responsibility. Visit www.high-purpose.com.*

46

Values-Driven Investing

by Carter B. LeCraw

What is the future of freedom—and, therefore, America? Will this lofty ideal, symbolized by our Statue of Liberty, survive and thrive in the near and distant future? If freedom and America are under massive global attack, what can we do to stem the tide? These questions must be addressed.

The concepts of liberty and freedom were probably best exemplified by America's fight for independence. The opening remarks of the *Declaration of Independence* clearly state a belief that the ideals of "Life, Liberty and the pursuit of Happiness" are self-evident, God-given rights. Thousands have given their lives to protect these freedoms.

The growth of freedom in the world since 1776 has been nothing less than phenomenal. One of the most dramatic examples was the fall of the Berlin wall in 1989. As a result of this world-inspiring event, Ronald Reagan became the poster boy for freedom; indeed, he and his administration were critical in the liberation of the USSR and communist Europe.

The advance of freedom has been well-documented and communicated throughout the media-connected world. As a result many, if not most, in this segment of the world have assumed that the continued advancement of freedom will be a foregone conclusion, and its success is merely a function of educating the rest of the world on its benefits.

Here's what we have not fully realized. There are millions, maybe billions of people living underneath the radar screen (almost invisible to those of us in the media-connected world) who are being led by those adamantly opposed to liberty, freedom and America. This group would not, had they seen it, have celebrated the triumphant fall of the Berlin wall.

Disturbing is the way their leaders have figured out how to become a significant force on the world's stage by using extreme violence. This type of violence goes well beyond the violence the world has seen, as it involves not only others but themselves. Never have so many been so willing to inflict violence on themselves in order to advance their agenda.

Compared to this real threat, conquering Hitler was a piece of cake. We knew exactly where Germany was and even who to shoot at because their soldiers wore uniforms! Many Nazis were willing to die for their cause, however flawed; but few, if any, were willing to strap on a bomb and walk into a crowded place filled with innocent people.

Freedom for the future world is no foregone conclusion. There is a titanic battle being waged against liberty by an incredibly fierce and formidable group of people. Furthermore, if we think our government, the strongest military power on earth, can win this war by themselves we are mistaken. We can be victorious, but millions of Americans must be empowered and engaged to confront this enemy. But how?

The future of liberty and freedom are dependent on how free people, especially Americans (since we are the leaders of the free world), use our freedoms. As Americans, will we choose to use our freedoms to do what is good and right? Our ideological enemy says that is poppycock, and the only way to get people, especially Americans, to do what is "right" is by force. They contend that iron-fisted enforcement tactics must be used to bend the will of the people to obey a strict moral code. Not all Muslims are of this opinion, but most making today's violent news stories subscribe to this belief. Thank goodness for the Muslim leaders who speak out against the rise of fundamentalist violence.

Benjamin Franklin said it well, "Only virtuous people are capable of freedom. As nations become corrupt and vicious, they have more need of masters." Some radical Muslim leaders believe America (and the rest of the world) is in need of a master to make its citizens do what they think is right. I believe, by the grace of God, we can become more virtuous and therefore become a stronger example of why freedom and liberty are infinitely better than tyranny and oppression.

A very special organization, The Statue of Responsibility Foundation, is trying to help the cause of freedom by encouraging Americans to use their freedoms to do what is good and right. The push for their inspiring project is coming at a very critical time. The goal is to construct a Statue of Responsibility on the West Coast of the United States as a bookend to the Statue of Liberty. Its fundamental message, "Liberty + Responsibility = Freedom." It will be a great reminder for all of us to use our freedoms to do what is good and right in order to maintain and strengthen America and this cherished ideal.

Investment Freedom

In keeping with the Statue of Responsibility Foundation's theme, some investment professionals have encouraged investors to use their freedoms to direct their financial assets to support what is good in America. This should help build a better America and strengthen the ideals of liberty and freedom.

Indeed, one of the most overlooked weapons in our struggle to build a better America, and defend freedom and liberty, is how we select our personal investments. To facilitate a paradigm shift in thinking about personal investing, we came up with new term for using investment capital for good. We call it "Values-Driven Investing." It requires not only a shift in thinking, but a shift in where we put our trust.

We take for granted that the main purpose of investment capital is to increase the wealth of the owner of that capital. It is reasoned, the investor will be a "good steward" of that capital, and the increased wealth obtained can then be shared with others. The fallacy of this argument is that investment capital can dramatically affect our culture for ill or for good. It *does* matter how the wealth is obtained.

Since more investors are realizing that investments in objectionable industries are harmful to society, portfolios are often being "screened" to eliminate certain "objectionable" categories of stocks or other investments in industries considered detrimental to society. This is a reasonable first step in "sanctifying" investment capital. Still it does not address the question, "What is the ultimate purpose of investment capital?"

Henry Ford had an opinion about the purpose of capital. He said, "The highest use of capital is not to make more money, but to make money to do more for the betterment of life." So, what would happen if the average American investor changed the ultimate goal of investment capital from "building more wealth" to "building a better America"? If that paradigm shift in thinking were to happen, then investors would target stocks and bonds of companies that best reflect good principles and values, and add to the goodness of society. The focus on stock-picking would change from eliminating objectionable companies to targeting noble and honorable ones. Calvin Coolidge spoke to this concept when he said, "Little progress can be made by merely attempting to repress what is evil; our great hope lies in developing what is good." (For more risk-adverse investors, church bonds are a great way to contribute toward building places of worship all over America.)

What about profitability? What about investment return? What about the financial stability of the companies or organizations in which stock or bond investments are made? Should questions such as these be disregarded? No, not at all, but they would become secondary questions. They would be asked *after* more important questions like, "How will my investment portfolio contribute to society?"

A way to begin a paradigm shift in our thinking about capital is to adopt the new term "Values-Driven Investing" and its definition, "An investment strategy that uses principles and values as the main criteria for selecting investments." There are millions of values-driven people in America. If these people would merely choose to align their values with their investments by adopting a values-driven investment strategy then trillions of dollars of investment capital could be used to build a better America and a better world. And, with the enormous "baby boomer" wealth transfer, a whole new group of investors could be challenged to adopt this exciting new vision for investing.

Here's the scary part. In order to adopt the concept of "Values-Driven Investing," we must "dethrone" money and financial return as the main investment objectives. Good financial returns may, in fact, materialize, but they become a result of focusing on values and not the main objective. We must *trust* that the return will be acceptable without trying to control it. The word *trust* is a significant part of our national motto—printed on the very thing in which we are tempted to put our trust!

One of our best *offensive* weapons against our current enemy is to export our values to the rest of the world via corporate America, and one of the best ways to do this is to direct more investment capital to those companies that best reflect American values; values like integrity, humility, diligence, and caring. Increased financial support for these companies will allow them to be stronger ambassadors for us here and around the globe and show others the goodness that is at the heart of most Americans. Skeptics might be surprised to learn that values-driven companies, as a general rule, have solid financial performance (of course, there is no assurance of future financial results). More important, they reflect the principles and values upon which America was built.

The Founding Fathers became some of our country's first values-driven investors when they signed the *Declaration of Independence* as evidenced by the last line which reads, "And for the support of this *Declaration*, with a firm reliance on the protection of Divine Providence, we mutually pledge to each other our Lives, *our Fortunes*, and our sacred Honor." These brave and visionary men committed (invested) their entire fortunes to *build* America; therefore, let us pledge our fortunes, our investment dollars, toward *building a better* America and thus strengthening freedom and liberty around the world.   ᔕ

Carter B. LeCraw is CEO of American Values Investments, Inc. Email carter@americanvalues.com, call 423-722-1776, or visit www.americanvalues.com.

47

Ethics in Action

by Charles Garfield

A company's ethics determines its character, its health, its performance, and ultimately, its bottom-line success.

Ethics, a company's moral code, is one of those "soft" concepts that are often relegated to Corporate Affairs or the legal department. Often, ethics are viewed as peripheral to the company, as an issue that will be dealt with only when a flagrant abuse of ethics arises or when such an abuse becomes public knowledge.

But ethics, far from being peripheral to the company, is its very foundation. Ethics is the set of written and unwritten moral principles by which a company operates at a core level. A company's ethics determines how it treats employees, customers, and suppliers; how it develops products and processes; and how it participates in the larger community.

The Body Shop Example

In 1976, at the age of 34, Anita Roddick launched The Body Shop in Brighton, East Sussex, England, after her husband, Gordon, announced his desire to spend two years traveling in South America. Her interim way to make a living has blossomed into an international success story.

The Body Shop was founded on five principles: To sell cosmetics with a minimum of hype and packaging; to promote health rather than glamour, reality rather than the dubious promise of instant rejuvenation; to use naturally based, close-to-source ingredients wherever possible; not to test ingredients or final products on animals; to respect the environment.

By the time Gordon returned from his travels, The Body Shop was well on its way to becoming a thriving concern. Today there are over 1,000 Body Shops in 50 countries, and the number is steadily growing.

The Body Shop is not only a phenomenal economic success but also an international symbol of corporate social responsibility, waging campaigns that have ranged from saving the whales to rescuing the rain forests. Anita Roddick

181

notes, "We take seriously our product development, the ingredients we use, how we source them, and then how we educate our customers about our choices. And so our customers or our investors are able to make informed decisions about whether or not they want to do business with us. Customers crave knowledge; they want honest information. They want to feel an affinity not only with the products but with the company.

"Many people work at The Body Shop because our values, our goals, our causes are every bit as valuable to us as our products and profits. What moves the spirit is not a moisture cream. Our employees don't dream of soap when they go home. It's all the noble purposes we put our energies into."

Putting Context Back into Business

"Ethical behavior" means doing what is right, what brings the greatest benefit or the least harm to all involved. We may argue about what is right (for example, some contend that disinvesting in South Africa hurts those it is meant to help) but not about the fact that doing what is right is at the core of ethical behavior.

Ethical is different from "legal." Installing a minimum of pollution control devices may be legal, but it is not necessarily ethical. A commitment to healthy progress requires a genuine sense of responsibility for the results of our actions, not simply taking actions that will meet the minimum requirements of the law.

Levi Strauss spent a fortune to reduce the formaldehyde levels in the finish of its Sta-Prest pants beyond the government standards, even though there was no evidence that merely adhering to those standards would cause any harm to consumers or employees. It did so because it had a policy of monitoring all chemicals used by suppliers to discover any potential for harm. Levi Strauss goes beyond the legal requirements to ensure that it is "doing what is right." This is ethics in action.

Ethics is the spiritual glue that binds the organization. A company's ethics determines its character, its health, and, ultimately, its success. Says Robert Haas, past CEO of Levi Strauss: "A company's values—what it stands for, what its people believe in—are crucial to its competitive success. Indeed, values drive the business."

Not all corporate leaders are so enlightened, and not all corporations operate so ethically. To a great extent, American business has been separated from the value base that would humanize it. This lack of a strong ethical foundation has sometimes allowed corporations to pursue heartless and destructive actions with impunity and to justify them in the name of "good economic sense."

Because we have minimized the ethical dimension of business, there is little open discussion of ethics at work, despite the fact that we all face ethical choices every day. By ignoring or minimizing the ethical dimension of business, we unwittingly encourage or condone ethical abuses and produce a work-force that is literally de-moralized. Instead of being hushed up, ethics must be talked about openly, brought onto center stage.

Mixing Profits and Social Responsibility

When Levi Strauss patriarch Walter Haas, Jr. gave a speech in 1990 to introduce 40 owners of small businesses in Emeryville, California, to the idea of philanthropy, he said: "Some people argue that doing what's right is some-how contrary to doing what's good for business. I find this view both puzzling and wrong. We have learned that when we do what we believe is proper, the company gains. I can't translate that value into a number that appears on a financial statement, but I know that we wouldn't want to be in business and we would not be the leader in our industry if we did not enjoy this relationship with our people."

It is not that profits are unimportant to Levi Strauss, The Body Shop, and other socially concerned companies; it's just that they are not the central prior-ity. Says Anita Roddick: "Profits are an integral part of business, but you do something more, beyond your own accumulation of material wealth. You do something more which spiritually enhances you or educates you."

Paradoxically, companies that focus on values instead of profits often end up enhancing their profit picture as a result. UCLA business professor Bill Ouchi observes: "Among the fastest-growing, most profitable major American firms, profits are regarded not as an end in itself nor as the method of keeping score in the competitive process. Rather, profits are the reward to the firm as it continues to provide true value to its customers, to help its employees to grow, and to behave responsibly as a corporate citizen."

Rewriting the Book on Business

Charles Hampden-Turner writes: "Corporations have great power, and where that power is humanized, lasting and significant changes can occur to the very fabric of our society." As we come face-to-face with the negative con-sequences of our old ways of doing business, we can, by shifting our thinking, embrace a new way of doing business, one that will contribute to the health of the global community instead of profiting at its expense.

Anita Roddick believes that The Body Shop model of social responsibility will be adopted on a wide scale: "I think it will be the norm. We will have businesses where the bottom line is absolutely where it should be, at the bot-tom. Far more socially responsible products and services will be demanded from the marketplace. Business does not have to be the science of making money. It is something that people—employees, customers, suppliers, franchis-es—can genuinely feel great about, but only on one condition: The company must never let itself become anything other than a human enterprise. I think you can trade ethically; be committed to social responsibility, global responsibility; and empower your employees without being afraid of them. I think you can rewrite the book on business."

A small but vocal minority of leaders are showing the way to an enlightened partnership between business and society, a partnership in which economic, environmental, and social ends merge rather than compete. Such a partnership mutually optimizes the needs of all stakeholders—employees, customers, suppliers, the community, and the environment—as well as shareholders.

Charles Garfield is CEO of the Charles Garfield Group in Oakland, California, and author of Second to None *and* Peak Performers. *Call 510-272-9500 or visit www.shanti.org.*

48

The New Corporate Responsibility

by Anita Roddick

Let us remain awed by our responsibility, excited by the possibilities, and engaged in good *works*, not just good *words*.

Over the past decade, while many organizations have pursued business as usual, I have been part of a different movement—one that has tried to put idealism back on the agenda. Business can and must be a force for positive social change. It must not only avoid hideous evil—it must actively do good.

This movement is growing. We are forming our own networks and exchanging best practices. We are creating new markets of informed and morally motivated consumers. We are succeeding and thriving as businesses and as moral forces, and we are here to stay.

Business is now entering center stage. It is faster, more creative, more wealthy than governments. However, if it comes with no moral sympathy or honorable code of behavior, God help us all.

According to the theory some call free trade but I call licentious trade, we should all be happy that the globe is quickly becoming a playground for those of us who can move our capital and our projects quickly from place to place. We businesspeople, according to this theory, will make everyone better off if we can roam from country to country with no restrictions—in search of the lowest wages, the loosest environmental regulations, the most docile and desperate workers.

But I agree with Franklin Roosevelt who said, "Goods produced under conditions which do not meet a rudimentary standard of decency should be regarded as contraband and not be allowed to pollute channels of interstate trade."

There is always someplace in the world that is worse off, where the living conditions are a little wretched. Just look at industries in search of even lower wages and looser standards—from Europe or the U.S. to Taiwan to Malaysia to China—each country is just another pit stop in the race to the bottom, where wages and environmental standards are still lower, and human rights abuses are even more sordidly suppressed. The new nomadic capital never sets down roots, never builds communities; it leaves behind toxic wastes and embittered workers.

You may think this is hyperbole. Please go out and check. Visit the cities capital flight has left behind. Go to the places where capital has newly and temporarily alighted.

If this blind pursuit of licentious trade continues, political instability will return. The rise of fascism, brutal nationalism, and ethnic racism are no accident. Demagogues prey on insecurity and fear; they breed in the darkness of poverty and desolation. If we do not build an economic growth that sustains communities, cultures, and families, the consequences will be severe. Even if our politics somehow survive, our globe will not.

From Free to Fair Trade

Ah yes, you say—but free trade brings growth and jobs. That's the rub. I don't believe that unfettered free trade inevitably brings growth in anything but short-term transitional profits and long-term environmental destruction. We need a broader model. I call it fair trade; I call it sustainable trade. The label doesn't matter—the content does.

We need trade that respects and supports communities and families. We need trade that safeguards the environment. We need trade that encourages countries to educate their children, heal their sick, value the work of women, and respect human rights. We need to measure progress by human development, not gross product. Right now good political leaders in struggling countries are faced with a choice—lower your standards or lose our capital. This must stop.

So what's my alternative? Corporate responsibility—plain and simple. We have to rethink our approach to these issues. And then we have to act in ways big and small to bring sustainable and healthy growth across the globe. Our political postures must change—we have to stop endlessly whining for easier rules, lower costs, and fewer restrictions. And our business practices must change. We have to take longer-term views, invest in communities, and build long-lasting markets.

The new corporate responsibility is as simple as just saying no to dealing with torturers and despots. Consumers are expecting moral decisions. The new corporate responsibility is as complex as changing our basic notions of what motivates us and what our corporate goals should be. We, as business leaders, can and must change our views and our values.

Why do moral business decisions work? Because people understand that their purchases are moral choices as well. Today people want to like not only the product but they want to like the company. Customers crave knowledge; they yearn for information. Customers want to know the story behind the product.

We at The Body Shop believe not only that business should be held environmentally and socially accountable, but also that we should go beyond the law and exercise exemplary behavior.

I would rather be measured by how I treat weaker communities I trade with than by how great my profits are. There are trading networks out there that espouse a gentler, kinder way of doing business, where core values of community, social justice, openness, and environmental awareness are flourishing. Businesses can have a vital, driving sense of responsibility to people and the planet.

I urge you to keep your spirit independent and fertile—and challenge everything you've been told as a fact of business life. Far more important than free trade is the freedom we have, as leaders, to define and build a healthier and stronger world.

Anita Roddick is founder and CEO of The Body Shop. Visit www.thebodyshop.com.

49

Corporate Responsibility

by Mark Albion

Socially responsible corporate programs are critical strategic tools for sustaining competitive success. The cost-benefit analysis of business has been altered. Global economic imperatives, socio-demographic shifts, and the importance of human values to executives and consumers alike have created a new competitive climate—a shifting landscape of possibilities and opportunities for enlightened business leaders, but one with many pitfalls and traps as well.

The definition of *corporate responsibility* is rapidly changing. It is no longer simply a question of wanting to do the right thing. Instead, an increasingly complex set of social imperatives are being generated from the marketplace of employees, consumers, investors, and interested communities.

Chief executives need to organize effectively their various strategic resources (physical, financial, informational, and human), constantly improve the position of their products and services in the marketplace, and adapt to internal and external changes. Managing change may well be the executive's most important task.

Socially responsible actions play a critical role in creating competitive advantage and expressing corporate culture. In this article, I focus on what some companies are doing, how they are implementing these programs, and why it makes sense for the long-term financial bottom line. The purpose is to help you improve the quality of life and financial well-being.

Making a profit no longer depends simply on traditional business strategies and management of resources. It also depends on paying close attention to a variety of groups of people who are thinking and acting very differently than in the recent past. In their roles as your employees, consumers, investors, legislators, and the public at large (media, public interest groups), people are expressing their values in the marketplace—a marketplace that has changed. How is your company responding to the demographic and psychographic sea change in our society?

Managing the Five Es

The marketplace in many ways is about five Es: Employees, Education, Ethics, Environment, and Externalities.

Employee issues. As reported in the *Wall Street Journal*: "Workplace shortages may accomplish what activism could not: getting corporations deeply involved in social issues." Social issues will be at the heart of a company doing well. Having focused on slashing the workforce, senior executives now must do an about face. Recruiting, retaining, managing, and promoting the rapidly rising number of women and people of culturally diverse origins in the workplace is critical to sustained competitive success.

The aging workforce also consists of many two-career families (about 75 percent), some of the "sandwich" generation (adults taking care of their elders and children), whose values have evolved from those of ambition, acquisition, and accumulation to concern with fulfillment, family, and fun.

Those companies who recognize the Workforce 2000 imperatives, and are sensitive to the needs of these groups, will flourish. They will be better equipped to deal with problems of worker shortages, turnover, poor job skills, low morale and productivity. To date, most have not been so attentive. Why has readjustment been so slow? Says one workforce expert, "Senior executives (mostly white males) still think like Ozzie and Harriet." The price of insensitivity and discrimination will go up.

Education. Just as our concern grew in the 1980s about how we could compete with the Japanese in business, today we recognize the imperative of better primary and secondary education. The extent of illiteracy (20 million functionally illiterate adults), the lack of basic reading and mathematics skills in new business recruits (expressed as a serious problem by 70 percent of firms), and the shortage of skilled labor is threatening our competitive position in the global economy. Yet less than one percent of our major corporations spend 95 percent of the training dollars. Companies that become involved in education can influence the quality of job candidates, protect and develop local talent, demonstrate community leadership, and improve the business climate in their communities. The price of poor education will go up.

Ethics. "I wonder about the value of sending my kids to college if the price I pay is not knowing my kids well," expressed one senior executive. The aging or "maturing" of our society has seen these issues of balancing life reappear. Time has become the cultural currency. Moreover, the values of Wall Street have turned into the values of Main Street, as we have gone from a mergers and acquisition era of the Boomtown to a return to the Hometown. The family is back. The caring individual has replaced the rugged individual of the Right and the collective individual of the Left.

Companies that tap into those values can bond—not just brand—with employees and customers alike. Attracting and retaining workers and consumers, building corporate reputation, and sustaining corporate growth has always been a function of giving people what they want at a fair price. That "price," if in terms of too much time away from the family, if in terms of fuzzy product/company images in a crowded marketplace, may be too high. The price of this missed opportunity is going up.

Environment. If you doubt that corporate social responsibility is a requirement of being considered a good company, just look at the 180-degree change in approaching the environment. The return to our environmental concern—galvanized by closed beaches and the Exxon *Valdez* tragedy—followed naturally from our concerns about our health, which rose rapidly (look at the meteoric sales trend of bottled water). Now, environmentally sensitive, "green" products are becoming the "lite" products.

An image as an environmentally responsible company is becoming an essential part of a competitive strategy. Environmental responsibility is now a key factor in making *Fortune's* "Most Admired Companies" list. Some companies even include environmental measures in their compensation systems. Certainly, there are real costs associated with non-compliance (litigation, liability, imposed restrictions, fines, a damaged reputation). And the costs of environmental irresponsibility are going up.

Externalities. Externalities are behavioral outcomes not directly accounted for by the marketplace, such as the freedom to pollute at no direct cost to the polluter. These market failures need to be corrected by changing the "pricing" of the behavior, for example, by charging the polluter. Some of these behaviors have a "hidden subsidy" behind them. Social and political forces are now working to remove certain subsidies.

In many ways, externalities summarize the first four Es. The price of excessive time away from family, of a workplace that does not fit employees' values, of a poorly educated workforce, and of a polluted environment has not been fully accounted for by the market system. Companies will obtain competitive advantages by recognizing that these changes in values translate into changes in the economics of business.

Will this broader definition of corporate responsibility evolve further? The westward shift in the population into more liberal states indicates that it will. And with skilled workers in demand, consumers offered more product choices than ever, and global competition increasing, social and business interests should continue to converge. We are seeing a redefinition of what constitutes good (and profitable) business practice.

Redefining Boundaries

Are you listening and responding only to your stockholders or to all your company's constituents? Everett Dirksen, former U.S. Senator, once said sagely: "Sometimes you have to realize that the people have spoken, and that it's time to get on with it." Has the definition of your corporate mission and objectives changed in the last three years? The last five years? If not, you might take another look. Does it pay attention to all those groups of people who can significantly influence your company's future?

Often, we concern ourselves with the financials and the investment community. When thinking about how we operate, we may say that "If we take care of our employees and they take care of our customers, the market will take care of us."

Today, more than just these three groups have a stake in how you do. The government can have a say through legislation, and public interest groups, the media, and local communities also may influence your well-being. Moreover, these groups have made it clear that their thinking has evolved on the role of the corporation in society. It is no longer just vague notions about corporate responsibilities—it involves a list of activities with direct bottom-line impact. To include the interests of these five stakeholders in your corporate activities requires a broader view of a corporation's role in society. And the corporation has to adjust to meet this challenge.

Stakeholder Strategy

The essence of corporate strategy is to develop a broad formula for how to compete, based on corporate strengths and weaknesses within the context of the competitive environment. A successful strategy capitalizes on these strengths and anticipates important changes in outside forces.

With a stakeholder view of the world, a firm will assess its relative competitive position, evaluate its strategies, and monitor changes with each of its five stakeholders: government, investors, consumers, employees, and society at large. To compete successfully, a firm must deal with its rivals and with changes in the interests of its suppliers (investors and employees), its buyers (consumers), and the external forces of legislators and other societal groups. Few firms explicitly recognize, measure, and monitor their positions with each of these stakeholders.

Strategies that strengthen relationships with these five groups of stakeholders create opportunities for sustainable competitive advantage and long-term profitability. These strategies can dramatically improve the cost/benefit relationship of doing business.

Investors. Economics catch up with social conscience. Rather than marching in the streets, private and institutional investors are using their dollars as market power. Social responsibility is a key indicator of the great companies.

Individual examples of shareholder pressure on social issues, such as South African involvement and environmental responsibility, abound. One company was forced to rethink its marketing of plastic packaging because the institutional giant CALPERS called every couple of weeks to see "what are your environmental policies going to be." Divestment of tobacco company stocks by Harvard University and the City University of New York have led Massachusetts to consider doing the same. But the cost of equity capital decreases for the socially responsible.

Employees. We all dream of noble purposes. Diversity is the nature of today's workforce. If you can not attract the best minorities and women, and create a culture in which they are comfortable and productive, your costs from excessive recruiting, high turnover, and low productivity will skyrocket.

There is a real cost to not being on *Business Week's* list of the most "women-friendly" companies. For top MBAs of color, the third criteria for job choice was whether the company had a volunteer program to help educate minorities in the inner city. And if you are not involved in education and training, you will suffer from a skills shortage.

When business people are asked what issues bother them the most at work, the top three replies are: lack of career purpose in life, little free time and high stress, and a poorly balanced professional and personal life. The employer that can help fulfill these needs will have a productive, innovative group of employees. The cost of human resources decreases for the socially responsible.

Consumers. More people than ever based their product choices on how a company rated on: pollution prevention efforts, efforts to hire minorities, community events sponsored, charities supported, and employee volunteer efforts encouraged.

The shopping cart has turned into a vehicle for social change. The publication *Shopping for a Better World* rates supermarket products (by company) on eleven social criteria of good citizenship. A reader survey indicated that 70 percent of respondents had changed their buying habits, with 52 percent saying that corporate giving was very important when deciding among brands.

Consumer boycotts have made international news due to their regularity and efficacy. Whether its dolphin-safe tuna, fast-food beef imported from South Africa, or "cruelty-to-animals" cosmetics, consumers are making their voices heard. The success of companies like The Body Shop, who are socially and environmentally responsible, testifies that consumers are looking for the good in companies as well. Responsibility leads to customer (and employee) loyalty that goes beyond branding in a crowded marketplace. The cost of marketing decreases for the socially responsible.

Government. A wave of legislation is just beginning. The expanded rights given to the disabled, the new Civil Rights Act, new clean air requirements, better food labeling, potential bans on cigarette machines, further restrictions on beer advertising, and potential diaper regulations—all indicate the growth in legislation to engender more responsible behavior. The benefit of being ahead on these issues will increase for the socially responsible company.

Society at large. Political and social realities. As a business executive, these constituencies are important to acknowledge in dealing with social issues. They offer opportunities for good press and good community relations. The media is looking to change society, and stories of corporate social "negligence" make good copy. Public interest groups have grown stronger, with excellent publicists and established ties to city halls and regulatory agencies. And local communities where you do business are the homes of your employees and customers, and their families. The benefits of addressing their needs increase for the socially responsible company.

Good values complement good economic results. Managing internal and external change means addressing the needs of your business and society. It requires a corporate culture that is responsive to societal changes and can attract and retain qualified employees. Corporate strategy should be set to recognize these many corporate stakeholders. Done properly, a charitable giving program can then be implemented to help the company meet its strategic objectives.   ❧

Mark Albion, Ph.D., is chairperson of Apple Brook Farms in support of social causes, president of Children Against Drugs, author of three books on marketing, consultant to Fortune 500 companies developing programs that address social needs, a member of the Social Venture Network, and former faculty member at the Harvard Business School. 617-0235-8923.

50

My Responsibility

by Arthur Blank

As a values-based company, we are sustaining and preserving both our business and our environment. At first glance, our performance in 1998 might not look much different from trends in previous years: Consistent sales and earnings growth, a steady rate of new store openings, strong comparable store sales performance, all resulting in the 13th consecutive year of record earnings delivered to our stockholders.

But 1998 was a pivotal year for The Home Depot—a year during which we firmly positioned our company, competitively and strategically. However, as Will Rogers once said, "Even if you're on the right track, you'll get run over if you just sit there." We agree, so we remain aggressive in our drive to develop key strategies for longer-term growth. Longer-term, increasing our sales in other segments of the industry will become progressively more important to supporting a consistent growth pattern.

Leadership is not just measured by sales and profits—it also entails certain responsibilities. Our long-term plans also address alternative methods of distribution to attract more customers, enhance their shopping experiences and obtain a larger share of the total market.

We are proud of where The Home Depot is today, and of how we got here—through an unwavering commitment to our stockholders, customers, associates, and communities. We have built strong and lasting relationships—a pattern of consistently strong earnings growth—and the foundation is solid enough to keep building.

Our long-term plans are all threads that weave into our vision of providing total solutions for our customers—offering the right products and services at the right price, when they want them, how they want them, and where they want them. We believe that, by doing business on the customers' terms, we will continue to enhance our leadership position in the industry.

Leadership Entails Responsibility

Leadership is not just measured by sales and profits—it also entails certain responsibilities. These responsibilities begin with our associates and extend to the communities we serve and the environment in which we live.

One of my primary responsibilities as CEO is the development of our people. Life has taught me that if you surround yourself with people who are different from yourself, your life is enriched. We are enriching our organization through our recruiting, succession planning, and training.

As we extend our reach, we will be serving a more diverse group of customers. This dictates a broader skill set—a need to build a workforce that reflects the customers and communities we serve. And, we have a commitment to our associates to train, nurture and provide opportunities for professional growth.

Giving back to our communities is not only a responsibility, it is part of doing business at The Home Depot. Through many corporate giving programs, we strive to have a positive influence on today's youth and to make housing more affordable. In addition, countless hours are volunteered every year by representatives in all our stores to worthwhile projects of their choice.

We're also taking a leadership role in protecting the environment. How we treat the environment is an issue of values. Preserving the environment is one area where we are willing to share the leadership position. There's plenty of room at the top, and the only way to make a meaningful difference is to gain the support, wisdom and foresight of our suppliers and other retailers. By working together we can have a greater impact in making our world a better place.

Arthur Blank is co-founder and CEO of The Home Depot. This article is adapted from Home Depot's 1998 Annual Report.

51

Corporate Social Responsibility

by Ken P. Cohen

The foremost component of social responsibility is fulfilling our mission. At ExxonMobil, we take corporate social responsibility seriously. We view social responsibility as more than just doing good works. The foremost component of our social responsibility is fulfilling our basic mission: finding and producing oil and gas in a safe, environmentally responsible and cost-effective manner—and then providing petroleum and petrochemical products at competitive prices to markets worldwide.

I would like to make five points:

1. Well-run companies are far more socially responsible than is usually conceded by critics—simply when they fulfill their basic function. Successfully fulfilling the conventional role of a corporation is extremely difficult, and also extremely beneficial to society. If a company can't do what it is designed to do—reliably provide products at reasonable cost while making enough money to ensure its investors earn a return on their money—it goes out of business. Its employees don't have jobs. Governments don't get tax revenues. Suppliers lose their trade. Competition is reduced, and consumers lose choices. If a company can't run its business well in the first place, its social role is compromised.

2. By producing energy at competitive prices, ExxonMobil contributes a great deal to social welfare in ways that few people appreciate because they take a steady supply of clean, affordable energy for granted. A reliable and affordable energy supply is vital for economic viability and growth. Even with the emphasis on conservation and the efficient use of energy, worldwide energy use is growing rapidly. Over the past 10 years, global demand for energy has grown two percent per year. This rate of demand growth is expected to continue over the next 20 years and keep pace with projected world GDP growth. But energy is not simply some disembodied productive input. It is the source of enormous benefits. Oil has revolutionized transportation. It has permitted complex machines through its powers to lubricate moving parts. Through diverse products, it has promoted safety and saved untold lives. In agriculture, it has permitted huge increases in productivity. All the people who benefit from these uses of energy are hugely advantaged by obtaining energy at reasonable prices.

3. How we conduct business—our standards of business conduct—is an important factor in contributing to social change. ExxonMobil does business worldwide; however, despite our global size and technical competence, we are an invited guest of host governments wherever we do business, and we must comply with all of the applicable laws and regulations. We also adhere to our rigorous standards of business conduct wherever we operate. Many of these countries are extremely poor, several have governments that do not conform with Western norms, and some have traditions and views that are not acceptable in the developed world. But wherever we do business, we follow some common approaches of business conduct that telegraph our values and promote beneficial change by our actions. For example, when we insist upon legal protections for our investments, including legal due process, in some places we are among the first to introduce their use.

Another practice that can be transforming is to train local nationals, and then to promote them based on their abilities. Not every society promotes on ability rather than ethnicity, race, religion or sex, but we do. And we train people. We are a pacesetter in developing and using leading-edge technology and processes. Technology is our lifeblood and the key to our competitiveness. We must invest in the abilities of people.

4. The special programs that we develop and support as we work in the poorest countries are closely aligned with the social and environmental needs of the people there. We are usually among the highest paying employers in countries where we operate, and we put a premium on training, safety, and skill. When we have a project in a developing area of the world, one of our primary preoccupations is protecting the health of the people who work for us and protecting the surrounding environment. In those situations, we provide quality medical care for our employees and their dependents, often working with health care professionals to improve basic sanitation practices in the area.

We also take steps to protect the natural environment as we conduct our operations—no matter where we are located. We recognize that we need to be sensitive to the concerns of local citizens and communities about our operations. We try to involve local citizens and community groups in the development of projects that affect them. This community outreach process can be new in some countries. While we are, of course, guests of the national government and cannot undermine their prerogatives, we can do things that promote citizen involvement.

We put our most advanced knowledge to use in developing countries. For example, our expanded refinery in Thailand is world-class. The Thai nationals who work there are obtaining cutting-edge training and skills. In Angola, we are working with the U.S. Agency for International Development on a public education program to combat the spread of HIV/AIDS. Also in Angola, we are partnering with health organizations to wipe out malaria—a scourge that impacts almost every family. This is only a small sampling of what we do.

5. We productively work with many non-governmental organizations (NGOs) for the common good. Despite the value we bring as a company to the many places we work, we still are accused by some of being socially irresponsible. Usually the attacks come from activists within a few special-interest NGOs. These groups represent a variety of interests and concerns. In many places, we welcome their help. We have worked closely with CARE, UNICEF and AMERICARES on health, environment, and poverty programs. We find these and other NGOs to be willing and helpful partners. They have a track record of expertise and accomplishment in the local areas where we work. They tend to be diversified with an established donor and financial resource base. They know how to operate efficiently in difficult circumstances. They have a reputation for ethical behavior, and they have solid financial controls to track funds. These NGOs want to work with businesses that are trying to alleviate real problems.

But some NGOs tend to be single-issue focused and made up of uncompromising activists. They can be ideologically hostile to business, unwilling to accept tradeoffs, and unrepresentative of public views. They are splinter groups, front groups, and phony coalitions. The criticisms wielded by NGO activists adversely affect business and countries. Some NGOs are hostile to oil development of any kind.

Too often, worthy projects are placed under threat of cancellation from the costs of delay and expense creep. NGOs have important roles to play in addressing issues related to the environment, public health, and the development of poorer countries. But these roles need to be responsibly played.

Corporations that operate ethically, sensitively, and cooperatively should not be victimized by baseless charges that they are socially irresponsible. Despite the challenges posed by uninformed attacks on what responsible companies do, we are optimistic that over time there will be a greater public appreciation of the role that corporations play. We hope we can communicate the enormous benefits that flow from the way we conduct our business.   ✍

Ken Cohen is vice president of public affairs with Exxon Mobil. Visit www.exxonmobil.com.

Be Transparent

by Mike Farriss

My company makes a dangerous product that is addictive and causes serious diseases. Cigarettes cause lung cancer, heart disease, emphysema and other serious diseases. There is no such thing as a safe cigarette. And, with all that is known about cigarettes, some question whether it is possible to market them responsibly at all.

I'll share with you some of our past failings and actions we are taking to demonstrate a responsible approach to marketing our products. Some would say that our experience is unique because of the health effects of our products. We do face unique challenges. But today many industries face some of the same challenges we've faced as they struggle to address the public's concerns about their actions and products. So, the tough lessons we've learned may be relevant for your company and industry.

For many years, Philip Morris USA defined success as: following the law, achieving our objectives, respecting our employees, and giving back to the community. That worked for a long time. But over time, society's expectations changed, and we failed to keep pace. Society was sending strong messages to our industry and company.

We saw this in many ways—increased litigation, legislation, regulation, and taxes. In the face of increasing pressure, we receded into a "bunker" mentality. We failed to listen to the many voices that criticized our products and actions. We spent too much time debating the precise relationship between smoking, disease, and addiction and not enough time listening to people to understand their points of view and concerns. Our conduct, in many cases, was wrongheaded, mistaken and regrettable.

When we did look outside of our bunker, we saw many people lined up with concerns, among them the President of the United States, the United States Surgeon General, the FDA Commissioner, attorneys general, the public health community, and many in the public at large. This was a sobering reality.

We had a choice to make. We could keep doing business as usual and risk being put out of business. Or, we could change to more closely align ourselves with society's expectations of a responsible company. We chose to change the way we do business.

First, in 1997, we developed a new mission statement: Our Mission is to be the most responsible, effective and respected developer, manufacturer and marketer of consumer products, especially products intended for adults. Today, every business decision at Philip Morris USA is guided by this mission.

A second milestone was our public agreement with the medical and scientific consensus that smoking causes serious diseases and is addictive. Today, we communicate broadly and openly about the risks associated with smoking. We do this on our website (philipmorrisusa.com), in advertising, in testimony before Congress, in forums, and in many other ways, including our voluntary advertising about the serious health effects of our products (see our TV ad on Addiction, Causation and Quitting).

Another example is the testimony our Chairman gave before Congress: *"We are mindful of the critical need for manufacturers to work with the public health community to emphasize the fact that all smoking is dangerous, and that the best option from a health perspective is to quit or not to start in the first place."*

Even though there is no such thing as a safe cigarette, people continue to smoke. So, as a manufacturer of a product that is harmful and addictive, part of our mission is to develop new methods and technologies with the potential to reduce the harm associated with smoking. We have devoted $2 billion in the past decade to fund scientific research and new products and processes to reduce the risks of smoking. We are making progress.

Another defining moment was when we signed the State Tobacco Settlement Agreement, forever changing the way cigarettes can lawfully be marketed and sold in the United States. Gone are tobacco billboards, transit ads on the top of busses or taxis, branded merchandise like caps or t-shirts, and product placement in movies and TV. We all agree that kids should not smoke. To address the rise in youth smoking, we started our Youth Smoking Prevention department. In the last seven years, we have spent more than $600 million dollars to help prevent kids from smoking. First, we prevent kids from getting access to cigarettes by not selling cigarettes over the Internet, by paying retailers to keep cigarettes behind the counter, and by being the major supporter of the "We Card" program that has trained 87,000 retailers to verify age, so that cigarettes are not sold to minors. Second, we try to prevent kids from starting to smoke by working with child development experts to create resources that help parents talk to their kids about not smoking. We provide brochures, such as *Raising Kids Who Don't Smoke,* in both English and Spanish, to retail stores and at The Parent Resource Center on our website.

We've also become one of the largest corporate contributors to positive youth development programs. We support things like mentoring and health education programs. The good news is that national youth smoking rates have been declining in recent years. According to the Centers for Disease Control, cigarette smoking by high school students is at the lowest level in a generation, down 38 percent since 1997.

As a manufacturer of an addictive product that has serious health risks, we also help adult smokers who have decided to quit. We launched QuitAssist, a resource guide, to help smokers who have decided to quit to get the support and information they need to quit smoking for good. The guide gives specific and practical tips from smoking cessation experts and former smokers. We promote this resource through advertising, brochures placed on our cigarette packs, and by placing this information on our website. To date, we've had over 160,000 visits to our QuitAssist web site, and have sent out over 128,000 brochures. In addition, we have also provided a three-year $15 million grant to Duke University Medical Center to research about new quitting methods.

Perhaps our most far-reaching effort to meet society's expectations of a responsible company is our support for meaningful and effective regulation of tobacco products by the U.S. Food and Drug Administration. Americans want a trusted government agency to oversee tobacco products. So do we. Tobacco products are the only products that you ingest that are not now regulated by the FDA. All medication, food, and cosmetics must be approved by the FDA. And yet cigarettes, which are dangerous and addictive, are not regulated by the FDA. This make no sense.

Yet, Philip Morris USA is the only major cigarette manufacturer that supports legislation that would give FDA regulatory authority over tobacco products, giving the FDA the ability to require full disclosure of all ingredients in cigarettes, ban the sale of candy- and fruit-flavored tobacco products, set standards for products that could reduce the harm caused by smoking, and do more to prevent youth smoking.

The American Cancer Society, American Lung Association, American Heart Association, Campaign for Tobacco Free Kids, and other health organizations also support this legislation. Unfortunately, FDA legislation before Congress last year was unsuccessful. This was a bitter disappointment—not just for us, but for everyone who hoped to see a coherent, comprehensive national tobacco policy. We will continue to support FDA regulation of tobacco products because it is the right thing to do.

These are some things we're doing to address society's concerns about our products and actions. We're taking the right steps in a responsible way.

What Have We Learned

So, what have we learned that might help you?

First, you need to seek input about what is expected of a responsible company and listen. You can't live in a "bunker" and succeed. Looking outside your walls means engaging and listening—not just to the people who support you, but to everyone who has an interest in or is affected by your products and actions, especially your critics. You may not always like what you hear, but you need to hear it.

Second, you need to act on what you hear. You can't lead with talk. You must have the courage to act on what you learn. This is the only way to show society that you are listening and responding to their opinions and concerns.

Third, you need to be open and transparent. Be open about what you are doing, why you are doing it, and how you are doing it.

I invite you to visit our website philipmorrisusa.com to learn more about us, our policies, positions and actions.

Mike Farriss is senior vice president of communications & government Affairs, Philip Morris USA. Visit www.philipmorrisusa.com. This article is adapted with permission from his speech to the Houston Forum. 804-484-8897.

53

Never Give Up!

by Bill Marks

A t the Coca-Cola Company, our commitment to corporate social responsi-bility is integral to the way we do business. Through our actions, we strive to earn the world's continued trust in our company and our brands.

There can be no better evidence of how we view our responsibility to our communities than the timely, direct response of the Coca-Cola Company to the events of September 11, 2001. We made a gift of $12 million dollars to the national United Way fund immediately after those attacks, making sure we did not get any publicity for that donation. Why? Because helping is simply the right thing to do!

I believe that act demonstrates the heritage of The Coca-Cola Company as one rooted in relationships—a company our communities can count on for support in the worst of times as well as in the best. Thousands of our people, working tirelessly with our bottling partners, rose to the occasion and deliv-ered whatever was needed most.

These are essential, enduring principles—serving one's community, build-ing credibility, building relationships of honesty, integrity, and forthrightness.

And, let's not forget some human qualities that serve us well: optimism, fortitude, perseverance, confidence, commitment, and leadership.

In truth, these principles and qualities rise above and help raise us above life's sometimes sordid parade. If we let them, such ideals can help put even devastating experiences, like terrorist attacks, into a perspective we can deal with. Having principles and aspiring to ideals can help us prevail during trying times.

In business, one essential function is the "pitch." As practitioners, we pitch stories to the media. What happened to the pitch after 9/11?

First, the media changed. The assignment of reporters, crews and resources—human, electronic, and financial—to the biggest story of our day literally stopped "the pitch"! Our media sources dried up; they were off report-ing the BIG story.

Now more than ever, corporate CEOs understand the value of corporate reputations. But, what about Enron and Arthur Andersen? I'm certain the PR teams at those companies had crisis plans. But, did those plans help them? In a crisis, it's not the plan that helps you get through the problems. Instead, it is the integrity of your relationships that pulls you through. Obviously, relationships like those take years to build. But, they are worth every ounce of the effort. Because relationships are the fuel that make crisis plans work!

Preparing for the crises is no mystery. You just do what we've always said to do: Be honest, be straightforward, and build relationships of trust with constituencies.

Public relations professionals need to ensure that their skills, abilities and experience fit their clients' needs! Believe in yourself and in what you offer. Refuse to compromise or quit! When you believe in something passionately, you learn never to take a "no" as the final answer! In the words of Sir Winston Churchill, "Never give up! Never, never, never, never, never give up!"

We have been struck a terrible blow. The tragedies of 9/11 can never be forgotten. They changed us, our lives, and our sense of security. Immediately. Immutably. Immeasurably. But we are adapting and recovering, emerging from a recession. Unarguably, terrorism deepened and prolonged our economic pain. Yet, as a people, we are recovering by following the injunction: "Never give up!

Bill Marks is vice president of public relations at Coca-Cola North America. This article is adapted from his speech to the University of Northern Iowa, PRSSA Chapter, and used with permission of Vital Speeches of the Day.

54

Are We Doing Enough?

by J. W. Marriott, Jr.

Is our company and industry—and yours—doing enough to fulfill its social responsibilities? Obviously, we can all do more. It's not just a responsibility—for us it's a business imperative. When we work to make our communities more vibrant, beautiful and prosperous, we're investing in making them more attractive to our visitors and giving them a reason to travel. Of course social responsibility is not just about investing in places—it's also about investing in our people.

A guiding principle at our company is when we take care of our associates, they take care of our customers. When we provide a community's young people with education and training, we enhance the quality of the labor pool. And when we do our part to make entire communities or countries more prosperous, we broaden and deepen a global middle class so people can afford to buy the services we sell. For instance, as the new middle classes in China and India begin to travel extensively, all of us will benefit.

Community service initiatives are laboratories for leadership. They help identify and develop promising leaders, build teamwork, and improve loyalty. And obviously, when our companies demonstrate social responsibility, we add to our industry's reservoir of goodwill from governments, customers, and the general public.

Real and effective social responsibility is not just the responsibility of the community relations staff—it is an entire company's responsibility. Although we set policies for Marriott's "Spirit to Serve Our Communities" program from our corporate headquarters, our leaders across the globe are strongly encouraged to get involved on a personal level in their communities.

Knowing what a community needs is critical to social responsibility. Just swooping in and offering some global cookie-cutter program and acting as though we know best just doesn't work. Our communities know best what they need—and how to achieve it.

In 47 cities around the world, our general managers form business councils representing all of the brands in their market. One of their top priorities is to pool their capital and human resources to serve the unique needs of their communities.

Of course, there are many needs, and we can't meet them all. So, we try to leverage our core expertise. That might mean offering ballroom space for charitable fundraisers, or donating surplus furniture to housing programs, as most hotels have done.

It also means tapping the experience of our leaders. For instance, 50 percent of Marriott's managers come from the hourly ranks, and those people personally know how difficult and rewarding it is to climb the economic ladder. And those same leaders have helped to bring thousands of chronically unemployed people into the work force. Our leaders are the spirit behind a program we call "pathways to independence"—where people learn to find and keep good jobs.

In our pathways program, we match participants with mentors, train them in the classroom and on the job, and help them with solutions to problems that get in the way of work—like childcare and transportation. When they complete the program, they're guaranteed a job offer.

Environmental protection is another example of social responsibility that meets communities' needs and our own. In environmentally fragile areas, we might support the community and its tourism-reliant economy by protecting endangered species.

Take the JW Marriott Phuket Resort, for example. Recently, nearly 2,500 guests and locals gathered at sunset to release 10,000 baby turtles into the ocean—helping to raise awareness about the plight of these magnificent creatures.

Sometimes meeting local needs means building a roof over someone's head. At a recent Habitat for Humanity project in Costa Rica, associates and top executives from Marriott worked side by side to help build several homes for local families. We're doing the same in Washington, D.C., and many other cities.

We also need to invest in our communities by investing in our people and improving their lives. Travel and tourism is a 24-hour, 7-day-a-week business, and we put real effort into helping our people deal with this. Every parent knows childcare can be a challenge, but when you're working the overnight shift at a hotel, it can be almost impossible. That's why we offer several resources to help families. One example is our associate resource line, which provides access to local services for help with family, legal and other issues. We also coordinate closely with our people to find flexible and creative solutions to childcare needs.

At our Desert Springs resort in California, for instance, six housekeepers with 11 children formed a "childcare cooperative" where they take turns caring for each other's kids. The property helps coordinate their work schedules—and it works!

Now, all of these ideas are fine, but they're meaningless if we don't address our industry's challenges. So we need to work together to get people traveling again.

Travel and tourism's "perfect storm" has created challenges greater than we've ever experienced. Yet, in every dark cloud there is a silver lining. The events of the last two years have significantly raised awareness about the vital importance of travel and tourism in the world economy.

It's the role of the WTTC to work with governments, world, and community leaders to revitalize our industry, not further damage it with unnecessary restrictions and regulations. For instance, the effect of September 11 on the airline and hotel industry in the U.S. was a defining moment. So much so, that President Bush allowed us to use parts of his speeches to film a commercial to get Americans on the road again.

The travel advisory from the World Health Organization due to the SARS outbreak in Toronto brought a storm of protest by Prime Minister Chrétien and almost every government official in Ontario Province, prompting us to realize that Canada clearly understands the benefits of tourism and travel.

Because of the effect of terrorist events and the SARS outbreak, our industry has top-of-mind awareness among world leaders. We must continue to educate our leaders about the tremendous value of our industry. They will be more receptive than ever before.

We need to be active champions for our industry and continually ask, "Are we doing enough to make travel and tourism work for everyone?"

We are doing a lot, but I hope we never allow ourselves to believe it's enough. In social responsibility, as in leadership, success is never final.

J.W. Marriott, Jr. is chairman of Marriott International, a leading worldwide hospitality company. This article is adapted from his remarks at the World Travel and Tourism Council Global Summit in Portugal. Visit www.marriott.com.

55

Shaping the Way Things Are Done

by Barbara Ley Toffler

While there are some simple principles at play in ethical management, business applications can be complex. "Ethical" derives from the Greek word "ethos," which means both "character" and "sentiment of the community"—what we might call culture. For me, "ethical" has to do with a general conception of right and wrong in the attitudes and actions of individuals, communities, and organizations.

Principles such as honesty, promise-keeping, and doing no harm are held by most people, allowing us to make statements like "that's unethical" about a given action with which most people would agree.

In business, ethically questionable situations are either practices involving outright illegal activities—such as the application of personal expenses to contract budgets, the stealing of company products, or practices which compromise a recognized corporate policy—or practices that result in physical harm to a person or group (like producing a gas tank vulnerable to rear-end collisions or dumping of toxic wastes into a local river).

Ethical concerns in business are pervasive and complex. In fact, ethical concerns are part of the routine practices of management; they are characterized less frequently by legal issues than by concerns about relationships and responsibility; and while they deal with right-and-wrong decisions, they frequently involve factors that make the right and wrong less than patently clear.

One thing, however, is clear: How managers define ethics certainly affects how they perceive and handle problems.

One has responsibility to deal with a situation if one has capacity to do so.

Explicit and implicit roles. "Roles" usually refer to the activities, responsibilities, and level of authority specified by the formal job description. As managers talk in detail about what they do on the job, however, they describe an "implicit" role, which is different from the "explicit" role of the job description. They talk about implied responsibilities and about activities they see as part of their roles that are neither written nor formally verbalized.

Three Kinds of Responsibility

Responsibility is the link between the manager, the job, and the organization. While we might say that "managing" means taking responsibility, no manager is responsible for everything. Good managers know when and for what they are responsible. Generally recognized are three kinds of responsibility: Role, causal, and capacity. Understanding them is critical to understanding how the organizational/individual relationship creates and resolves ethical dilemmas.

Role responsibility. Simply stated, role responsibility is all of the activities and obligations specified by one's formal role. In the course of getting their jobs done, however, managers frequently find that a particular problem may not come under their formal responsibility to act. That is where causal and capacity responsibility come in.

Causal responsibility. The basic notion is this: If one has caused harm or a problem, one has the ethical responsibility to attempt to correct it. Straightforward as the notion may seem, the experiences of many people suggest otherwise.

In management, causal responsibility gets intertwined with role responsibility. The manager who gives an assignment without providing resources or access to resources might well respond to an accusation by insisting that the subordinate's role was to find the way to get what was needed to get the job done. If personal causal responsibility is redefined as someone else's role responsibility, the role occupant may be forced to choose between acting unethically or being seen as derelict in taking responsibility. The issue becomes even more complex when the notion of capacity is added.

Capacity responsibility. This notion says, simply, that one has a responsibility to deal with a situation if one has the capability of doing so. Of course the use of capacity responsibility raises a number of questions about the consequences to individuals of assuming such responsibility. Sometimes the reactions can be negative, ranging from the co-worker's angry "mind your own business" to the supervisor's punitive action for "interfering" with production.

The ongoing debate about whistle-blowing is really an argument about the exercise of one kind of capacity responsibility and is a microcosm of the pros and cons of assuming responsibility outside of one's appointed role. The taking of capacity responsibility can create ethically sticky situations or provide energy and creativity toward their resolution.

Barbara Ley Toffler, Ph.D., is a professor of business administration at the Harvard Business School and a consultant for a number of Fortune 500 firms. This article is adapted from her new book, Tough Choices, *and used with permission. Visit www.barbaraleytoffler.com.*

56

Great and Good

by Jeffrey R. Immelt

We have moved from an era of individualism to an era of personal and corporate responsibility and citizenship. If you want to be a great company today, you also have to be a good company.

What can business leaders do to create a great and a good company—*great* in the sense of tremendous results for investors and customers, growth and profitability, and *good* in the sense of connection to the world, adding to the quality of our workforce, customers, and communities?

Ten Principles

I apply 10 leadership principles to create both a great and a good company. The first five form the foundation of a company, and the last five describe the behaviors of a company.

1. Set high standards for performance. Strong performers are the best corporate citizens. Once I was having dinner in Washington, D.C., with a prominent politician from the state of California who was complaining to me that corporations don't do any good any more in California. They don't give any more in California. And then this person named 10 companies that used to do a lot but now do nothing. Why? Because, in fact, these companies don't even exist any more! The 10 companies that this person picked all failed in the marketplace. So, cynicism can't be battled through mediocrity. Great and good companies start by setting high standards for performance.

2. Make compliance a core operating process. The way you do things can become a key competitive advantage. If you treat compliance using all the best process tools you have inside your company, because it's a central artery of the company, you will be able to take on tough challenges. Don't be afraid to do this. It starts with having clear rules. Have strong and clear processes, have transparency, have openness. While you have to treat compliance seriously, you're not perfect. But you can make compliance a core process and a competitive advantage for your company.

3. Build exceptional governance with a strong board. Companies need strong oversight with people whom investors or any constituent can trust. Often, it is hard for the board to be experts on any particular topic, but they smell the culture and feel what's going on. Such openness is very important.

4. Make a real commitment to openness, both internally and externally. It's called transparency. Essentially what transparency means is to talk about your company externally the way you run it internally. To allow people inside, to allow employees to touch and feel what's going on, to give people voice.

5. Have a culture where the company always comes first. Learn to believe in great people. Become bound together by a common set of values. In our company, we have a values card with four words on it: Imagine; Solve; Build; and Lead. They are inspirational words that bring people together and tie them together. It gives people freedom and commitment to achieve values we hold dear. But if you want to have good corporate citizenship, you must have a culture that places the good of the company ahead of everything else.

6. Develop great leaders that have the right incentives. In our company, we believe in promotion from within. Our top 600 leaders, on average, have been with the company for 19 years, and 13 of our top 30 leaders have served on the corporate audit staff. So nearly half of our top 30 leaders were one of those 500 people that were trying to build processes, trying to figure out what was happening inside the company. That gives them tremendous perspective. In addition, every manager, every person in our company, gets measured on two dimensions, financial performance and values. If you are financially strong but have bad values, you'd be asked to leave the company. So this two-dimensional metric is how we build people and develop leaders in our culture.

7. Be very committed to people, to developing people and building trust. Focus on merit. Have compassion when people are impacted. Occasionally, from a competitiveness standpoint, you have to close a plant or downsize in an area. But in that case you can either retrain people to make them employable, or help your people bridge to retirement. Stay competitive so that your employees know that they can count on something over the long term. Your people are your best ambassadors and your most important asset.

8. Make a business out of solving the world's toughest problems. There is business (money) to be made by helping solve the world's toughest issues. The last 25 years were really about the development of information technology. The next 20 or 25 years will be about technology around the economics of scarcity—about how you get more health care into people's hands, about how to get more energy into the system, about basic commodities like water, about how to make the world more secure. The economics of scarcity will be important both to help solve the tough issues and to provide big profit opportunities.

9. Give back to communities, through philanthropy and volunteerism. Volunteerism, combined with the company's generosity, gives us a critical one-two punch, because we don't just give money, we make it work. If you want to have impact, add the element of volunteerism. It will make your people feel better, and giving back to the community is important for the company.

10. Focus on teaching people to compete. Making people confident instead of afraid. Confidence ultimately comes before compassion. Today nobody is guaranteed the future. So, to be good corporate citizens, give your people the self-confidence to think about the future—by training, selling every place in the world, having tremendous capabilities, and inspiring people. Confident people think about the future, dream about the future, build your reputation, give back to the community, and make a real difference.

Companies have to stand for compliance, competitiveness and compassion. But ultimately a corporate citizenship group helps build institutional confidence that you are doing things the right way, that you'll be around for the long term, and that people should not feel afraid. So, every day, focus on these 10 steps: High standards, making compliance a process, having exceptional governance, having a commitment to openness, having a culture where the company comes first, supported by strong leaders, supported by a real commitment to people, having business innovation that can solve tough problems, by giving back to our communities, and by teaching people to compete.

Good business leaders have the breadth and depth to know how to solve problems—*breadth* meaning what products are you in, and what customers do you have, and what regions do you want to sell to; and *depth* meaning risk management, and how do you do financing, and how do you make the company run, and how do you generate cash? I find that there is a third dimension—understanding context, or how you fit in the world. You can't train for it. It's a sixth sense you need to run a company—any time you lead people. And that's something that you learn on the job. How does my company fit in the world? What is our place? How can we be a better company? How can we use it to make more money? How can we use it to be a better recruiter? How can we use it to improve our reputation?

Ultimately our job as leaders has to be the triumph of confidence over fear. In this era when fear permeates almost every city, we need to rebuild confidence that companies stand for something, that they can be both great and good, and that they can create the future. Strong companies that care can help create the future. Ultimately this journey is much more about action than words. Actions speak loudest. As Emerson noted, "What you do thunders so loudly that nobody can hear what you say." It's really about actions.

Jeff Immelt is the CEO and chairman of the board at General Electric. This article is adapted, with permission, from a speech given to The Boston College Center for Corporate Responsibility.

Bill of Rights

Amendment I

Congress shall make no law respecting an establishment of religion, or prohibiting the free exercise thereof; or abridging the freedom of speech, or of the press; or the right of the people peaceably to assemble, and to petition the government for a redress of grievances.

Amendment II

A well regulated militia, being necessary to the security of a free state, the right of the people to keep and bear arms, shall not be infringed.

Amendment III

No soldier shall, in time of peace be quartered in any house, without the consent of the owner, nor in time of war, but in a manner to be prescribed by law.

Amendment IV

The right of the people to be secure in their persons, houses, papers, and effects, against unreasonable searches and seizures, shall not be violated, and no warrants shall issue, but upon probable cause, supported by oath or affirmation, and particularly describing the place to be searched, and the persons or things to be seized.

Amendment V

No person shall be held to answer for a capital, or otherwise infamous crime, unless on a presentment or indictment of a grand jury, except in cases arising in the land or naval forces, or in the militia, when in actual service in time of war or public danger; nor shall any person be subject for the same offense to be twice put in jeopardy of life or limb; nor shall be compelled in any criminal case to be a witness against himself, nor be deprived of life, liberty, or property, without due process of law; nor shall private property be taken for public use, without just compensation.

Amendment VI

In all criminal prosecutions, the accused shall enjoy the right to a speedy and public trial, by an impartial jury of the state and district wherein the crime shall have been committed, which district shall have been previously ascertained by law, and to be informed of the nature and cause of the accusation; to be confronted with the witnesses against him; to have compulsory process for obtaining witnesses in his favor, and to have the assistance of counsel for his defense.

Amendment VII

In suits at common law, where the value in controversy shall exceed twenty dollars, the right of trial by jury shall be preserved, and no fact tried by a jury, shall be otherwise reexamined in any court of the United States, than according to the rules of the common law.

Amendment VIII

Excessive bail shall not be required, nor excessive fines imposed, nor cruel and unusual punishments inflicted.

Amendment IX

The enumeration in the Constitution, of certain rights, shall not be construed to deny or disparage others retained by the people.

Amendment X

The powers not delegated to the United States by the Constitution, nor prohibited by it to the states, are reserved to the states respectively, or to the people.

Appendix II

Bill of Responsibilities

With Rights come Responsibilities—As Americans, we must accept responsibility with the gift of security of our rights. As the Founding Fathers of our nation set down the Bill of Rights, the first ten Amendments to the U.S. Constitution, to establish certain rights of American citizens, the Freedoms Foundation has outlined responsibilities of American citizens in a free society:

Preamble.

Freedom and responsibility are mutual and inseparable; we can ensure enjoyment of the one only by exercising the other. Freedom for all of us depends on responsibility by each of us.

To secure and expand our liberties, therefore, we accept these responsibilities as individual members of a free society:

1. To be fully responsible for our own actions and for the consequences of those actions. Freedom to choose carries with it the responsibility for our choices.

2. To respect the rights and beliefs of others. In a free society, diversity flourishes. Courtesy and consideration toward others are measures of a civilized society.

3. To give sympathy, understanding and help to others. As we hope others will help us when we are in need, we should help others when they are in need.

4. To do our best to meet our own and our families' needs. There is no personal freedom without economic freedom. By helping ourselves and those closest to us to become productive members of society, we contribute to the strength of the nation.

5. To respect and obey the laws. Laws are mutually accepted rules by

which, together, we maintain a free society. Liberty itself is built on a foundation of law. That foundation provides an orderly process for changing laws. It also depends on our obeying laws once they have been freely adopted.

6. To respect the property of others, both private and public. No one has a right to what is not his or hers. The right to enjoy what is ours depends on our respecting the right of others to enjoy what is theirs.

7. To share with others our appreciation of the benefits and obligations of freedom. Freedom shared is freedom strengthened.

8. To participate constructively in the nation's political life. Democracy depends on an active citizenry. It depends equally on an informed citizenry.

9. To help freedom survive by assuming personal responsibility for our nation's defense. Our nation cannot survive unless we defend it. Its security rests on the individual determination of each of us to help preserve it.

10. To respect the rights and to meet the responsibilities on which our liberty rests and our democracy depends. This is the essence of freedom. Maintaining it requires our common effort, all together and each individually.

"Personal responsibility is the cornerstone of a civil society. Each of the more than 3,000 high school students attending our Spirit of America Youth Conferences receives a copy of the Freedoms Foundation Bill of Responsibilities which is incorporated into the underlining message of the Statue of Responsibility. The Freedoms Foundation is proud to be associated with the Statue of Responsibility Foundation, which furthers the awareness of this important concept."

—*Aaron Siegel, president/CEO of Freedoms Foundation at Valley Forge. Visit www.ffvf.org.*

Reflections on Responsibility

by Gary Lee Price

As I see it, responsibility is two-fold: We must lead a responsible life personally in order to be responsible to others.

That is why I sculpted the Statue of Responsibility with two hands reaching. One hand represents ourselves (Man); the other hand represents humanity (or God)—those we wish to serve or those we wish to be responsible to. In my mind, it's comparable to the *yin* and the *yang*—one can't exist without the other, and it takes both to fully exist.

We can't give what we do not have. We truly must nourish and school our own souls before we can give to and teach others. This is one of the great conundrums of life: In order to fill our own reservoirs, we must first serve others. Which is more important, and in what order? I'm not sure. I do know that both are vital for a complete and fulfilled life.

I believe that true fulfillment in life comes with the relationships we create. That is why I've chosen to depict the two hands clenched together in assistance and fellowship. It is that connectedness that makes great things happen. It is those friendships that engender respect, honor, and the dignity that we all seek and deserve.

The reaching hands, representing ourselves and others, serves as a gathering place for other interpretations and discussions of responsibility. I envision a park, a beautiful pathway at the foot of the Statue of Responsibility, where artists from other countries around the world will display their creative interpretation of responsibility in the form of sculptures. Visitors will get a truly international message that the principle of freedom, as supported by liberty and responsibility, is a universal message for freedom-loving people the world over.

In November 2004, after spending time visiting with Viktor Frankl's wife, Elly, and their family in Vienna, I found myself waking up in the middle of the night going over our discussions about the Statue of Responsibility. My head was abuzz, trying to work out all the logistics and challenges of creating such a monumental work that, when finished, will impact and inspire the world. I picked up Viktor Frankl's book, *Man's Search for Meaning,* which was lying by my bedside and read about suffering (pages 80 to 86).

I started thinking about how much Viktor and I shared in common. Neither of us likes to dwell on the past, and both of us not only survived our suffering but have risen above it. I thought about how, in general, people are optimists, and how we gladly forget about the negative, sad, and ugly parts of life in exchange for the beautiful memories. I thought about the inconceivable suffering Viktor and the Holocaust victims went through. It caused me to dredge through some of my own personal, painful experiences—such as, at age 6, being awakened by gunshots and running through our apartment in the Heidelberg, Germany, Army barracks, to find my mom lying in a pool of blood, having been shot at the hands of my stepfather. I vividly remember standing over my mom and crying while she looked up at me with her beautiful green eyes but couldn't utter a word. I remember hearing my stepfather falling against the silverware drawer as he shot himself in the head. I remember that horrible, terrifying event as if it were last night. I remember the intense ache and feeling of loss as I kept asking my mothers' friends, who were taking care of me, when I would see my mom again.

I remember as though it was yesterday the beatings and abuse I received for the next five years from my new stepbrother in America who resented my intrusion into his life. I was 6; he was 12. He had witnessed an abusive father beat his mother and sister and was dealing with conflict by example. I remember being slugged in the stomach over and over until I couldn't breathe, being allowed to catch my breath only to be forced to hold up my hands high above my head to be slugged again. After several years of his abuse, I remember holding a knife to my stomach and trying to get the courage to push it hard enough to take my life so I could escape his torture. I was in the 3rd grade.

I, like Viktor, am an optimist. There is not one thing I would change in my life, or cancel, during those years of tragedy and suffering. Not one thing! I feel that I have truly been taken care of, and that everything that has happened in my life has been divinely orchestrated.

Reading Viktor Frankl's book that November night in Vienna renewed and re-energized my feelings about life and how suffering can truly be a positive force if we let it work for our good. I think of Viktor and how, through overcoming his trials and hardships, he has positively influenced millions of souls on this planet. He gives me hope and inspiration. That is why I metaphorically place my hand in his hand to lift millions more through creating the Statue of Responsibility. I view it a great honor and responsibility to fulfill Viktor's vision of creating an inspirational work that will complete the story of freedom and stand as a bookend to the Statue of Liberty.

Viktor's own words ring out to me even now, *"Freedom is not the last word.*

Freedom is only part of the story and half of the truth. Freedom is but the negative aspect of the whole phenomenon whose positive aspect is responsibleness. In fact, freedom is in danger of degenerating into mere arbitrariness unless it is lived in terms of responsibleness. That is why I recommend that the Statue of Liberty on the East Coast be supplemented by a Statue of Responsibility on the West Coast."

I envision the Statue of Responsibility very simple in design and yet very powerful in its meaning and symbolism. I see the statue in a gleaming stainless steel, radiating light in order to be a visual beacon of inspiration, hope and enduring freedom. I see the silhouette of the statue unmistakable in its meaning and message. It is a design for the 21st Century, just as Lady Liberty was a design for the 19th Century. Together they'll stand as beacons of freedom.

I believe the suffering Viktor and I endured was for a reason. It brought each of us to a place in time where the Statue of Responsibility will become reality, and as such, will inspire millions who come after us to understand that the ideals of freedom will survive as liberty and responsibility are meshed together.

Gary Lee Price is the sculptor of the Statue of Responsibility. Visit www.garyleeprice.com.

The Statue of Responsibility Foundation

Our Volunteers

The Statue of Responsibility monument project will be completed through the dedicated work of the Foundation's many committed volunteers. Their passion for promoting the *message* of the monument (Liberty + Responsibility = Our Freedom) is most appreciated. Volunteers are represented by 19 U.S. states and 16 foreign countries. We regard each volunteer as a true "Friend of Freedom." They invest their valuable time and energy in this cause, knowing that their investment will pay high dividends.

Staff

To organize the activities of the Statue of Responsibility Foundation, we have staff based in Utah. Once the host city on the West Coast is secured and the land is acquired, the Foundation will establish a staffed office in that community.

Trustees, Councils, Committees, Volunteers at Large

Overseeing the staff is our Board of Trustees. Our two Honorary Advisory Councils, several Steering Committees, and many Volunteers at Large offer new ideas, create buzz about the monument project, and provide advice, support, and energy. Once the monument is dedicated, the advisory councils and steering committees will be dissolved.

Organization

The objective of the Foundation *is to organize people to build the monument.*

What Next?

Here's a brief overview of what has been accomplished and what lies ahead.

I. Start-Up Phase (1997 through 2007—completed)
- Artist commissioned in 1997, organizational work initiated in 2002
- 501(c)(3) Non-Profit Foundation (incorporated in Delaware)
- Over $500,000 donated in product and services
- 195 Foundation volunteers in 19 states and 16 foreign countries

- 98 Foundation members sitting on committees, councils and boards
- Website and introductory DVD release 1.0 completed
- 3-D computer animation of monument viewable on website
- Sculpture design approved and 13-foot clay prototype finished
- Marketing and presentation materials developed and distributed
- Architectural renderings completed
- Four potential West Coast port city locations researched
- Fundraising and PR strategies researched and planned
- Operational cash-flow projections completed for monument and Visitors Center by Randall Bell of BellConsulting.com.
- Honorary Advisory Council members: Heinz Fischer (President of Austria), Mrs. Viktor E. Frankl, Jack Canfield (*Chicken Soup for the Soul* author), Senator Orrin G. Hatch, Senator (ret.) George S. McGovern, Paul Rusesabagina (Hotel Rwanda), Claudio Pintos (Catholic University, Buenos Aires, Argentina), Nabyl Eddahar (Senior Fulbright Scholar, Morocco), Paul Wong, and others.
- Trademarks applied for and awarded by U.S. Patent and Trademark Office.

II. Pre-Launch Phase (start date—January 2008)
- Engage fundraising strategies with goal of $5.7 million in 18 months
- Confirm which city will host monument and secure location
- Commission an archetype study on Responsibility (Dr. Clotaire Rapaille)
- Appoint a VP of PR and Development and fill Development Council
- Implement Phase I—Educational Awareness Campaign Freedom Tour
- Complete 30-foot tall clay scale model of monument and confirm cost
- Retain construction company and foundry
- Complete detailed architectural, engineering and landscaping plans
- Publish Foundation book, *Responsibility 911*
- Appoint new Board of Trustees members
- Expand staff of Foundation and open office in host city
- Complete release 2.0 of DVD and enhance 3-D computer animation
- Promote "Pennies for Freedom" school-based fundraising program

III. Capital Campaign Phase (start date—TBD)
- Appoint National Spokesperson(s) and engage all fundraising strategies

IV. Construction Phase (start date—TBD)
- Build the monument
- Film crew documents the process for later production of documentary
- Foundation photographer captures images for his commissioned book

V. Operational Phase (start date—TBD)
   • Monument is unveiled and dedicated
   • Create endowment fund to sponsor its educational scholarship program
   • Contract with a company to manage monument operations
   • Research, plan and market corporate educational/motivational retreat
seminars to be held in the Visitors Center and in top floor of monument
   • Fund operational expenses through ticket sales, concessions, bookstore
sales, sales of monument replicas, corporate leasing of top floor, restaurant
leasing, participation of countries in the International Monument Pathway, etc.
Between 3 and 4 million visitors per year are projected to visit the Statue.
   • Foundation will maintain private ownership of the monument property
for years. Eventually the property may be offered to the National Park Service.

Have More Questions?
   Visit our FAQ section of our website at www.SORfoundation.org.

About the Editors

Ken Shelton, for 25 years, has been the editor of *Leadership Excellence* magazine and CEO of Executive Excellence Publishing. He is one of the most sought-after thought leaders on leadership development and corporate responsibility. He is the author or editor of 72 books, and has been the ghostwriter, content developer, or publisher of many well-known authors, speakers and consultants, including Stephen R. Covey, Denis Waitley, Brian Tracy, Lou Tice, Warren Bennis, Chip Bell, Larry Davis, Hyrum W. Smith, and Kerry Gleeson, as well as for leading executives, including Ken Melrose (The Toro Company), Al Stubblefield (Baptist Health Care), and Robert Spitzer (Gonzaga University). His company is co-host of the annual Best Practices in Leadership Development conference and expo. He has a bachelor's degree from Brigham Young University and a master's degree from San Diego State University. He has spoken to audiences all over the world, including the United Kingdom, Spain, Turkey, United Arab Emirates, China, Japan, and Korea. Ken and his wife Pam live in Provo, Utah, and are the parents of three children, with one grandchild.

Daniel Louis Bolz, a native of Marquette, Michigan, grew up appreciating the joy of good art and the beauty of nature. His background encompasses the worlds of art, education, and business. His passion for the arts was developed at a young age through his mother's work as a playwright, actress, and director of a children's television program, while his interest in nature was honed through his father's work as a forester and conservationist. Bolz is a third-generation military veteran. His professional training comes from universities in Michigan and Utah, where he studied art, political science, community education administration, and business management. He has lived and worked in New York, Michigan, Utah, Germany, and Scotland. A writer, inventor, teacher, and business entrepreneur (his electronic invention can be viewed at www.PillowPhonix.com), he has, since 1987, headed his own management consulting company, Paradigm International, providing executive-level management and marketing consulting to private businesses, government entities, and nonprofit foundations. Daniel and his wife Ingrid are the proud parents of four daughters, with three grandchildren. He has worked on the Statue of Responsibility monument project since 2002.

Executive Excellence Publishing

Since 1984, *Leadership Excellence* magazine has provided business leaders with the best and latest thinking on leadership development, managerial effectiveness, and organizational productivity. Each issue is filled with insights and answers from top business executives, trainers, and consultants—information you won't find in any other publication.

CONTRIBUTING AUTHORS
INCLUDE:

Warren Bennis
Marshall Goldsmith
Meg Wheatley
Marcus Buckingham
Dave Ulrich
Jim Collins
Peter Block
Tom Peters
Peter Senge

"Excellent! This is one of the finest magazines I've seen in the field."
—Tom Peters, speaker and management consultant

"Leadership Excellence *is an exceptional way to learn and then apply the best and latest ideas in the field of leadership."*
—Warren Bennis, author and USC professor of management

For information about *Leadership Excellence*, *Personal Excellence*, or *Sales & Service Excellence* magazines, or for information regarding books, audiotapes, speakers, training programs, events, CD-Rom products, or our *Instant Consultant* archives, please call us at:

1-877-250-1983
or visit our website: www.leaderexcel.com

Executive
Excellence
Publishing